TO BUILD A LIFE

A LIFE WITH NO DECISIONS

JACK SIMPSON

To those who built my life.

CONTENTS

WHO IS RESPONSIBLE?

Who is responsible for a life? A criminal argues that he could not help committing a crime because of his upbringing or falling in with bad company. But I had a good upbringing and good friends. What could I not help? Who is responsible for what I did and became?

My life was determined by circumstances, chance, people I met along the way, and a few disabilities. These either decided things for me, created one way to go with no sane alternative, or presented "deals I could not refuse." I just added hard work for whatever task presented itself. I don't know when I made a significant decision in my life, but it worked out pretty well.

I took part in Silicon Valley's software industry boom as well as its accompanying sharp rise in real estate prices. Among several physics Nobel Prize winners, some helped me, one almost took me down, and another won the prize while I stood a few hundred feet away. One decision from a well-known venture capitalist changed the course of my business. I dealt with one of the largest computers in the world, foreign politicians, slum lords, terrorists, a saint, and one of the richest men in the world (before he was rich). I worked with the doctor who had cured one type of always fatal cancer to try curing some other types. I built companies and NGOs and did business with people at the very highest level in Korea. I've worked to improve education in exotic countries when they were still exotic.

All these things just came my way; I did not plan, or intend any of them. I just did the work that presented itself. Thankfully, I could not escape my father's influence, and my wife kept my rashest impulses in check.

Did I build my own life or did my life build me?

INTRODUCTION

Fiction is obliged to stick to possibilities. Truth isn't. – ***Mark Twain***

The case for individual freedom rests chiefly on the recognition of the inevitable and universal ignorance of all of us concerning a great many of the factors on which the achievement of our ends and welfare depend. It is because every individual knows so little and, in particular, because we rarely know which of us knows best that we trust the independent and competitive efforts of many to induce the emergence of what we shall want when we see it. Humiliating to human pride as it may be, we must recognize that the advance and even the preservation of civilization are dependent upon a maximum of opportunity for accidents to happen. — ***Friedrich Hayek***

Our family at MacBain, a few months before we left for North Idaho.
We had a cat, Buddy, also, but he did not do pictures.

The coronavirus has had my wife and me in lockdown since we returned from India on March 16, 2020. Another week and it will be nine months. What am I to do with the time? My software company has continued to do well. Actually, it's been doing better and better in the ten years since I left. I don't think that's because I left, although I have heard comments from some of the longer-term programmers on occasion. Some of that may be from irregularities in our software code due to my lack of the formal computer science education they have. Their complaints are not serious. They do fix these issues and appreciate the job security my lack of knowledge provided. Anyway, they don't often call for advice.

My wife, Sue's, unusual hobbies in India and elsewhere have led to foundations that keep us busy some of the time, but like my company, those projects are now managed by capable people who require less input and ignore some of that because they think they know better. In fact, they often do.

With less I can do outside, I'm now reading a lot about subjects other than the hard sciences where I have worked so long. I had a pretty good overview of these things from college, except for one thing. My other subjects like math and physics I learned as I worked on the problems at the end of the chapter. Subjects outside the hard sciences do not have such problems in their textbooks. I met those problems later in life.

I have worked these problems in our family, friendship, religion, and business areas. I've completed most of them correctly, if not optimally. Some were judged incorrect. Most of those were recoverable with one total disaster narrowly avoided.

So I have some perspective on what I've been reading now about economics, social issues, history, and other things. I like learning new things, but at this late date, what can I do with this knowledge? Run for government? Give everyone tons of advice? With good health and maybe ten to fifteen productive years left, hopefully, I'll think of something.[1]

After reading as much as I wanted, the idea of writing about incidents Sue and I had in our lives came to me. Some we've had were unusual and formed stories I like to tell. I tell them too much, according to Sue. Instead, I'm writing them down, and letting you read them here. Writing, not speaking, has always worked better for me.

How My Life Went: No Decisions

Looking back, I cannot see a time when I had to stop and make a real decision about anything in life. There are small things, not important, and Sue says I usually waffle around until she decides those. Maybe I could be decisive on big things if it were necessary. I just can't remember when it ever was. Situations have always presented themselves with, at least to me, only one sensible way to go, or a choice between ten things I could not tolerate doing and one that I could.

My parents decided my high school, Mom and my pastor my college, and my great dislike for cold and snow dictated a graduate school. Accidentally falling into computer software in graduate school determined the kind of job I sought. The one company interested in talking to me, after searching for as long as I could tolerate, decided my first job. Losing that job made me start my first business.

I had no acceptable alternatives or real decisions to make and ran into major events because of someone else's decision or, more likely, accident. I have been at the right place at the right time, even taken advantage of that, but still may not have known that I was until years later. I've read stories about people meeting the way Sue and I did. Stories like that are interesting because they are so unlikely, even miraculous, that you can't expect them to happen — except when they do. It's like Mr. Twain says above. The possibility was vanishingly slim, but it did happen, just like you'll be reading.

I don't believe in fate. I have often heard, "God opens some doors and closes others," or "God has a plan for your life." I grew up in evangelical Christianity, but I don't think the Bible verses they use to back these statements apply to individual choices such as choosing a school, occupation, mate, or finding a parking place when you really need one, but instead to being responsible for your family, telling the truth, not misleading others to their disadvantage, helping others as you are able, etc.

So how does that work, with neither decisions nor fate? I do believe in circumstances. You could call it chance or accidents. They always kept me busy. By the time I was done with one thing, another task had presented itself. I just kept going. I did have a few life plans. I'm glad they never happened.

~

Hey, nothing's my fault! Things happened as they did. I blame my parents, especially my dad. It's his fault. Maybe I should blame the system. It supplied me with some opportunities but not others. I happened to meet certain people who influenced me in certain ways. I did not meet others who might have sent me in a different direction. How can I know? Then there was my wife. That whole thing was her fault. I had no plan or intention of running into someone who looked like her and later spoke and acted like her. Not when I did and not later. Once again, I was left with no other sensible course of action. Our fifty years of marriage is all her fault. Don't blame me about…

~

The big things in my life really did happen unexpectedly, but you just can't expect things to happen to you the way they did to me. What do I say, "Work hard but if that work ends, just sit and wait for something to happen? Fate will intervene?" I was never able to sit. Well, maybe once for two days when I lost my last contracts in my first business. A phone call out of the blue fixed that one.

On the other hand, maybe you can expect things to happen to you the way they did to me. Not the same things, of course.

I don't think we can be responsible for the accidents and circumstances that come to us, just for our response to them. Without education, we won't even recognize them. With it, there may be something we know, hopefully several somethings we can put together to make the most of what accidentally confronts us.

I firmly believe in luck or accident. You may wish to call it providence or opportunity. I think there is more of it than we realize. The chance of a particular accident that came to me to come to you is negligible, but there are nearly infinite ways for accidents to happen, so you'll have your own. It could be some inconvenience or something that goes wrong. That might be the very thing your interest, education, and background have uniquely equipped you to fix.

If you have the right combination of skills and knowledge, you can respond to the right accident. You don't know what those skills and that knowledge are, but you can follow your interests and learn all that you can about as much as you can. There are enough crazy accidents and things that could be better out there, with new ones coming. You just need one, and to be ready when it comes crashing through.

I didn't realize any of this back when it was happening to me. If I had thought this way, maybe I could have responded faster and better than I did to a few of the circumstances that came my way. As you look back with me, maybe you'll see where, if we can both be more observant, we can make some of our encounters with chance less likely to fail.

We'll also look at two very different disabilities that were advantages for me. More generally, must a disadvantage we have really be a disadvantage? To what might it lead?

The one thing I'll come back to several times is how important my father was in my life. He was a huge part of my education, the part I could not have learned in school. He was different from most people, and perhaps would not have been the best father for some boys, but was certainly right for me. You'll see the contrast between my father and Clarence, who was like a brother to my mother and an uncle to me, but for Clarence to have been a good father for me would have required me to have been born a different person. My later best friend Warren, who you'll also meet in these stories, was like Clarence. Both were truly wonderful people, but very different from me or my dad. I could never hope to have the qualities that made these two people stand out.

I was different, like my dad, who was also a wonderful person. I was able to be like him. If anyone says, "A boy can do fine without a father," there may be something to that, but they must be talking about a boy very different from me.

[1] One good thing did result from my reading. Two of my grandsons, ages fifteen and seventeen, have taken up my reading list. One is starting the third book, this one about worldwide cultural disparities. These are substantial books that have had a great effect on me, already widely read and with graduate degrees. I'm not sure how well I could have understood these books when I was their age, but they are taking it in. Their enthusiasm may be influenced by small financial incentives. Given what they are learning and the price of a college education, this is a great value.

DAD

*The chief thing that fathers are to look to is that they themselves become effectual examples to their children, by doing all those things which belong to them and avoiding all vicious practices, that in their lives, as in a glass, their children may see enough to give them an aversion to all ill words and actions. — **Plutarch,** On the Training of Children.*

*Good is better, because it's nicer. — **Popeye the sailor.***

The William J. Bryan, out from Beni Saf, Algeria, arrived off the Port of Baltimore on December 16, 1945. In the midst of the US moving eight million men across the oceans for World War II demobilization, a liberty ship had little priority and would have to wait to dock. This would not do. If his next assignment was to be completed on time, the former chief engineer of the Allied radio relay station in Algeria had only a few days to get to the other side of the country. He went up to the pilothouse and continued to pull horn blasts. A harbor pilot came out, and he talked him into a ride to the into port. He hitched a few military rides and arrived nine months, plus a few days, before I was born. Without his quick and determined action, I would have missed my birthday and many things in these stories would have come out differently.

Dad and I at our house in Campbell CA.

As kids growing up, my sister Sharon and I were a little afraid of Dad. Sharon and I just "knew" that stepping too far out of line would bring a response from Dad that we could not withstand. We could misbehave some and push things a bit, but if we went too far Dad would go off the rails and …

He never did. Either we were always sufficiently well behaved, or Dad controlled himself a lot better than it seemed he could. All the times he ever hit me, my sister, or Mom add to zero. If it's all the times he just raised a hand or acted like he might hit someone, it's still zero. I am excluding the three or four times I got a well-controlled and explained spanking, the last around eight years old. Sharon never got spanked. To most of Dad's "greatest" generation, hitting a woman of any age was beyond imagination. Mom could do that, but not Dad.

Dad's bark, while sufficient for keeping things in line, was far worse than his bite. Neither Sharon nor I ever rebelled or had any of that sort of behavior as teenagers. We never had any thoughts in that direction. Neither of us was that kind of kid, and we could not imagine Dad ever tolerating such a thing.

From my child's point of view, Dad provided absolute security. All needs were supplied all the time without fail, with no hint it could ever be otherwise. Always having an owned house, a working car, food, clothes, shoes, or other items needed for school or normal activities was a given, with any other way of life only seen in stories or movies. Of course, wants were another thing, and we quickly learned the difference between a need and a want.

Everything worked, always. I used to watch Dad fix our car, washing machine, TV, work on the house, and other things. He might take the car to the garage, but that was it. I'm trying to remember when something did not work. Maybe a leaky faucet, a toilet that would not flush (bad since we had only one), something that could really use some paint, or a car that Mom could not take too far because it might break down? I'll keep thinking…

Dad could embarrass Mom in public. There were times he just said what he thought without thinking, or did he always just say what he thought without thinking? Later, when Sue was with us, there were a few times when she would keep her distance and not seem to notice anyone or anything in Dad's general area. Mom never embarrassed Dad, me, Sharon, or anyone else in public or anywhere else. Dad did cause distress this way to others, especially to Mom. He could have done better there.

When Sue first met Dad, she thought he didn't like her. He was somewhat gruff and was quick to say something about what he liked, but more often about what he didn't like. Her dad was a good man and father but nothing like mine. Among other things, he did smile more, went to church, and wore a suit when he did. Sue did come to know how Dad really felt about her and fully became one of the family a few months later when Dad sent her a letter. In a few lines he said he would always consider her the same as me and my sister, Sharon: at any time he would do anything she needed and help her any way he could.

Dad and I at age 14. Our '60 family truck (Suburbans weren't cool then) in the background. Mom didn't like going to church in that truck.

Years after Dad was gone, I began to understand him better. Dad often was not nice, and I never viewed him as a nice man, let alone a polite man. From church and elsewhere, I formed the image of a nice man as gentle, soft-spoken, always pleasant and polite, always a kind word, well dressed – maybe in a suit at times, attending church and always smiling. Dad fit none of that. I did not then think in terms of telling the truth, putting your family first, always supporting their needs, not borrowing so much you can't handle an unseen turn for the worse, and keeping your promise. Dad never made excuses. For example, a loan was a promise. You had to pay it back. His method of dealing was from straightforward to overly blunt.

With all the businesses Dad started and worked, I noticed him doing a lot of dealing. In all this, there were things I never got the slightest hint of from anyone or anywhere: a deal where Dad "cleverly put something over on" or "got the better of" someone, was unfaithful to Mom, or did anything significantly regrettable to a friend or anyone in our community. Rough and impolite, making jokes but never mean, but anyone could trust Dad with anything, anytime.

How long before you can look back and place an accurate definition on past life? For me, it was well after Dad was gone. I lived by standards I had not defined nor understood. I now know more as I near the age where Dad died. "Good" and "Nice" are not similar. I wonder if in some cases, they might be opposite. The general impression was that Dad often failed at being nice, but how good he was is a whole different animal. To me the idea of Good was not as apparent as Nice, but it was still there, maybe just unconsciously absorbed in the family environment. On the surface when I was young, I might have appreciated Nice more, but from where I sit now, there is no contest.

~

So how did all my great upbringing turn out? Ideally, the next generation should be an improvement on the previous. I have improved over my father in several areas and kept even in a few. There are areas, some important, where I have not measured up. I was not so bad but could have done better and have no decent excuses. I certainly can't fault parental abuse.

Poverty might fly, except no one told me I had any deprivation until I was in college.

Dad was nine when his father died gasping for breath from black lung, known as miner's disease. After that, Dad developed a quick "boarding house reach" to get enough food in the establishment for miners his mother had to run. Later, a much less-than-ideal stepfather added to the mix. Whatever excuses I might have, I can't match what Dad never complained about.

I am college age with long hair. Dad cut it at home-always a butch.

What about Mom? The Chinese curse, "May you live in interesting times," comes to mind. Mom was not so "interesting," a good thing. She was both good and nice, a great combination, but giving me less to write about. Her contribution was more obvious. She supplied the foreground while Dad was the background. She left me no space to write about seeming contradictions or the surprise of her appearing this way when she was really that.

Most explicit instruction came from her. She took us to church. She got us ready for school or anything else. Of course our family would not have worked without her. Her influence was immediate while Dad's was more long-term. She could not have been more different from Dad, just as it is with Sue and me.

Why Dad was in a hurry to get back from Algeria.

Mom attended the Coeur d'Alene Bible Church where Sue and I also went once we moved up north. Dad attended a few times. He was friends with an elder there, one of the few black men in town. They talked during Dad's last weeks and Dad had a change of viewpoint. When Dad's funeral was held, the sermon from Matthew 20, about the landowner hiring workers throughout the day, fit perfectly.

NO FOOLING AROUND

I was three years old and on a bed. It had wheels and a man was rolling the bed and me down a long hall. He had a big sheet or something around him, a mask on his face, and some kind of thing on his head. Mom wore a thing like that when she took a shower, but his was big and hung down around the sides. I couldn't see much more of him than his glasses. He was strange looking, but I wasn't afraid of him. Mom was walking right beside the bed and had her hand on me.

We went a long way, and then came to a wide doorway. Mom stopped but the man kept rolling me down the hall! This was wrong. I had to get back to Mom. I got off the bed, except the man picked me up and walked even faster. I could see Mom over his shoulder, but she was already a long way away. I yelled for her, but she just stood way back there. She was so far away.

He took me into a room full of people that were dressed like him and sat me down on a table in the middle of all of them. The room was full of metal and white things. What were they? I'd never been in any place like this before. I was crying a lot.

They were talking but I couldn't understand what they said. Someone pushed me down and put something over my face. It was white, really bright, and there were strange sounds. Then I breathed the most horrible stuff. I had never smelled something like that. It was everywhere. I yelled for Mom and thought I heard crazy noises.

Mom was there and was talking to me as I slowly woke up in a completely dark room. She told me it was dark because my eyes were covered. I was all better now, but I should not touch near my eyes. They would take the cover off and I would see in another day. She assured me that no one would take me away from her again for a long time. I felt safe. She told me again how my eyes "rolled in." We had to fix them so I would see better.

Mom explained everything, especially why she could not go with me when they took me away from her. She said she did not know when they would take me away from her that first time, and so could not tell me what was happening. Surprises can be bad. We talked until I understood everything. This was before anyone thought of a "patient's bill of rights," or doctors made it a priority to explain themselves to their patients.

Mom said from then on she would learn everything she could about anything that would happen to me, and then she would tell me.

A year later, I was a much older age four, and they operated on my other eye. It was still scary, but now I knew what to expect. Mom walked with me as before. My dad had previously visited and made it clear to the doctor in charge that everyone involved was to explain to me at each point what was coming next. Dad could speak in a way that made people realize that they could either listen to him now or they would end up listening to him a whole lot more later. The man wheeling my rolling bed stopped and told me that this was as far as Mom could go. I said goodbye and we rolled onward. When we got to the operating room, I started to move myself from the bed to the operating table, but they stopped me. They said they would soon pick me up and put me there, and so they did. I asked a few questions about some of the things I saw, and someone told me what they did. Most impressive was the light right over me. I had not seen anything like that before.

The only thing I was dreading was the ether. It really was awful stuff, but I knew one deep breath was the only one I would have to take until I was asleep. They told me and then put the mask on. I took the horrible-smelling breath and that was it. Knowing was everything.

Dad told me we were once in the doctor's office when the nurse sneaked up behind to give me a shot in the rear before I could cause a fuss. Dad stopped her. He told the nurse to come around, show me the needle, and then she could give me the shot. I came through without fuss. Dad did the same for my sister Sharon. Dad tolerated no fooling around his kids.

If a doctor, dentist or anyone else told me something like "This won't hurt a bit." with Dad present, a more detailed explanation was immediately requested. Mom would never interrupt someone like that. She would explain things to me before we went. If later I heard different it was OK; even little kids know that some people may not tell the truth.

We had few surprises in life, except for anticipated ones such as a Christmas present. There was never a reason not to believe everything my parents said. Mom and Dad made few promises, but they kept every one. It seemed odd when I later learned that teenagers often rebelled against their parents. I knew what was true. My parents told me. Against what part of that was I going to rebel?

FOR MY OWN GOOD

. . . the only purpose for which power can be rightfully exercised over any member of a civilized community, against his will, is to prevent harm to others. His own good, either physical or moral, is not a sufficient warrant. – ***John Stuart Mill***

How old should I be for this?

The incident I remember most from all of primary school is a long important talk with Mom after finishing the second grade. She and the teacher thought I should repeat the next year, and of course, were dead right.

Mom tried to talk me into repeating second grade. She took time and explained everything but wanted buy-in from me. No way. It was failure. No doubt, with some expert psychological approach, I would have gone for it, but Mom, to her great credit, was straightforward and honest with me, an example of both my parents' behavior that gradually built into me an absolute trust of their complete honesty in anything they said to me. I would usually agree with them, but not this time. Having the choice of failure or at least some success was no choice at all for me. I would not be a failure.

My academic performance was just good enough to pass. These abilities remained marginal for another six years. My September birthday got me into school just under the wire, age-wise. My small size, even for that age, lack of physical coordination, and bad social skills were all issues. I wore glasses, and the kids called me "goggles Simpson" from second through fifth grade. Lenses of glasses were breakable back then, and mine were broken several times. After surgeries at ages three and four, the glasses were a futile attempt to correct my lack of binocular vision, which took away depth perception and messed up any game involving a ball. My flat feet required corrective shoes. They were heavier and must have had some effect on running and game-playing.

These things piled on to each other, making play and interaction with the other kids that much worse. High-functioning autism added to my social interaction issues as well as adding its often-attendant physical coordination problems.

No one would be aware of the autism for a long time to come. I think it made social interaction harder but also made my need for it less. This remains true today.

I was not a total mess. I knew things did not work as well for me as they did for the other kids, but I never felt overwhelmed. I was different than others, and the difference was not in the best direction, but I felt I was just a little bit disabled, just a little different.

I graduated to third grade. My third- to ninth-grade experience was an unpleasant slog, with me bringing home "capable of doing better" or "C" report cards, daydreaming in class, and wiping out in any gym or PE class. Mom often told me, "Your IQ is so high; you should be doing better." I was not aware a number was attached to IQ, never did know my score, and have not taken another such test. Best guess it was above average, but not to where any teacher treated me differently, or at least not that I was aware of.

Other than daydreaming, I was not a behavior problem. A reprimand from the teacher in front of the class was the last thing I wanted. Not being noticed for anything, good or bad, seemed best. I kept my head down. I did not raise my hand, or did so sparingly if the teacher was the kind to notice consistent non-participation. My worst classroom moments were when the teacher called on me, possibly because I was daydreaming and not paying attention. I don't know what I daydreamed about, but I do know that Mom was always telling me I daydreamed too often in school.

I was successful in staying out of team sports, which was good, especially when a ball was used. I was always chosen last for any PE class team, which was not the best thing. While that disappointed me in class, I got used to it, and it was forgotten once outside. I think I was OK because self-esteem had not been invented yet.

Short term, I think life would have improved if I had repeated the second grade. That year of maturity from being six months older than the average age in my class, instead of being six months younger, should have made things easier for me. Long term, I have no idea. It was certainly the sensible course except for one thing: Mom was honest with me: I knew exactly what I was looking at, not an edited or slanted version. I made the choice, I lived with it and learned one more time I could trust Mom, even when she wanted what I did not.

THE MAGIC PANTS MYSTERY

When I was two and a half, Dad brought home a German shepherd puppy. Sandy and I grew up together for five years. A neighbor kid liked to tease Sandy over our fence until one day the dog got fed up, jumped the fence, and bit him. There was no further damage. Sandy was used to being around me and my friends. He'd made his point and stopped. Even so, we had to give Sandy to a family out on a nearby ranch.

One Sunday, Dad had time to visit Sandy and took Sharon and me along. I was about seven at the time. We changed out of our church clothes, but somehow I was not able to change shoes, so Dad gave me special instruction not to get my shoes muddy. He promised a "licking" if I did. Of course I did get them muddy, a fact recorded in the picture we still have of that occasion showing me, Sharon, and Sandy. My expression there shows that I am thinking about what is to come.

When we got home my shorts were also muddy in the rear and Mom put me back into my wool Sunday pants. A little later, Dad got out the heavy leather dog leash he had used for Sandy. I knew that leash would hurt but did not realize how much damage it could actually do, even to an adult, if wielded with any strength at all by my dad, who was six feet and often worked hard outdoors. He had me bend over something, probably a table, and gave me about twelve whacks.

Note my shoes are muddy. I'm not too happy here.

It hurt, but surprisingly less than I expected. Why was that? Dad was clearly angry about the muddy shoes, and I heard the leash as it hit me. Still, the whole thing was most unpleasant, and I was upset, scared, and crying. I was really going to try to remember to obey better. The excitement of seeing Sandy again, with him so active, jumping all around and over us, just made me forget everything.

Evaluating the situation afterward, I decided it had to be the wool Sunday pants I was wearing. I had never before been spanked while wearing those. Somehow that fabric, even though it seemed thinner than my jeans, protected me from that leash. I used that knowledge on at least two subsequent occasions, since spankings were never sudden, but discussed and then later given, so I had a chance to change. The pants did their job well; the leash still hurt but was bearable. Dad never seemed to notice that I had changed pants before getting spanked. I congratulated myself for cleverly bringing the spanking pain levels down from catastrophic to bearable.

Two years earlier in Dad's '49 Buick. Behind is our Campbell, CA house.

Spankings never were frequent with Dad and died out soon after we had moved up to Idaho when I was finishing the third grade.

Mom kept the pictures she took in an album that was always accessible, so when I saw that picture of Sandy, Sharon, and me again, the whole story would come back — especially the most important part of all, the pants. After a few years, I realized how a heavy leash like that would have felt regardless of the pants, if Dad had taken any kind of reasonable swing at me.

I had thought the licking was at least partly unjustified due to both my and Sandy's excitement over seeing each other. Was I not the only one who thought that? Dad had promised that licking and had to carry it through. Dad did not break promises to anyone, and certainly not to me.

I wonder if he practiced. He did get the cracking sound right when he hit me, and that added a lot to the effect.

What about those subsequent spankings with the leash? Dad was still holding back; those pants weren't the reason the spanking hurt less. Even so, they were still bad and were all the motivation I needed to do my best to correct whatever had brought them on. What made him hold back? Mom saw the majority of my misbehavior. I'm now thinking these subsequent spankings were "Wait 'till your father gets home" situations. After just a few of these, they must have discussed it together and decided to just end the spankings and perhaps move to imprisonment. I did have to sit on my bed on occasion. Was it one of them that pushed for that end? I'm betting it was Dad. I wish I could have thought to ask one of them when they were still here.

Dad used to tell me how his dad used the razor strap on him for misbehavior. That's how things were done back then. Sure, there were fathers back then that had a violent streak and went too far with physical punishment, and there still are today. There are many more fathers who, angry or not, control themselves and make sure everything they do is for their child's best interest.

Did I carry trauma into later life from the spankings Dad, and Mom, gave me when I was young? No. Was I traumatized fifteen minutes after Dad finished spanking me? As best as I can remember, not at all. From my viewpoint now, what happened then was fine. Whether the same would apply for a different kid and different dad I have no idea.

There is one punishment that I remember over any other. It was the worst one for me. Four months before I turned five, Mom, Sharon, and I flew from California to visit Grandma and Grandpa in Clarkston, Washington. Dad later drove up to take us back home by car.

Mom took me to a dime store on Main street, gave me some money, and I picked a few small plastic trucks out of a bin having various types and colors. During our visit, I was free to roam the area and later walked the two blocks to Main street, went back into the store, and managed to take a few more trucks to complete my collection. In due time, Mom noticed I had more trucks than she remembered and soon had me admitting what I did. Mom then dropped the subject, but Dad was there. He told me what would happen the next day.

It was a long walk to the store with Dad. He went into the store with me but stood back. I had to walk up to the storekeeper, give him the trucks, explain I had stolen them, say I was sorry, and promise him I would never do anything like that again. It was embarrassing in the extreme. A spanking would certainly have been preferable, but that or any additional punishment never happened.

I cannot recall stealing anything from anyone since.

SCHOOL AND MOVING NORTH

*People who get nostalgic about childhood were obviously never children. — **Bill Watterson***

In 1954, Dad and his twin brother Jim decided to move up to Coeur d'Alene in north Idaho, near where they grew up and where both lived when first married. Jim went first, and we followed a few months later. We first lived with Mom's parents in Clarkston, Washington for three months while Dad bought a house and otherwise made things ready for us in Coeur d'Alene.

Irascible as he could sometimes be, Dad was always good with Mom's parents and got along great with both of them. They were as close to parents as he would ever see. He lost his dad to the black lung miner's disease at age nine, and his mother two weeks after I was born. I think my grandfather respected my dad for being 4F but going overseas anyway, even though he was never in the kind of danger my grandfather faced in the trenches at the WWI battles of St. Mihiel, Meuse-Argonne, and Ypres-Lys.

I went to the first third of the third grade in Ventura, California, the second third in Clarkston, and the last third in Coeur d'Alene. We had moved from a southern California climate to spend the middle of winter in Clarkston, near sea level and in what was called the "banana belt" for its mild climate. By the time we moved to Coeur d'Alene, the worst of winter was over. It would be winter next year before I would feel the full shock of the much colder climate and lots of snow at a hundred miles further north and two thousand feet higher elevation.

At Parkway Elementary School in Clarkston, the major issue was the two bullies who always tried to catch me during recess — a somewhat larger guy and his sidekick. The big one may have had some issue with his legs. He seemed more stiff than normal when he ran. His friend stayed with him, which allowed me to outrun them, orthopedic shoes and all, so they never did lay a hand on me. Only once in the three months did they corner me. The sidekick said something like, "We're going to get you now," whereupon I ducked between him and a wall and ran off. They must have had opportunities to hit me or otherwise cause trouble when we were moving in and out of class or to lunch, but they never did.

A few months after moving to Coeur d'Alene, we returned to visit my grandparents and I went over to spend a day with my old class. The two "bullies" and I walked around the school and visited during recess like old friends. The whole bully chase game was just that to them, a game. It may have been a game to me as well. I thought they were genuinely out to get me on one level, but had no concern for it outside of recess, and did not think to mention it to my parents or anyone else when it was happening for three months. It was nice to see them again, and good to have had something for the three of us to do for all those recesses.[1]

From Google street view. It's still there. The back of the Central School building is little changed. Even the asphalt play yard may not have been updated. The AC units seen at the building's base have been added along with the concrete steps to the back.

In March 1955, I started Central School at 602 E Garden Avenue in Coeur d'Alene for the last third of the third grade. It was a typical neighborhood school in the town. I'm surprised its small building, old when I was there, has not been torn down. Today it houses a few small businesses, although I can't imagine it ever rising to the status of historical landmark. It had six classrooms for kindergarten through fifth grade, four upstairs and two down, along with some downstairs offices. We were called in from recess and lunchtime with a large brass handbell. I had my turns ringing it. I walked the half-mile from our house at 920 Montana Ave. to school. Now Coeur d'Alene has fewer, larger elementary schools, just like the rest of our nation. They still call them neighborhood schools. Maybe they are for the parents, but not for the kids.

I learned many of the popular songs that played on the radio at that time, since the radio was on as we ate breakfast every morning. I can't tell you how many times I heard *The Naughty Lady of Shady Lane.* Bing Crosby often sang *Straight Down the Middle* as well as *Dear Hearts and Gentle People.* The first song was about golf and the second about a place in Idaho, because Bing had a summer home by the golf course in the town next to ours.[2] We listened for the weather report, which would say whether school was closed due to the school buses being unable to run. It snowed often in north Idaho but the plows were efficient. The bus routes were cleared first, so we normally did not miss more than one day at a time. If the buses could run, they assumed the rest of us could walk. I don't think I ever heard of a parent driving their kid to school back then. The one exception was when we had more than a week of twenty-below-zero weather. Uncle Jim would come by in the TV repair truck to pick up Dad so he wouldn't have to get the '51 Buick started. Its straight-eight engine did not run well in the extreme cold. I went with them and was dropped off at school.

Montana Avenue ran up a hill in front of our house between 9th and 10th streets. Our entertainment on snowy mornings was watching cars slide past. Most of them were headed west and upward from 10th Street. They would make it partway up before sliding back down and taking 10th Street to a better place to travel westward. Going the other way was OK and most north Idaho drivers knew enough not to get into a wheels-locked downhill slide. With no garage or driveway, we had to park in front of our house. Dad must have had some worries about someone colliding with our car, but it never did happen. If he was going to use the car in cold weather, he would run a long cord out to the car and plug in the engine block heater beforehand.

On a winter Saturday, I might take a long, quiet, cold walk to visit my cousin Jim, my dad's twin's son. Mom helped me to get bundled up to walk the more than half-mile to his house. Our first Christmas there, I got a sled and used it on St. Maries Street, in back of our house, which was often closed in the winter for sledding. Sledding times were few, and I never did like the cold and snow.[3]

I learned to ride a bicycle our first summer in Coeur d'Alene. A local friend brought his smaller twenty-inch bike and I learned coasting it downhill on the grass in our front yard. Shortly after that, at my cousins' house, I was able to call everyone out to the back to show them how I could ride my cousin Dianna's full-size bike. At that time, I could not have straddled the crossbar on a boy's bike. When Christmas came, I had enough height to ride the new bike I got but could not sit in the seat if I was pedaling. I started riding it to school when the snow was not too deep.

The visiting music teacher caught me not singing in our once-a-week music class and made me sing a song all by myself during the class. I mumbled through it somehow. The various embarrassments that came my way usually caused little problem once they were over, but after this one, I learned to move my mouth and appear to be paying attention. I never again made a sound while singing in school, church, or anywhere else after that.

I liked my fourth-grade teacher, Mrs. Hatch, more than most teachers. One day I was feeling more and more sick as I sat in class until I finally had to do something. I walked up the center of the room to the other side of the teacher's desk where she sat facing the class. I could only say, "Mrs. Hatch, I don't feel so…" What I let loose easily crossed her desk and covered a good portion of her. The crowd went wild. Maybe every teacher gets something like that at least once? Of course, physically I felt better after getting all that out. Anyway, someone called my dad and he came and took me home. Someone might also have had to take Mrs. Hatch home after that.

In fifth grade, a science kit in a big wooden box was delivered to our class and sat on the teacher's desk in front of the room. I do not think I had performed well in any school subject at that point but was always interested in what passed as science for kids my age. The teacher must have noticed that interest and she elected me to unpack the items from the kit and store them in a cabinet in the room. The notoriety from this earned me the name "Science Happy Simpson," which was bandied about for a week or two. I looked at and understood the items I transferred into the cabinet. I never saw any of those items again.

One time, after the fourth grade in summer, Mom decided I needed to learn to play baseball. She got me a ball and a mitt and had Dad go out in the backyard to play catch with me a few times. Neither of us liked it, and when Dad saw that I would rather not play, he let the issue drop. Mom then signed me up for Parks and Recreation Department summer baseball. I would take my mitt, go to Pearson's Field, and sit down against the fence and watch the play. After a week of this, the coach came over, found out my mom had sent me there, and put me into the game. I was equally good at missing the ball with my mitt and the bat, and am uncertain whether myself or the rest of the team appreciated my presence less. When I got back home I told Mom I would play no more baseball, and that was that.

I never saw my dad play any sports. He did have some golf clubs he must have used in the past, but I never knew him to go golfing. He watched old movies and shows such as *You Bet Your Life* with Groucho Marx on TV, but never any sports. He did tell me how he and his landlord Dan Matthews used to beat all comers in croquet in the early '40s when he taught at the Naval Radio School at University of Idaho.

My family of three boys maintains the Simpsons' nonsporting habits. None of my three sons have ever played any sports. A grandson, at eight years of age, likes playing sports with his friends but shows little interest in any sports outside of that participation. Other than that, I've heard no mention of sports associated with any of my four grandsons. I didn't know that was inherited.

~

[1] I did not realize this until I wrote this chapter.

[2] It was a few years later that Dad's outspokenness had an effect on him at this radio station. Dad was chief engineer at our local KVNI radio. He soon hosted a weekly "Sportsman's Show" primarily about fishing. He also reported news from KVNI's "mobile unit," did announcements, and occasionally played music, until one time on the air, he said, "I don't know what people see in this singer," about a new singer, Elvis Presley. In an early example of "cancel culture," the station's constituency had changed, the town's teen age girls were enraged, and Dad was removed from DJ duties.

[3] Much later, when I moved my own family back to Coeur d'Alene, Sue decided we should all take up skiing. We did not take the kids for our first time and went to the Lookout Pass ski area where we rented equipment. I took the lift up and managed once to come down the easiest route, although not in

fine form. The snow was crusty that day; it might have been more fun in "powder." Meanwhile, a somewhat distant relative who had come with us took Sue over to the bunny hill. "I've been a ski instructor for years," he said and proceeded to give her too many instructions to remember. As she went down, her legs started separating. She was working on getting them back together when she looked up, saw all the people, and yelled. She was too close for anyone to move out of the way but still far enough to alert everyone so all could enjoy the moment. She managed to plow into a reasonably sized group of people at a speed sufficient to cause severe inconvenience to quite a few of them but knock only one completely down.

We never got around to going skiing again.

A number of my company's employees love skiing and are pleased with the number of ski areas close by. I'm glad it works out well for them.

SEA HUNT EDUCATION

I'm ten here, with our small swimming pool I used as a raft. I took all this to the lake on my bike. It would be four years before I used SCUBA.

Sea Hunt was my favorite show with its first season in 1958. Mike Nelson, played by Lloyd Bridges, spent most of his time underwater and had many adventures. He would retrieve a lost satellite, find a wrecked boat, or fight off bad guys underwater. A voice-over by Bridges gave a running commentary with an explanation of how he got out of his various fixes.

I picked up a lot of instruction about diving from watching every week and, by its next season at age thirteen, I was ready to start diving in Coeur d'Alene Lake just north of downtown. Mom had made me take Red Cross swim lessons after third grade and I continued through lifesaving. I had enough earned from my paper route to buy all the basic equipment. Diving was just starting to gather popularity, some of which came from the *Sea Hunt* show, so a small dive shop had appeared in Coeur d'Alene. At that time, there were no rules and restrictions about training or who could dive.

I got the tank, regulator, mask, fins, weight belt, etc. It was another year before I could get a driver's license, so on a weekday a friend helped me transport my equipment down to a little-used public dock near the boat launch area. I hauled everything to the end of the dock where I had previously checked a twenty-foot depth. Mike Nelson had sometimes gotten stuck where he had to remove his equipment, untangle everything, put it back on, and get away. Bad guys would rip off his mask or get behind him and turn off his air. He would handle the situation and quickly put the mask back on or turn on the air and go on. I would do something like that, except for the bad guys.

I put on the weight belt, since I didn't want to do all this while thrashing around on the surface. I put an arm through the straps for everything else, jumped in, and sank to the bottom. I located the regulator, got it in my mouth, turned on the air, got the mask, etc. Once outfitted, I moved out into the lake. Beyond Mike's lessons, that was my diving instruction.

At the end of the show, Mike always gave a little talk that was often a useful lesson. He would emphasize the few things a diver should never do. On the few occasions the bad guy did one of those things, the results were predictably disastrous.[1]

The "pits" for the '58 Diamond Cup races was the center for all the excitement.

Mike did dive alone nearly all the time. I knew this was not good, but I was also alone since none of my other friends got into diving. Mom was usually in the kitchen when we watched *Sea Hunt* and may not have had a complete idea of what I was doing. Dad was fine with it. After high school, he worked a few years for the Bunker Hill mine under conditions far more dangerous than anything I ever did, so he may have had a different idea about risk than others.

Every summer starting in 1958, the Diamond Cup unlimited hydroplane races were held on Coeur d'Alene Lake. Race week was our high point of the summer. Dad set up radios, PA, and other electronics for the race and always got me a "pit pass" badge, which allowed me into the area where the boats stayed and were maintained when not in the water. Pit boys ran errands, did other odd jobs, and hung around the boats and drivers. It was exciting stuff.

I worked off the back of a tug from the same company. It was a sister to this one.

Somehow, maybe through Dad, I got the job of hooking up the course buoys for the 1961 and 1962 races. I worked off a tugboat whose back deck held the buoys. Each was a stack of orange-painted inner tubes with large tractor tubes at the bottom going up to car-sized tubes at the top. Each was eight or nine feet tall. I would take a buoy's line and jump into the water. Surveyors miles away on three surrounding mountain-tops sighted the yellow top of my wet suit hood and told me where to move via CB radio through a speaker on the tug. Their OK sent me down to find the big white tie-on buoy "floating" thirty feet underwater. Dad and others contributed their work to the race, and I was no different. It was fun. As a fourteen year old, I felt important because it was an important job; the race would not run without those buoys in place. So, just a year after I started diving, I was an essential part of a team with a tugboat crew and professional surveyors.

A few times, the tie-on buoy wasn't there, and I had to go down, often in the pitch darkness past eighty feet, feel around and find the concrete anchor placed for the original 1958 race. Once, this was over 170 feet down and they got a diver from the small Coast Guard detachment there to monitor the race to go down with me. We felt our way around in the pitch dark, soon found it, and tied on. I had read about the disorientation caused by the very cold water playing tricks with inner ear balance canals, which were magnified in the absolute darkness below eighty feet, and so was prepared for a bit of that. I didn't know the deep-diving rules but could follow them just by finding the anchor and tying on within five minutes and staying with the other diver on the way up. This was a great time for me, and I was not in unsafe situations, but legal and other standards of today would have never allowed me these experiences.

There really was not much interesting to see in Coeur d'Alene Lake. Lake fish are skittish, fast, and rarely seen. The water may seem clear at the surface, but visibility is usually only twenty or thirty feet and the water is a uniform four degrees centigrade beyond about thirty feet down. Past sixty feet, it starts getting dark. So diving was not fun unless there was a job to do.

Later at Seattle Pacific College, I had a job diving in Puget Sound and on the Washington coast with a marine botany professor. I held the bag and he selected plants to stuff into it.

He specialized in plants that lived in highly oxygenated water, which often meant diving in areas with extreme current or wave action. This led to interesting dives carefully timed so the currents would not carry us off or the waves beat us around. That narrow winding canyon off the coast was maybe the worst. It was often less than five feet across and lined on both sides with sea urchins. The current was not so heavy but still enough to require my complete attention while the professor hunted his plants.

With graduate school and work, I got away from diving except for a wonderful Hawaiian adventure with my two older sons.[2] When I took it up again in my sixties, I had to take a course and get certified, none of which was done when I had stopped diving. Since then, I finally fulfilled my dream to dive around various Caribbean and South Pacific islands. The clear water, exotic fish, and coral forests have been great. There's also been a number of times snorkeling with Sue in the Caribbean and South Sea Islands.[3] We've got friends living by the Great Barrier Reef in Australia, and hope soon to dive on that reef and explore another amazing underwater environment.

~

[1] The basic rule in SCUBA diving is "Never hold your breath when rising in the water. Breathe out as you go up." This is often translated to the easier to remember "Never hold your breath at all." Break this rule and you will die quickly. Mike Nelson was fighting one bad guy who had lost his mouthpiece, had to hold his breath for a bit more fighting, and then get away to the surface. As Mike's voice-over explained, he kept holding his breath! He essentially exploded from an "air embolism" on the way up. I did not forget that lesson.

This was a coming-of-age experience. There were some mistakes that I could not make, ever. Diving could be dangerous if not done properly. I was careful. I made sure I knew what I was doing before I tried anything. I did trust Mike but would still double-check what he said in books.

[2] When my two oldest kids were twelve and seven, Sue and I took them on a Hawaiian vacation. We all went out to Hanauma Bay at six in the morning. This was before the extreme popularity and tourist restrictions they have now. The kids and I put on our snorkeling gear and sun protection shirts and swam out from the beach. We left Sue, who was not a snorkeler at the time, alone on the beach on a large towel.

We all saw clear water, abundant fish, and other marine life for the best water exploration ever. The three of us had previously been in the water together a lot, and even with Nathan being only seven, did not come back into shore until afternoon.

When we returned, the beach had changed. Sue was immediately visible on her towel, completely and closely surrounded by a sea of smaller identical towels, each with a Japanese tourist on it. Tour buses had dropped hundreds of them off while we were out. Their darker towels tiled the central area of the beach completely, with Sue's big white towel standing out prominently right in the middle. They were friendly, and Sue had a more interesting time on the beach than she thought she would.

[3] Once when snorkeling with Sue at a South Pacific island, we swam out over a coral bed extending between thirty and a hundred feet offshore. The entire bed was only a few feet down from the surface and beautiful. All the colors, fish, and other animals were close up the entire way out. We were swimming along the far end of the coral bed when it was time to go back. The tide had gone out and now the coral bed was less than a foot below the surface. We would scrape ourselves raw swim-

ming over it, and trying to walk over it might have hurt the coral but would have hurt our feet a whole lot more. We could only swim along the far edge until we found a break a maybe a thousand feet down the shore. That was a little scary, but Sue had gotten pretty relaxed in the water when we were in our sixties, and we got back to shore without much worry.

SCHOOL GETS BETTER

In 1957 I attended Coeur d'Alene Junior High School, which was only two blocks from my home. There were two buildings, a red brick one built as a junior high where I completed sixth and seventh grades, and an older tan brick building, the former high school, for eighth and ninth. Both were torn down years ago to make Seventh Street Park. I had a young male teacher for sixth and did well. He even showed me a little about algebra.

In seventh grade, we started having different teachers and classrooms for each subject, so I had PE for the first time. I was the "always chosen last" kid you've heard about, which was unpleasant while in class, but not so much that I thought about it when it was over. The only game I really liked was dodge ball, which we called "soak 'em." Apparently, this game has long been banned because it was unfair to kids like me, hurt self-esteem, or some other reason.[1] I was certainly not the best at it, but it required little skill and gave a lot of action.

I had been with good students in seventh grade, but did not

do so well, so I ended up with a rougher group in eighth grade. Some of the boys were pretty big, and pandemonium could rage in the homeroom. The female homeroom teacher would yell loudly to get the class's attention. Often it didn't work. One of the larger boys once bounced her off the wall. He tried that subsequently with the male social studies teacher and got himself soundly bounced off the wall. I didn't see him after that. I sat next to another fully man-sized boy who apparently had been held back several years or had been away from school for a while. He seemed nice enough but spoke slowly, and he clearly had problems with academics.

The small, somewhat elderly Mrs. Lightheart was our English teacher and also the school librarian. She never raised her voice but somehow maintained iron control in her classroom. I could never understand how she did it when the other teachers kept much less control and our homeroom teacher hardly any at all.

We had a whole hour for lunch in those days, whereas in today's schools, kids are lucky to get twenty minutes. This was the age of rock and roll, so after eating, many kids went to dance and socialize in the gym, where music played every day at lunchtime. I never participated, but the indoor track upstairs that surrounded the gym was a great place to watch the activities. I usually went to Mrs. Lightheart's library, where it was always quiet, and read the *World Book Encyclopedia.* I skipped most of the biographies, unless it was someone I'd heard of, but read much of the rest. By this time, we had gotten the same encyclopedia at home, a big expense for my dad, so I had that to read when I got bored.

Once, in eighth-grade science class, the teacher was explaining how a rocket worked. He said it moved because exhaust gas came out of its end and pushed on the air. I'd already been through most of the Q-R World Book and knew how rockets worked, but thought a simple way to show the problem was to ask, "If they push on the air, how can they work out in space?" He thought about that and said, "They don't." The next day, the teacher announced how rockets do work and ended with "I stand corrected." I realized how embarrassing the whole thing was for him and felt I had done the wrong thing. After that, I was careful and seldom asked questions in any class.[2]

My first encounter with electricity was years earlier at an outlet in our house in California. I was not grounded to anything, so the jolt was confined to my hand but enough to give me a solid memory. Later on, there were always various electrical and electronic parts available from Dad's TV repair business and left over from his ham radio days that I could use for "experiments." These were interesting and only a few verged on the spectacular. Damage to the house electrical system was minimal and easily fixed by Dad. He never seemed upset about any of this. He and his twin brother learned radio and electronics on their own when young. I should have thought to ask him if he had any experiences similar to mine.

Once, soon after moving to Coeur d'Alene, I turned on the bathwater and went to do something while the tub filled. The forgotten tub overflowed, of course, and there was a bit of redecorating, especially with the floor covering. Dad always saved a lot of money by fixing these issues himself.

I got a chemistry set for Christmas. The sets were different then, with thirty or more small bottles, each with a different chemical. These were the real thing and, I think, full strength. One time, I started a fire during one of my experiments down in the basement. The blaze stayed small due to limited material, yet created an unusually large amount of smoke. The forced air furnace then circulated that about the house and it settled on the walls upstairs, causing most of the rooms to get repainted. Dad did have something to say about that. I did hear something about an insurance settlement. I wonder if they got a discount on the premiums when I finally moved out for college?

I enjoyed my Erector set, which I got for Christmas when in the fifth grade. I was hoping for the 10½ Amusement Park set but was fortunate my parents could afford the 8½ Giant Ferris Wheel set. The first thing I built was a lit, rotating airplane beacon on a tower taller than I was. This was followed by an equally tall elevator and various trestle, cantilever, bascule, and other bridges. There were different types of motorized cranes, steam engines, and of course, the giant Ferris wheel. I also built model kits as I could afford to get them with paper route money. The largest of these was an entire nuclear power plant. I liked building things.

During my junior high years, I got an afternoon paper route that covered a few blocks of a residential area. I did this on my bike for several years and was free to spend earnings on things like model kits, model railroading, and SCUBA diving equipment. I later earned more from delivering a morning newspaper from Spokane. Early Sunday mornings in the dark, with snow on the ground, and below zero temperatures were tough. I could not carry all my papers for the huge Sunday edition walking, let alone on my bike, so halfway through my route, I had to trudge back to the drop place and get the rest of them. I've never liked cold weather and it didn't get colder than that. I was fortunate this was not a full-time job.

Dad learned they were hiring, and I became a box boy at Albertsons supermarket. Box boys bagged groceries, carried them to the customers' cars, swept floors, stocked shelves, and stamped prices on items. None of the other box boys were in my high school. They were different than any kids I had known. All of them smoked and were a pretty rough bunch, although they never bothered or teased me for being different. They frequently talked about their visits to prostitutes in Wallace, Idaho fifty miles to the east. I think they realized that visiting a prostitute for me was over the top, but they were always wanting me to try smoking. I had no intention of starting up with that, but I finally took a drag in the backroom when they were all around, had a coughing fit, and that seemed to satisfy their curiosity. They stopped asking me.

The box boy culture was strange to me, but while I could not have kept up with their activities outside of work, I had no problems working with them. Most must have dropped out of school; some had worked up to checking and perhaps were looking to a career in the store. Unlike them, I was having problems smiling, and at times was not so friendly with customers. I never directly said or did anything bad, but if I had a down day, it would show through. Once a customer even said in a nice way, "Hey, smile a little, things can't be that bad." He was right. They weren't bad, but I just could not smile and relate to people that way. After three months, the assistant manager took me aside and said they would have to lay me off.[3] Working with people constantly was hard for me.

I knew everyone had to work. A great concern at that time was what I could do. Mom took me to the local main street men's shop to get a shirt once. No other customers were in the store. I still remember Mr. Simon standing alone in the store, dressed in a suit, just looking across the room at nothing. It seemed that I would end up doing a job like that, maybe for the rest of my life. The same thing every day. The thought did not exactly frighten me. "Crush" would be a better word.

In ninth grade, I was back with a better, more academic

group. I had my homeroom with our algebra teacher. While arithmetic up to the eighth grade was not a great subject for me, I came alive in algebra. I learned it easily and missed no problems in tests or homework. This continued through the rest of high school for all math courses. Around this time, I woke up one day while walking through the halls and realized that I now actually liked coming to school.

I had only two real friends in grades ten through twelve at Coeur d'Alene Senior High School, but most all of the kids were fine. The "in group" of socially aware kids were nice enough but were definitely in another world from mine. The athletic jocks were also around but did not rule, and the few rougher types kept to themselves.

There were three or four of us who went around with slide rules on our belts. This was hardly a "group," and I didn't know my other fellow nerds that well. The school being three blocks east of my house certainly helped. I never went to games, although I did attend required pep rallies during school time. I joined no clubs, not even the science club, and was in no honor or other societies that I knew about. In my school annuals, I am in no pictures or lists except for the required headshot. This was not the way to get a good record for college acceptance.

Dad often transcribed Morse code with a typewriter as a ham operator and in his radio communication jobs in World War II. He wanted me to learn to type. Typing was considered a secretarial skill and not for those of us on the academic track. I had trouble with the many minor arithmetic problems in the test required to qualify for the class, so I did not finish or get enough of them right. This was the only time that Dad ever came to school to intervene on my behalf.[4] I did take the class in tenth grade. There was no more arithmetic, just typing, and I did OK. Of course, this ended up helping me a great deal when

I started working with computers in graduate school. I was an average physics graduate student there, but certainly the best on the keypunch machine and computer terminals. I punched 20,000 lines of code for one program I typed and maintained 80,000 lines of code when the terminals and machine program storage became available. In my subsequent jobs and businesses, I spent about 80 percent of my time at terminal or PC keyboards. Dad saved me a lot of time there.

Overall, high school was a good experience. I had two good friends and we learned a lot from each other. Those in the popular group were pretty good kids. They didn't lord it over kids of a different social class or cause us any trouble. Indeed, while I looked at them as a class above, I'm not so sure most of them looked at me or the rest of us as beneath them. I heard only one unkind word from a boy in the popular class and even that might have been a misunderstanding. Otherwise, every one of the "high class" kids behaved and spoke remarkably well. It's obvious now, if not then, that much of their popularity came from this. After all, they were more socially mature than us; I suppose you would expect them to do better.

[1] The experts that banned dodgeball to protect our self-esteem seem dense. Dodgeball was much easier on me because if I failed or succeeded, I did not mess things up for others in a team, like I did when I missed the ball in baseball or volleyball. Why didn't they ban those games? You can escape notice in a game like dodgeball and not be a critical part of anything. I didn't want a prize, I wanted to be ignored. A game where everyone gets a turn is the worst. You are on display when your turn comes, and you mess up.

[2] Causing embarrassment for someone else was the very worst thing I could imagine doing to anyone. I hated it more than anything when it happened to me, as when I returned the stolen trucks in chapter four or sang a solo in chapter five. I was so ashamed by what I did to that teacher I could not talk to him again. I used books for my questions and seldom asked them in class even in college. In a church Sunday school class today I will keep my mouth shut. I don't fear being wrong; I fear being right. I'll ask you if there's no audience.

[3] Besides my customer interaction, there may have been another reason. One night, when I was marking prices, the ink can on my shopping cart got tilted and the ink slowly ran out onto the floor. I was not in the aisles marking prices when this happened. My cart was right in the middle of the "up front" area where you waited to get to the checkout counters. While the floor had a neutral pattern to hide imperfections, it certainly did not hide the foot and a half wide black spot that appeared while I was distracted doing something else. You could see it from anywhere in the front part of the store. They finally got the ink out with bleach, leaving a big white spot, just as noticeable, that remained until they tore the building down years later to replace it with a larger store.

[4] While Mom always would meet with the teacher for the standard conferences, she never otherwise intervened or tried to fix anything for me at school. Parents didn't do that back then. Anyway, at this point, I can't identify anything else like this that either Mom or Dad could or should have done for me at any point in my schooling.

In my senior year, I learned that Dad was a good friend and a long time fishing buddy with the high school principal, my tenth-grade biology teacher, and my twelfth-grade physics teacher. Maybe he had a lot of pull at my high school.

TO BUILD A HOUSE I

The first principle is that you must not fool yourself, and you are the easiest person to fool. – ***Richard P. Feynman***

1104 N 15th St. today. Built as a duplex for my parents on the left, grandma on the right. The garage is right, entered from the end.

During my high school senior year, I designed a duplex for my parents and grandmother. It's that long, low house at Fifteenth and Birch in Coeur d'Alene, Idaho. I started a fourplex design with extra rentals after Dad's politicking changed the zoning for his lot, but funding realities changed our design to a duplex. We needed at least a duplex because Mom's mother, the only grandmother I ever knew (my dad's mother died two weeks after my birth) would come to live with us. Her sister, Aunt Sada, would go to live with her son Clarence. The sale of Grandma's house would help finance the lot purchase and construction of the new duplex.

I got interested in house planning from my junior high friend Rod, who wanted to be an architect. He was often doing drawings when I visited him. I worked hard to complete the plan and elevation drawings and thought I'd done a great job. I dropped by an architectural office just to show off my plans. The guy who invited me to the back was happy to take a look. The floorplan was OK, and then he quickly sketched some of the shapes he extracted from the front elevation view. They did appear convoluted when seen that way. Another minute or two and he rough sketched the start of a simpler, cleaner alternative.

Both deflated and excited by ideas for a much better front appearance, I finished up a modified plan and gave it to Dad. He knew I had significant help, even if it was only a few minutes of ideas. Additional details were also needed for city approval, so he took the plan down to the same architect and got it completed for an affordable amount. Dad didn't like the idea of maybe getting the better of someone. I got to pore over the architect-produced plans and learn more about the details needed to make a house plan set complete.

Construction started the spring before I left for college. I saw the completed house when I came home for Christmas. Grandma had moved to the other unit as well.

Once, I came by during spring construction to see most of

the walls framed and raised upright on the floor platform. As I wandered through, Mom and Dad's bedroom appeared larger than I expected and the adjoining living room smaller. I measured across the plywood subfloor and then checked the jobsite plan copy. The dimensions agreed; the plan seemed to look right, but the actual rooms still did not. Taking an architect's scale to the plan showed the problem. On the plan, the wall separating the bedroom and living room scaled differently by two feet from the dimensions I had written on the plan! The plan was drawn and scaled correctly but the incorrect written dimensions were easier for the builder to follow.

The builder was not happy but required just a couple of hours to fix things at that stage.

What a stupid mistake! Did anyone else do things that dumb? Consistency is important. What if I drew a window in one place on the plan and had offset it on the elevation? No doubt one of those views would represent what I wanted, and the other would direct what the builder did. Neither the architect nor the builder caught the error I made. The architect just copied it into his version. The builder just used it to position the wall.

There was a framing plan, an electrical plan, a plumbing plan, a plan for the kitchen cabinets, exterior elevations, interior elevations. Things could look right but be wrong. Did they all agree?

I got my plan set and spent some anxious hours. Nothing else came up.

In college, I forgot this experience in home design. I was going into physics and then into computers, not architecture. I was forty-four and learning a new way to write software when it came back to me.

Dad had bought a large lot for the new house and later sold the back portion to a homebuilder to raise some cash. The homebuilder did not build a home. The second time I came home for Christmas, there was a two-story apartment building that ideally would have been further from our back lot line. Dad's politicking for that fourplex came back to bite him.

COLLEGE AT SPC

When one asked him what boys should learn, "That," said he, "which they shall use when men." – ***Plutarch****, Morals*

On my first date except for that one almost date in high school, it didn't seem right to just sit there. The girl sat scooted right next to me from when I first got in the back seat of the car, so it was easy to just put my arm around her shoulders. That may have been the signal, because she turned and was on me. I had my traumatic first kiss: her smoking made her taste terrible. She persistently continued while I was thinking about how to reduce the activity while not being rude. Rude would have been appropriate then but knowing "appropriate" in social situations would not be one of my abilities for a few years yet.

She was starting to paw away at areas best left unpawed when I decided I needed to use the restroom. This took some time to find at a drive-in movie, and by the time I made it back after losing my way once, her passion, or my irresistibility, had waned.

I had a lot to learn at college. Not everyone graduating from my north Idaho high school in the '60s expected to go to college, but from when I first heard about college, I knew I would go. This originally came from Dad, although later math and science teachers also encouraged me. Dad had been valedictorian of his high school in Kellogg, a small north Idaho mining town, but financially and culturally was far from able to attend college.

Dad had become an amateur radio enthusiast at the beginning of that hobby and knew everything there was to know about radio. Somehow, he got enough money to buy parts and build equipment, some well beyond what is permissible today. He told me how when he pressed the key down to send Morse code, the neighbor's back porch light would glow. Six years after high school graduation, he was teaching naval radiomen recruits in all their future WWII tasks at the University of Idaho. Mom told me how awkward she felt at her first tea for faculty wives at age nineteen, so they both knew something about college.

I was not in shouting distance of our valedictorian but was good in math and physical science and above average in other things. I was glad to be going to an average college somewhere. I did not know of anyone saying anything about going to a big-name university except the University of Idaho.

I had never seen a college except for the small junior college / vocational school in my town. The school guidance counselor told me about some colleges in Idaho and Washington, but none of that information meant anything to me. The only other place I had heard about was the California Institute of Technology. I sent a letter to them which they were quick to return. I would not be going there. The pastor of our small Baptist church talked up his college to Mom and then took me there on his next visit to Seattle. Seattle Pacific College (SPC) was the only college I had ever seen and at 2,000 students, seemed plenty big to me. I was impressed. Further good feelings came when I met some physics professors. I already sent SATs and grades ahead and they told me I could get in.

The Free Methodist Church started SPC as a Bible school to train pastors and missionaries. Along the way, it added liberal arts and was known for its pastoral, education, and nursing programs when I arrived in '64.

Seven years after Sputnik, the space race was going strong and our country decided it had to have more physicists. I'm sure the big universities got most of the government money but physics at SPC got some. At seven professors, most at the PhD level, plus the engineering guy, the physics department was large for a college like SPC and was plenty adequate for me. I don't think I was ready for a large university.

It would have been interesting had SPC launched a computer science department, but it was too soon for that. Even Stanford did not have one until a year after I started college.

Discounting first-year and survey courses (astronomy, basic science, a science course for nurses, etc.) the physics student to faculty ratio was about 3 to 1, so if I wanted to see a professor, I'd knock on the door. When we could not decide something in his office, we might both go upstairs and work it out in the lab. I worked hard, did well in class, and worked through other physics texts outside the coursework.

I had interesting times with Dr. Anderson who would get so excited when talking about areas of quantum theory he was working on. Another student and I got together with him for a general relativity course one quarter and that was great. Dr. Crichton liked to talk about the basic foundations of modern physics and Dr. Ogden was really into educating incoming students and making sure they understood the basics.

Professor Hughson taught different types of engineering and was as close as SPC got to a computer science professor. I took a short Fortran class from him and wrote a program on fifty-three punch cards. It took maybe three runs to debug it and get it going. Each run required a trip over the University of Washington to feed in our punch cards to the IBM 7094 mainframe. We then came back several days later to pick up the printed results. Programming was interesting but at that pace not exciting.

The second floor of the boys' side of the Hill dormitory where I lived was the closest thing you could find to a fraternity at SPC. The "Nads" tried to operate at the limits of respectability and worked at appearing more disreputable than they really were. Given the conservative nature of our institution, they did not have to push very far to pull this off.

SPC had chapel every weekday morning at 9 in McKinley auditorium. The mix of religion, music, outside speakers, and our professors from all disciplines gave a great overview of the world's knowledge that was especially good for an overspecialized student like me. It was not long into my first year that all forty Nads worked through the wee morning to unbolt every bottom cushion from the traditional fold-down theater seating and stack them neatly on the stage. Even though there could be no chapel the next morning, it was satisfying that everyone came in to take a look.

A month or two afterward, just as a music professor placed his hands on the pipe organ's keyboard, a loud toilet flush, followed by "better flush twice, it has to go all the way to the commons," another flush, and finally Paul Revere and the Raiders singing "I can almost taste it now" blared from the PA system. What had been a solemn moment proved hard to recapture.

With many students going into music, church ministry, studying instruments, and singing in the well-known acapella choir, the start of chapel was by far the best "congregational singing" I've ever heard. A biology major on our second floor was able to get white lab mice by the boxful and procured an adequate amount. All were seated in chapel and singing when at various places someone suddenly stood up. Singing died away to other sounds as more stood until many were up looking down at the floor. This was before much of today's animal rights activism, but I can still say that everyone did what they could, even resorting to some unusual movements, to avoid stepping on or otherwise damaging a mouse. I heard no one talking about a squashed mouse anywhere and now assume those mice were better off than if they had gone to wherever lab mice normally went.

Our disruptions were a small amount of the total. Each college department put significant effort into presenting something worthwhile in chapel when its turn came. Little of this eclectic mix of the world's wisdom was targeted to my field of study, and I probably would have used my time for more career-oriented learning if I had the choice. Fortunately, the choice was not given, and so I learned a lot more than physics and math at college. After I left, when my sister was attending SPC, students started agitating to make chapel voluntary. I just looked at the college website, and chapel is now held once a week, is voluntary, and has significantly reduced importance and attendance. Another unfortunate example of institutions giving in to what the students want.

The Hill second-floor guys would often congregate in the room of one of the informal leaders and talk about things that interested college boys. A discussion of how best to make out with a girl somehow brought up my inexperience. Now I'm not sure how experienced some of them actually were, but at least I was not as experienced at hiding my deficiency. The consensus was that, since I had not had a date before, I was past due for development in that area in order to get up to speed with the rest of the group.

Bruce had a car and his girlfriend knew someone, so a double date to a drive-in movie was arranged which led to the experience at the start of this chapter. In the front seat, Bruce and his girlfriend quickly demonstrated knowledge of the main topic for drive-in movies. My date then pitched in and gave it a good effort, but things did not work out. She was not an SPC student (she smoked) and was not so attractive to me.

Upon my return to the dorm after this adventure, everyone was packed into one room and asked how it went. I still had not caught on that there was a plot and wasn't sure what to think about the date. The standard talk I had heard about blind dates came back to me, and I just thought that things could go wrong like they did that night. What everyone was expecting must not have happened, and neither side was interested in any more blind dates for me.

I had one arranged date in high school but did try dating in college, averaging maybe two or three dates per year. Sometimes I would go out a second time with the same girl. I never made three times with anyone, nor was passion, such as on that first date, encountered again.

I had a 1954 Plymouth from my sophomore to senior years.

When parked, its left taillight would come on for unknown reasons and run down the battery, so I would open the trunk and disconnect its wire when parking. Sometimes on a cold winter night, water would run in around the edge of the trunk lid, freeze, and stick the trunk shut.

On one date, my second with this girl, we went to Seattle Center to hear the famous pianist Arthur Rubinstein, who at eighty showed that a practice a day keeps the arthritis away. He was really good. It was cold when we went back to the parking lot and sure enough, the trunk would not open. I used my standard method of climbing up on the trunk and jumping up and down on it to break it loose. I never did slip and fall doing this, got the light reconnected fine, but somehow the girl was not impressed with my athletic ability. On the third try, she turned me down.

You'd think I had opportunities to date at a school that was 65 percent female. One year, the physics department asked me to run a weekly lab and some classes for a "physics for nurses" course. All I learned was that I was not good at teaching.

SPC was on the quarter system. I had a scholarship and a small loan, but nothing like today's big loans. Dad had paid for my first quarter. He said nothing about finances, but I knew I needed to help all I could. I found a job at night on the school's switchboard in the student union and occasionally assisting a marine botany professor on his dives. The physics department had government money for a few projects. I assisted with electronics and some telemetry antennas for a satellite project. All three jobs, especially the diving, continued into the summer, so I did not see home in Idaho except sometimes at Christmas and a week or two in the summer.

My first quarter was all Dad ever paid for college. Three years later, when my sister went to Seattle Pacific, Dad paid her first quarter. She made the big bucks at Alaskan fisheries (onshore, thank goodness) in the summer and paid for the rest of school that way. Had we not raised enough funds, I'm sure Dad would have thought of something. He thought of college for us as a need, not a want.

College graduation with Dad, Mom, sister, and Grandma.

Dad put me on his own checking account. He told me if anything came up to take what I needed and just write and tell him the amount. He was concerned when I wrote about the $10,000 check, but never called or said anything. He later learned from his statement that, in my letter to him, I had forgotten the decimal point for a $100 check. He never said anything to me, but my aunt Marge did mention that there was a small amount of consternation when my letter arrived.

I did study hard in college. I'm not sure why I didn't study in my dorm room. All my roommates were great and would not have been a distraction from work. It was months before I realized the one thing the whole school seemed to know about me. It was my place at one end of a table in the library. I was there a lot. I often spread other open books and papers to one side of me or even across toward the other side of the table, since there was always room to do that. Whenever I came into the library that place was always empty, so I went there without thinking. Had someone else sat there, I would have just gone to another place. They never did.

Dad and Mom came to graduation, and I was called up at the end for an award. I didn't have it for long. Dad kept that on the wall in his office until he died.

~

That blind-date girl certainly seemed willing. What if she had been cute, a good conversationalist, demure but available, and turned out to taste OK? Let's add we were alone in the car without the two in the front seat. What would have happened? I have no idea. I did have awfully high standards, even then, for what made a girl attractive to me. They were beyond anything reasonable for anyone, let alone for someone like me. I did not think of it like that. I just remember no girl I was ever around seemed particularly attractive to me. Anyway, studies, not a social life, were my priority. If I had put forth a more consistent effort at dating, maybe I would have done better.

CLARENCE

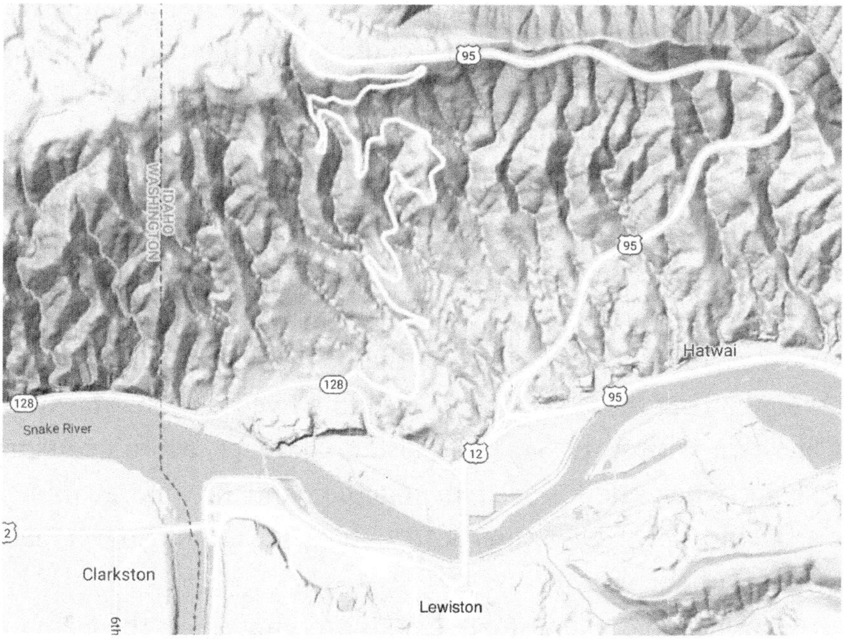

The zigzag white line is the Old Spiral Highway. The top at the north is 2000 feet above the bottom at the south. The new road (95) is to its right. Google Maps.

We had almost made it to the top of the steep grade cut into the side of the hill, but rising two thousand feet had made a difference in the road condition, slowing us down to a stop on the icy surface. Applying power just spun the tires, causing the back end to slide toward the drop-off at the outer edge. I told my passenger, a girl my age I had just met, that I would have to get out and put on the tire chains. Fortunately, other people had sense enough to stay off the hill in weather like this, and we saw no other cars on the hill that day.

I locked the parking brake and got out to get the chains. The car was sliding backward! With my foot on the brake, I had locked all four tires, but the parking brake held only the back wheels. Did she notice she was moving? Getting behind a car sliding toward me was not an ideal thing to do, but the car continued slowly enough that I could get to the trunk and get the chains out of it and throw them under the locked back wheels, stopping the slide.

It was Mom's cousin Clarence who had gotten the idea of me coming down to Clarkston, Washington and taking the daughter of his friend back to college after Christmas break. My mother's father died when she was five months old, and Grandma did not marry the grandfather I knew until Mom was seven. During those six years, Grandma lived out on a farm in Clarkston with Aunt Sada, her sister. Clarence, Mom's cousin, was six when they moved in together and became an older brother to her. They were both only children and never had other brothers or sisters.

Clarence told many stories about growing up on the farm in the 1920s and '30s. Older kids would strip him and his friends down to their shorts and trap them outside at night in the winter. He and his friends would get payback by trapping them in a barn and pelting them with rotten eggs from the hayloft until they were sick. There were many fights and rough stuff. That's how kids grew up then and they were accustomed to it. I loved hearing his stories. Clarence's mother, my Aunt Sada, told about the day his father had bought a Model T Ford. Clarence drove it into a telephone pole and knocked himself unconscious. Back then, they just took you home, put you to bed, and hoped you got better. After a few days, he did, but did not remember what happened.

Clarence knew I liked to swim and told me of his adventures in the Snake River with whirlpools, being swept way further downstream than expected, catching a sturgeon so large they pulled it out of the river with a car, etc. It was an adventurous time if you lived through it.

Clarence had a high school education, plus the education of being a Seabee in the south Pacific during World War II. He smiled all the time, was always "up" and friendly to everyone, all the time. He genuinely liked everyone, and they could tell that. It was hard to feel anything but good when you were around Clarence.

Clarence started working at the Lewiston pulp mill after the war and, despite his education, his personality moved him into the executive offices. He was the guy they sent out to smooth things over when there was trouble with the union, a major customer, or anyone else. It was just too hard to be mad and upset around Clarence.

Clarence and Evelyn, his wife, lived in Clarkston, Washington, 120 miles south of where we lived in Coeur d'Alene, Idaho. My grandma and grandpa also lived there close to Clarence and Aunt Sada. Mom, Sharon, myself, and sometimes Dad drove down every few months to visit all of them.

In my junior year at Seattle Pacific College, a friend of Clarence's at the mill had a daughter my age or a year younger who went to college in Kirkland, next door to Seattle. Clarence told me how cute she was and suggested we should get together. The chance came after Christmas break. I had my '54 Plymouth then and could drive her back to her school. I would finally get to meet this girl Clarence had talked about so much.

I drove down and stayed overnight with Clarence so we could get an early start the next day. The girl's dad brought her over the next morning. She looked fine and seemed a bit on the quiet side but was reasonably friendly and we soon were on our way. Just out of town, I would have to rise 2,000 feet, climbing the seven-mile-long Lewiston grade[1] to the plateau that went on all the way to Coeur d'Alene and from there on to the northern border of Idaho. It was a winding road with hairpin turns whose steepness could cause trouble even if it wasn't midwinter. This time the road turned out to be "compact snow and ice" as the radio reports used to say many mornings when we listened for the road and school closing reports at breakfast years ago in Coeur d'Alene.

After our adventure near the top of the hill, I got the chains on OK but came out of the ordeal with my pants mostly soaked and otherwise quite messed up. I'm not sure whether that experience gave my passenger a scare or not, especially the car sliding with her in it after I got out. It was a slow slide; I think from the pressure of my tires having to melt the ice before it became slippery enough for them to slide on the film of water. Anyway, we didn't talk further about it.

We talked a little, enough to avoid long silences, for the remaining 300 miles of the trip and I was able to drop her off at her school in fine shape. Our first time together was OK, although not anything special.

I didn't know whether I had made a good impression or not, but about two weeks later I got up the courage to ask her on a date somewhere. She was unable to go, so I took that as a signal she preferred not going out with me, which was the state I expected for such things. I did not call again and forgot about her.

Sometime later, while visiting Clarence, he mentioned that the girl was disappointed that I never called her back after that first time. I didn't know what to think of that. She did not seem to want me to call her back. When she turned me down in that phone call, she could have said something like, "I really would like to be able to go with you. I hope you can call me again," and I would have done so. Maybe that's what she would have wanted to do had she thought of it. Given my past performances, should I have expected her to say just the right thing on a sudden phone call? It's tough being young and learning the hard way how to do things correctly.

Anyway, summer had started, she was home in Clarkston, but I would return to Seattle and my jobs at the college, putting us 300 miles apart. I was just not interested enough to pursue her further. Before I originally met her, Clarence had made her sound wonderful, but everyone sounded nicer and more beautiful when Clarence talked about them. That's just how he was and how he saw things.[2]

Clarence was my dad's age but lived twenty years longer. It was great to continue to visit him for so long. Clarence died at ninety-five after a short illness in 2014. Mom died at ninety a month later.

~

[1] A new freeway now gets you up the hill in an easy drive with long gradual curves. The old Lewiston grade is still there but is now called the Old Spiral Highway. You can still drive it instead

of the freeway. I took Sue down it once. When I suggested we take it again a few years later, she said, "No way."

If you check, you'll see that I could have avoided that grade altogether and saved seventy-three miles off the trip by going a different route. I would have done that if Google Maps had been available then. Figuring that out the mileage difference with paper maps was possible but not often done. I just took the routes I was familiar with, driving from Clarkston to Spokane Washington, and then on to Seattle on Interstate 90.

[2] I don't want you to think Clarence didn't know real beauty when he saw it. His wife Evelyn was a true bombshell, knockout beauty. She did area TV commercials for car dealers, since back then a beautiful woman was expected to stand in front of the car with her arm extended toward it as if to say, "Now there's the real beauty." She turned down opportunities to go further in modeling and TV. Clarence saw her on TV, searched, found her, and married her. When I was five, I once watched her apply her red nail polish, something I had not seen before. Even at that age, I could tell she was a unique woman.

She had beauty and he had charm. What could go wrong? Nothing, as it turned out. She was like a movie star in most aspects except one: they stayed together, and stayed in love into their nineties.

WHAT GRAD SCHOOL?

By graduation, I had learned physics far beyond the single course I had in high school and it had kept my interest. I was ready to learn more, but as yet had not developed an interest in any one field of physics over another.

Everyone assumed I would continue to grad school; it was the only sensible thing to do. Physics departments at most major universities had government funding for their US students, so if I was accepted at one of them, chances were most of my tuition and even some living expenses would be paid. My professors all thought I would get in somewhere.

If you asked me then what my future career might be, I would have answered that I was uncertain, but thinking of teaching physics in a small college. I might even come back to SPC. I knew physicists also worked for companies, but I was pretty fuzzy about any details. A job as a professor at SPC seemed to come with a nice lifestyle. Most of them lived on Queen Anne Hill near the campus. One, actually a math professor, invited students to his home for get-togethers on a few occasions.

The first thing I did was to buy a bike, the best way to get around on campus. I could use it all year, with the weather being warmer than Seattle or Coeur d'Alene

I had no clue about doing research. I had yet to learn about the frontiers of physics and so had no way of selecting any one of them. Certainly, to work at a large university a research area was necessary, but I would have to learn about that in the future. About a third of the physics professors at SPC did research, but I was uncertain how serious any of that was, so teaching should work regardless. I had not thought about whether I would actually like working with a class of students.

I applied to at least ten physics graduate schools and also to scholarships and fellowships during my college senior year. I took standardized tests, some of which were specifically for physics. I first learned that I did well on the tests, then one or two acceptances came in.

It had been eleven years since the launch of Sputnik, but the government was still in the space race and had yet to reach the moon, so money still flowed to physics. One early acceptance was a National Science Foundation fellowship. This paid tuition to any US graduate school, plus living expenses for four or more years. It turned out this was the important acceptance.

Graduate school acceptances then poured in from every school where I applied. The schools also got notifications of the fellowship. The schools had government money to support their graduate students, but if they accepted me, they could keep that money. Several schools even awarded me prestigious fellowships named for some famous, or at least rich, donor. One was the Higgins Faculty Fellowship from Columbia. It did have a nice ring to it. They could hand out the award without having to back it up with the funding, so why not?

I was hoping for some acceptances but did not expect them from every place I applied. This did make the decision easy, however. I picked the only institution where it never snowed. I went to Stanford.

~

I disagree with those who today disparage standardized tests. They involve some unfairness, but what can replace them more fairly? When sociologists do their studies, SAT scores correlate better with later success in college than anything else available to colleges. IQ tests are not legal or are considered racist by many. Not that they're really great, but there is nothing better. Without them, we'd rely more on how someone in admissions feels after reading over whatever else is left to look at. Maybe their essay? They didn't have any help with that, right? I got my only college D on my first quarter's required literary term paper. I would have killed that essay.

My SAT results were among the top group in my high school. A couple in that group got a special scholarship award. My math scores could have gotten me that, but other subjects brought things down. Given my solid but not outstanding school grade average I think the SAT helped to get me into college. Where would even a great grade average get me, if it was from what at that time was a small logging town's high school? As my college studies ended, doing well on another standardized test, the Graduate Record Physics exam, certainly helped me a lot more. I was the top graduate for the physics department, but there were only three of us that year, so I did need that good test score.

THE DRAFT

You will kill ten of us, we will kill one of you, but in the end, you will tire of it first. — ***Ho Chi Minh***

I'd read how it made sense for the United States to fight, but it made sense to them to fight also. Did it make sense for me?

The Vietnam War was going strong when I graduated college in 1968. I stayed on after graduation to finish up some work I was doing for the physics department and continued with some other jobs I had with the school. I was pretty glum much of the time due to my likelihood of being drafted into the war.

I had a great opportunity for graduate school, but deferments were given only for undergraduate study, which I had just finished. I thought that, for me, slogging through the swamps in Vietnam was unlikely but I had little hope of avoiding some years of military service. By this time, even those of us with a conservative outlook had decided that this particular war was a pretty useless exercise but did not know how to avoid it. I still had a month at home before going to graduate school and I would not be hearing from my local north Idaho draft board until the end of the year or after.

My '54 Plymouth just barely made it home and was then found beyond reasonable repair. I had funds left over from school jobs and Dad offered to go halves for a new car, a 1968 Buick Skylark. It had the small six, and few cars in north Idaho had aircon then, but it was beyond anything I had imagined. To the extent a car can make a young man cool, I was suddenly cool. Getting a new car six months before getting drafted was not the most sensible thing to do, but Dad and Mom could use it if I had to go.

I went to the army recruiter in nearby Spokane, Washington to check out alternatives to the draft. I was a college graduate, so he suggested I take a few standard armed forces tests appropriate for that. I had gotten reasonably competent at that sort of thing and made him happy he met me. He suggested I take the one-year Officer Candidate School (OCS) and enter as an officer. Some officers did slog through swamps then, but he thought it unlikely I would be doing that.

My eyes did not work together due to a slight birth defect. I use both for peripheral vision but do not have normal stereo vision. I ignore my right eye for most of my vision. I had a note from the eye doctor regarding this. The recruiter checked and said I would not fly a plane, drive a tank, and probably not shoot a gun (Yay!) but would be fine with many other jobs in the army.

If I had to go, that made more sense. Going in as a draftee

could still be dangerous. I've had little experience but think some people close one eye when aiming a gun, and with one eye closed, my vision was as good as anyone's. The army wouldn't spend the time to train a two-year draftee for anything complex. Driving a tank and flying a plane would be off the table anyway. Shooting a gun with one eye closed, on the other hand…

Misery is better with company, so I talked my cousin Jim, the son of Dad's identical twin, into checking out the army. He was three months older than me, had just graduated from college, and was admitted to a great graduate school back east in physics. He had everything I had except my school had better weather. He took the same army tests with predictable results, so we could both go in and were likely to do our first-year OCS together. Once we signed up, two new officers might get our recruiter a bonus.

It was not to be. A week later, he said, "I've had it, I'm just going off to grad school and will see if I can think of something," and was gone. It looked different going into the army alone, and Jim did have a point about the difference between the uncertain future he faced and making it completely certain by signing on the line. It was fall and not only the local draft board but the coming north Idaho winter was weighing me down. I loaded up my new car and was off to sunny times in California, a thousand miles away from my draft board.

~

If Jim had not up and left me, I would have signed up with him and that would have been that. I had it all planned and that included Jim. After he blew everything up, my plans to be an army officer didn't look the same as before. What had seemed best one way now looked obvious the other way.

Some months later, the draft caught up with Jim, who arranged a last-minute interview with Admiral Hyman Rickover, the "Father of the Nuclear Navy." The admiral proved more than capable at dealing with our local draft board and Jim spent a few years (not all at once) underwater as a nuclear power officer. The draft caught up with me about the same time, but I never did enter the military.

OFF TO GRADUATE SCHOOL

*It's a dangerous business, Frodo, going out your door. You step onto the road, and if you don't keep your feet, there's no knowing where you might be swept off to. — **J R R Tolkien***

The first of my two best driving trips from my early life was my return to my second year at Seattle Pacific college in my "new" '54 Plymouth, my first car ever. There was that "D" in term paper class, but otherwise, I did well for my first year, and Dad got me a yellow four-door car with a white top. He looked it over and then, jerking the wheel side to side as he drove it, said, "This will do." He did have to get four new tires at the local hardware store. They cost more than the car.

The second trip was to graduate school in my brand-new Buick. I had taken that 1000-mile drive before. I was in the third grade when my family moved from California to Idaho. A year before that, Dad and I had walked halfway out on the Golden Gate Bridge. I wanted to cross that again.

At Stanford with my Buick Skylark in the lot near McFarland apartments, where I lived.

I was near Weed, California when I pulled over to sleep. I woke up to a police officer showing a light through the window. I told him I was on my way to grad school. When I got my registration from the glove compartment, he saw my dad's large, sheathed hunting knife in there and told me it was considered a concealed weapon since it was inside the compartment. He said I shouldn't be sleeping there but didn't need to move until morning. He told me to keep the knife in the trunk and drove off. Maybe he told the other police because no one else bothered me that night.

I woke up early, got on the road, and crossed the bridge into San Francisco. This was my first time in California since leaving Ventura in the early third grade, so I avoided risking my new car downtown and headed south after the bridge. The road soon passed through Golden Gate Park, which I knew nothing about. I turned and drove from one end to the other through the most amazing city park I had seen. I stopped at the Steinhart Aquarium, the first aquarium for me. This was getting better and better.

At the end of the 3/4 mile drive from downtown Palo Alto, with palm trees all the way. The church can be seen in the background.

Later that day, I turned off the main road into the university and was in the country on a palm-tree-lined road. After almost a mile, that corridor opened out, showing the old part of the university still a quarter-mile ahead. I'd heard Stanford had a big campus, but this was over the top. This was well before Google Maps could preview a trip. It was surprise after surprise. For a north Idaho boy, "big time" did not get bigger than this.

THEY GOT ME

*Whoever said the pen is mightier than the sword obviously never encountered automatic weapons. — **Douglas MacArthur***

*A survey just released by the Washington National Journal reveals that the Army's draftee GIs were killed in combat last year at nearly double the rate of the Army enlisted men — the volunteer GIs. – **Bill Downs**, ABC Washington, August 14, 1970.*

We had suspected that. I was getting down to the wire. If I lost, could I still get into that officer program? I'd heard that every fourth draftee went into the marines. I might become army tough, but marine tough? That Spokane recruiter might not have the clout that Admiral Rickover had for my cousin.

The October 1967 riot outside the Oakland induction station occurred two years before I visited.

"Draft graduate students; care enough to send the very best," taken from the old Hallmark greeting card commercial, was going around the physics department at Stanford. I was not the only first- or second-year student under the cloud.

I was soon researching how to use a new type of radiation for cancer treatment with a physics professor and Dr. Henry Kaplan at the medical school. Kaplan was most famous for developing the cure for Hodgkin's disease that was sure death for men around age twenty. Effects of his radiation program for a complete cure could end up causing death around age seventy, as it did for a friend of mine, but fifty years and change was still a good trade for him.

I received my draft notice saying I could appear before the board to explain any reasons why they should not take me. I had my first flight since age six and went back to tell them I was in an essential job developing a new way of treating cancer. They didn't buy it. I was going in.

The physics library was on the top floor with a graduate student lounge at one end where various conversations were held about the oncoming draft. I learned how the infamous Oakland induction station operated from several students who had already been there for their draft physical. It looked like there might be a way.

I needed to do something legal, straightforward, and honest: no lying about any condition, running off to Canada, or crazy stuff like wearing women's underwear to the physical. Perhaps the WHOLE truth might be worth trying? I made an appointment with an ophthalmologist in Palo Alto for a full eye exam.

While California was not yet so completely liberal, Palo Alto, as it has in so many areas, was running ahead in this respect, so finding a doctor who felt as I did about the war was easy. I explained my history, asked him to examine me, and then asked for a complete description of my condition. I was slightly farsighted, not enough to bother with correction, but he threw that in also.

I left with a paper that was thirty lines single-space typed. I started reading it and bogged down about four lines in. I had optics courses and thought I knew this stuff, but this doc was way ahead of me. I could have worked through it in a half-hour or so with some reference books, but never did.

I soon got called up and given a time at the Oakland induction station. I went through various tests in big rooms with a lot of other guys all stripped down to their skivvies. There were no eye tests. For the last step, we were in a long hallway lined up to see an army doctor so we could explain any remaining issues. These were the doctors who would evaluate medical conditions not picked up in the basic exam we had just gotten.

The others in the line had no papers with them; they would explain any medical issue they might have to one of the doctors. If I just explained my issue, as I did to the Spokane recruiter, I would probably go in. That's why I had the paper written up.

They surely would not take the time to read what I had. I hoped they wouldn't take the time to ask anything more.

Looking ahead from the back of the line I saw three offices on each side.

"Excuse me," I said. "I have to check something."

I walked past the line and looked in each office. All the doctors except one were young. They were sharp guys from the doctor draft. The other one had white hair. I thought that an older doctor who's any good should by now leading a surgical team or be in a lucrative private practice. Who would want to sit here day after day just listening to excuse after excuse from kids trying to avoid the draft? Maybe the army put him here to end his career here because he was not able to do something more significant. He would probably have the least patience, would not want to dig into the problem I would present, and would just get rid of me.

I started keeping track of when the old doc's office was empty. When I got to the front of the line, I just acted like I forgot something, excused myself, and let the guy behind me go until the right office called. I entered and handed over my paper. No one on earth could have read a significant part of that paper in the time he looked at it. He put it down and stamped me 1-Y: I could be called up only in a national emergency, which Vietnam apparently was not.

I was free to go on with life.

I don't know how proud I should be of that episode. What I did worked, and I did not spend a chunk of my life in the military. While maybe someone went in instead of me, no one likely went into combat or extreme danger in my place. Anyway, it's just as well, since I never wanted to run for office or do TV ads for the NRA.

I don't think any of the three generations after Dad will see a war or at least a war with a draft. I hope not. My dad came of age during WWII. He and his identical twin brother volunteered for the draft, even though they had deferments. They were both 4-F due to congenital holes in their eardrums. Dad found a way to go anyway. He hired on with Mackay Radio as a civilian radio technician, was given a uniform and captain's bars, was sent to French Algeria, and became chief engineer of the Allied radio relay station there.

My grandfather on Mom's side took part in WWI in trench warfare at the front. He never talked about war except to say he got his big toe shot while diving headfirst into a hole. I don't know if he was joking or not. Once he did mention something about Sergeant York. Later I heard from Grandma that in his younger days, he was a bit of a hell-raiser by standards of that time. One night, he rode his horse down the main street of Colfax in Washington, shooting his pistol several times into the air. The judge who gave him a few days in jail for that became the father-in-law of my Aunt Sada, who was sister to the woman he would eventually marry, my grandmother. After returning from the war, Grandpa was completely changed to quiet and soft-spoken. Grandma married him eight years after he returned.

Grandpa had kept two books from the war. One is *History of the 347th Machine Gun Battalion*. It's been on my bookshelf through our last ten moves. I've looked through the first part with pictures from the war. While doing this history, I looked in the back for the first time and found sections listing all the members. In the section for Company C:

Charles H Kirkland (2256136), Private, first class – Winona, Wash. Enlisted at Colfax, Washington, October 5, 1917. Joined at Camp Lewis, Washington, October 26, 1917. Actions engaged in: St. Mihiel, Meuse-Argonne, Ypres-Lys.

I CURE CANCER

Well, not quite, but it was an interesting, if not practical, try.

*If we knew what it was we were doing, it would not be called research, would it? — **Albert Einstein***

The contraption below came to be known as the Stanford Medical Pion Generator (SMPG). The original idea for this kind of device, for other purposes then, came from my advisor, Robert Hofstadter. I designed and did the calculations for the pancake magnet shapes and their positioning and numbers and produced their construction drawings, serving as the graduate student slave labor on this project. No one taught me anything about computers or programming beyond "use the medical school computer." What I was starting to learn about computers and computer graphics was most important to me.

Other than a fifty-punch-card program I wrote for a Fortran (an old coding language) class at Seattle Pacific, I started using computers with this project.

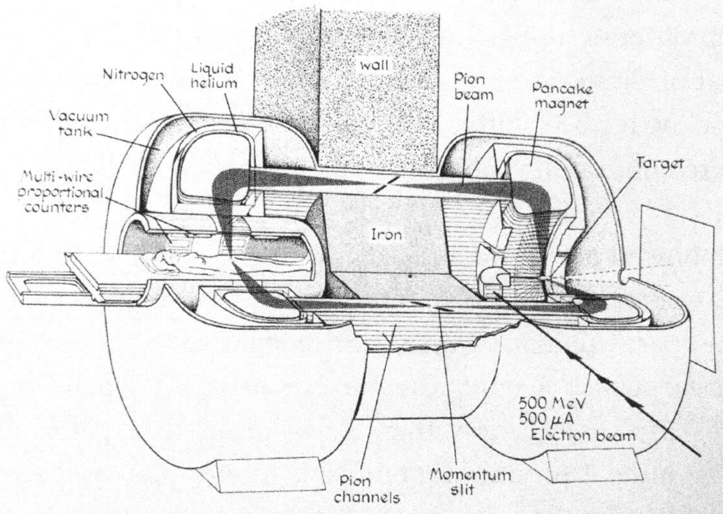

Fig. 1. Artist's illustration of the planned use of the superconducting pion channel.

Use of the pi-meson, or pion, particle, discovered in 1947, for cancer radiation treatment had been discussed off and on in the United States. The particle was rare and hard to produce in any quantity, but it was hoped that the new superconducting accelerator planned at Stanford would change that. The pion would start in an area of hellish radiation and have to be transported in a "channel" to a patient in a separate shielded place. Directing pions required large, very strong, and unusually shaped magnetic fields produced by many carefully shaped and positioned coils of superconducting wire. My design had windings contained in sixty aluminum plates, or "pancakes," at each end slotted into a frame like old photo slides into a slide carousel. The magnetic fields would direct the pions as they flowed between the plates.

This may be the only time I played a significant role in producing something with a widely known acronym. You can look up SMPG on the Internet. The acronym resolver finds sixteen different things for SMPG and lists the first six. We are the last of those six, so if you are going to look, you should do so quickly. It's been fifty years and any day some new thing is going to come along using our acronym and we will fall off the shortlist.

I followed one blind alley, if for longer than I should have. There were many tradeoffs. Improve one part of the design and another part would get worse, more expensive to build, or just a lot larger which would also be expensive. I'd spend a few months in one direction, then a few in another. After a few more months, I produced a buildable design that would work acceptably. Finally, the professor, research associate, and research assistant (me) flew to Boston to work out the details with the company that would build the two carousels.

The young secretary who took our lunch orders during our two days of meeting was memorable. While dressed conservatively in a long skirt and a long sweater, her lack of certain underclothing did not escape anyone's notice. A few jokes here and there along with comments about ever-present temptation were a minor topic of the meetings.

I was to stay an extra day to see Boston sights since I had never before been east of Idaho. Because it was my own dime, I would be moving out of our nice hotel to somewhere less expensive. There were comments like, "She might let you stay over at her place." She was quite fetching, but I had recently married Sue, also quite fetching. I ended up at the Boston YMCA.

This project had little to do with my eventual thesis project since they decided it was engineering, not physics. Even so, the device was built at considerable expense, tested, and worked, but the superconducting accelerator to produce its radiation source did not, or at least not enough. That's why they call it research, if not physics.

This gave me my start with computers, since this type of design work could not be done without them, and at that time the computers required were available at only a few places like Stanford. While I did get a degree for doing physics research, this turned out to be the start of my drift away from physics and toward engineering and computers.

The research associate later told me that the Boston company had lost money on our project. It had closed, but that was only part of the reason. Two wives of people in top management found out about affairs with an employee and sued their husbands and the company into bankruptcy.

This was the project involving Dr. Henry Kaplan, famous for his Hodgkin's disease cure. He was involved at the start and wrote a nice letter to my draft board. This, along with my in-person performance before the board, did not convince. We were at the beginning then, with no papers or drawings for show and tell. Do you think the above story and pictures would have turned the tide?

I was hitting that blind alley as I was entering a relationship with Sue. Dr. Kaplan had found a professor's office for me with a terminal and plotting equipment hooked to the medical school's computer. Sue would come after her school, sit there doing lesson plans and grading papers while I puzzled over a design that would transport the beam so nicely but appeared impossible to build. Sometimes she would nap on a table in the office. I wish I had a picture, but we didn't do that so much then. With all the concentration required, you'd wonder if her presence there was a benefit. It depends on how you define "benefit."

I'm sure you're all wondering about that blind alley where I spent so much time.

WARNING: The following physics involved may be upsetting to some.

To get the magnetic fields right for focusing the pion beam (dark grey in the first picture in this chapter) and still allow space for the beam to get through required the wire windings to follow a complex path. Making the "pancake" forms for these windings required computer numeric controlled (CNC) machinery. CNC technology was being researched at MIT and by that time huge, expensive, hard-to-program machines were just starting to appear at aerospace and a few other large companies.

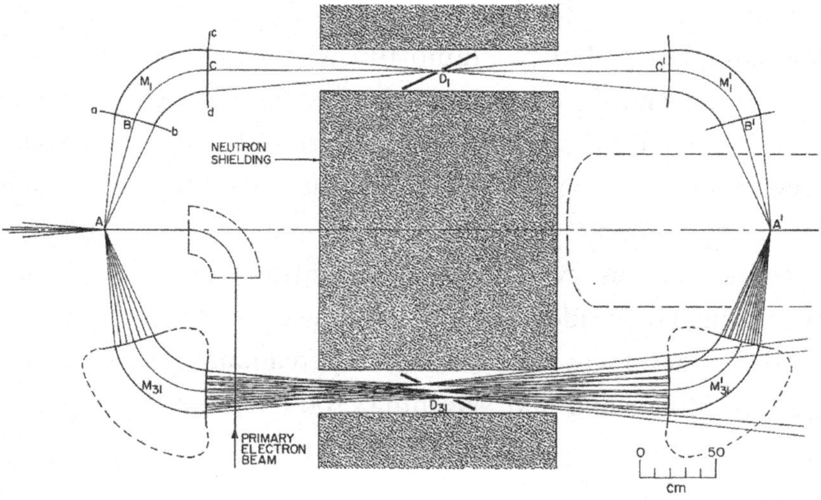

Output from the plotter, with labels added. Lines representing paths of pi-meson particles. The lower half shows how different energy beams are selected in the middle by angular barriers but come back together on the right.

I had no idea CNC or the like existed. I ended up duplicating previous research when I test manufactured prototype parts. I made printouts with five columns of numbers, which I read to tweak five different cranks in sequence over and over. Two cranks were for the rotate-tilt table I fastened to the bed of a milling machine in the Physics Department's large basement shop. The other three cranks moved the bed in the three dimensions. All the cranks had calibrated numeric readouts that had to match the numbers on my printouts. I did manage to make some prototype parts. If Stanford would have sprung for a few million for the huge CNC machines of the time and hired their specialized help, we could have produced those winding forms. It was good they did not, since I could not figure out how to get the niobium superconducting wire properly wound on those complex forms that I had made.

I finally solved that problem by (fortunately) making the windings follow a simpler path in 2D only (the simpler pancake was completely flat) but (unfortunately) extending the outer edge of the pancake outward. In the first picture, notice how far radially outward the pancakes extend from the edge of the dark grey beam, making the entire machine larger. This whole machine operated at liquid helium temperatures and was contained in an even larger super-insulated tank. Making everything larger added a lot of expense to the federally funded project. When I was younger, Dad talked about various government programs and said, "Nothing's too good for the taxpayer," so I knew everyone would be fine with this.

GIRLS

Some things are straightforward for me that might be pretty difficult for others. Other things that were common and easy for most others, required for me the utmost in thought and detailed planning along with constant observation and care while performing.

I wanted to date and meet girls just the same as other boys. Yet, no girl went out with me in high school. I did read a book on how it was done, but my few invitations were rejected, eventually leading me to try less. One girl, who I thought was no higher than me in overall school social class, lived not far from me, so I tried intercepting and walking home with her a few times. She preferred to be alone. I did take a girl to the senior ball dance, but we were put together by the event organizers. They made arrangements for any girl not asked. A week after the dance, I tried asking her out on a normal date. It was no go. In my college, there were maybe seven girls I dated. Some of those went out twice with me, but that was it.

An unmeant but too blunt word could kill things. Once, when I was a college sophomore, a girl hosted by her older sister came during college visit day for prospective new students. She actually noticed me and got her older sister to find out who I was and call me to arrange a meeting.

Wow, that had never happened to me.

So, I walked into the dorm lounge and sat across from them. The older sister just introduced herself and her sister. This was not her conversation; she expected me, as the older sophomore, to pick up a conversation with the younger high school senior. She did not realize how many years ahead of me socially the younger girl must have been. This situation was too new to me and I couldn't handle myself.

"Cringeworthy" best describes my speech from there. I long ago repressed the words that came out of my mouth, but I was thinking for weeks afterward how stupid, idiotic, supply your own words here, I felt. The young girl was not particularly attractive to me, but pretty and nice enough. "Losing" the girl was not the issue. Acting that stupid anywhere, for any reason was just, well, too stupid to imagine.

I had one date during grad school. She was from my church, I think. Some kind of car rally. Like a scavenger hunt on wheels. Not memorable for me, and I'm thinking not for her either.

While the girls I tried dating were somewhat attractive, I had never met or even seen anyone I had the slightest thought of marrying. I assumed that sooner or later I would get married, since, as far as I ever thought about it, everyone did. If it always happened, it would happen to me, right? Perhaps if I ever found a girl that would want to have more than two dates with me, things might continue for a while and we would marry. I was so busy with school and projects that little time was left to worry in that direction.

Mom had often told me I should marry a "nice Christian girl" with never a hint that her denomination would make any difference. Once, while my cousin Jim and I sat around in their TV repair shop, my dad and his twin brother pontificated on how one should marry. "Looks, a nice personality, and being a good church girl are all important," they both agreed, "but, though it might be the last on the list, don't forget the bucks." I think they were joking. When Dad taught me to drive, the first time I encountered a pedestrian, I braked a little late and a lot hard. Dad just said, "Run over her." No one believed everything he said.

Cousin Jim didn't seem to take the advice either. He also ended up marrying well, certainly checking all the boxes outside of wealth. As for her being from a rich family, I have never heard of or noticed anything of the sort in the fifty years they have been together. From what I knew of my aunt Marge, her advice to Jim had to be a lot closer to my mom's. Jim and I did take a lot of advice from our dads, but not all of it. In fact, I've never run over anyone, either.

Sue turned out to be the first girl with whom I had ever had any kind of a close relationship. Was "saving myself for marriage" a result of my relatively conservative upbringing and moral character or simply due to my lack of opportunity to do anything else? I really don't know.

AT FIRST SIGHT

Some enchanted evening, you may see a stranger, you may see a stranger across a crowded room — ***Rodgers & Hammerstein***

Yes, exactly that.

More than ten guys formed a noticeable circle a distance away out in the large room. In the center was a girl talking easily with some and then turning to talk to others. All the guys appeared to have equal footing; she did not seem to be with any one of them. I had not had a good view yet, but she soon turned to full view and ended all doubt. I had not seen a girl like that. Not at any school. Not out anywhere ever. Not in pictures, movies, or TV. I had thought every guy's standard of what is attractive is different. She hit me 100 percent. She also had hit a considerable percent with all of the guys in that circle. Others standing off a further distance, if hit with a percent or two of what I saw, would be looking too. Maybe my standard wasn't so unique.

When I came to Stanford, Peninsula Bible Church was where the students of my persuasion were. It was large and somewhat famous, its pastor having published a number of popular books. The church had a large singles group of young professionals and some grad students.

Christmas my second year, the group hosted seven other Bay Area churches at a Christmas party held at a large Palo Alto home. The living room holding the party was the largest I'd seen, and furniture was moved back. Hundreds attended.

Once I saw her out in that room, I had nothing else to do or think about. I had to find out whatever I could about that girl. If she proved unattached, as she appeared, then I had to go after her. I could not approach her yet. I was a north Idaho boy among Palo Alto – San Francisco Bay area people who were socially well ahead of me. I was not ready to compete with even one of those guys surrounding her, much less the group. Months later, I came to know some of them and knew that was a wise decision. Success seemed unlikely, especially given my track record. If I got her in a comfortable situation with just a few (not boy) friends or alone, she might even like me. You never know. She did not attend my church, so that left seven others.

I looked around the room to see where I could get as much information as I could about where she might be from, who else might know her. She was dressed more conservatively than most all the girls there, and these were church girls. The miniskirt had just come into fashion, or maybe it had been around for a while since I had previously been at a small conservative Christian college. Anyway, nearly all the girls wore them. Only a few had skirts a little below their knees. She was one of them.

I found one of the event organizers from my church and asked which churches were in attendance. I learned they were our community church, a Baptist, an Episcopal, another community church, a Methodist, a Conservative Assembly – BINGO! Understanding the situation, I found another girl in a long skirt and asked about her church.

Even I was not so crass to ask this girl about another girl who was likely a friend of hers. I could later find out more about my new interest without being rude. I would need all the help I could get and everyone who had anything to do with her had to be on my side.

Some double-checking to confirm things (there were more than two girls with long skirts, all easily approachable except that one), and I spent the rest of the time looking for clues and trying not to stare. Concentrating on anything else for a while was going to be tough. Having Christmas vacation time now was great. I had broken through a difficult part of a project and classes were off for a few weeks. The draft was behind me, I wasn't going home to Idaho and had nothing planned, until now.

~

She was both beautiful and cute according to my view of these words, which is not in full agreement with dictionaries. Her appearance came out and overwhelmed any thought of "sexy." Her overall dress and appearance were easily described as demure. Sexy did turn out to be fine but was not for public view and was not what I was noticing when I first saw her.

She did not have a "hard-edged" beauty I associated with

well-applied makeup or movie stars. She had no problem with makeup and used a little. Its presence or absence never seemed noticeable, however. She was the kind to look at every morning when getting up, the end of every evening, across the table at every meal, all the time and everywhere, year after year. I had not before seen her like.

The closest I've found to my first sight of Sue was Leslie Caron in her first movie, *An American in Paris,* when Gene Kelly first saw her across the restaurant, although I saw this movie much later. Now, before you make any comments, let me say this: any comparison between Gene Kelly and me, or the way he took quick action in that incident, would not even start to make any sense to Sue, let alone anyone else.

I GO TO CHURCH

He had heard that women often love plain ordinary men, but he did not believe it, because he judged by himself and he could only love beautiful mysterious exceptional women. — ***Leo Tolstoy***, *Anna Karenina*

Suits and decent clothes were not needed at school and optional at my somewhat informal church. Some of the guys this girl seemed to know in that circle at the party wore suits, however, and Bay Area Conservative Assembly culture was not my strong point. The next day I hit the high-end men's store at Stanford Shopping Center. I knew nothing about getting clothes; my mother did that. The dummy in the window looked good to me, so I went in and asked for that. When the clerk said that suit would look great on me, I said fine, but I meant the suit, shirt, tie, vest, and anything else on the dummy. What shoes and socks go with that?

The only picture I can find that shows my "original" suit, shirt, and tie. This is after we were married. Sue is in her "going away" dress & jacket.

I can't wear the same thing all the time, so I needed a second set, but there was no second dummy. He found a second shirt and tie he assured me would go with the suit.

Before I went to her church, I had thought about advertising. I would need all the help I could get. I knew you normally don't go about name-dropping, but the Stanford grad student status should be helpful. Back then it was common for students and even their proud parents to have a decal of their college's name across the back window of their car. The university bookstore had two "STANFORD" decals. One was on the small side and the other seemed maybe just a little too large. I have had few points in my life where a decision was required, but this was one of them and did take some thought and time. I finally decided my car's back window was pretty sloped, which would make a decal harder to see. I already had the bright shirt, so might as well go all the way. I chose the large one. I had good clothes, a new Buick, and a nice if not so subtle advertisement in its back window. I was good to go.

The next Sunday, I showed up for the singles group Sunday School class at Sunnyvale Assembly. All the guys wore suits. I was a bit nervous about my somewhat bright shirt. It looked great on the dummy but not quite as good on me. Colored dress shirts turned out to be in, at least at this church.

She wasn't there. I still thought it was the right place, and the people there were great. I wasn't sure, but maybe one or two of the guys had been in that circle at the party. There were maybe fourteen there, about the same number of girls as guys. All were warmly, but not overly, friendly so I relaxed more quickly than I would have expected. Her not being there, while disappointing, relieved much of my tension. Over the next month, I used this "opportunity" to get to know her friends. Ages ran similar to the singles group at my church and all were well educated. If her friends were any indication of the kind of person she was, things were looking good.

We all went to church afterward, and there she was in the choir. She looked as good there as she had at the party. I wondered if she sang alto. Mom did and I always liked her voice.

The church was not huge, so a new boy, especially with that shirt, would be noticed by most of the unattached girls. I was watching my behavior. I was new so they would speak first. It was safest for me to be as quiet as possible, but friendly and ready to respond. I had worked on smiling, which was not natural for me.

I was prepared to just say "hi" to her as if she were anyone else when I saw her after church. She would be just as likely to first greet me. Remember, I was the new one here.

When the service let out, she was nowhere to be seen. The

singles group always went out to a restaurant for lunch together so of course I was invited. Again, she was not there, but I had more good times with the group. They were closer than any church group I had seen. Many had been in this church from childhood. Others started with the church when in a Bay Area college and stayed afterward. Nearly all were college graduates. I was not at my best in group social settings, but this was the easiest group I had been in. I was careful, and all went well.

I did not know why she was missing but made no inquiries. I was not hurried. I didn't think she was paired up with anyone here, but there still could be someone who was away at this time. Too soon to start asking.

The next week was the same. The third time, the same again with one exception. After the church service, we carpooled to the restaurant and this time, Beverly invited me in her car. I was always agreeable so off we went. Beverly was the most flamboyant of the girls in the group, but flamboyant against this church's standards was not so far out. I was surprised at her two-seat sports car. This was the first two-seat dedicated sports car I was ever in.

As we drove across the church parking lot, we went right by her. This was the first time I had seen her outside of the choir. She may have seen me: that sports car was open top. This was not an ideal situation, but at least she might be at the lunch this time. She wasn't.

Then a month had gone by. I had not thought it would take this long. Most of the girls in the church must have known about me and most in the group had spoken with me. Girls always talk. She had to know what the other girls knew. I was getting to be part of the group, so it was natural for me to ask about various others, not limited to but including her, that I had seen around the church. Conversations here and there revealed that: Her name was Sue. She and Paulette were teachers at the primary school the church ran. Each was part of the singles group but for the last month, they came to church from the county jail and had to go back afterward. They would continue like that for the near future.

No, they were not let out to attend church. They were let in to sing and hold church services at the county women's facilities. My estimation of her character continued rising. Her voice was better than average even for the choir. Regarding that, she and her jail mate sung a duet the previous Sunday. She was an alto like Mom. I was somehow sure she did not drive around in a two-seater convertible sports car. She did not seem like that kind of girl.

The idea was to meet her casually along with others in the group — an easy and natural way to get familiar with each other. My errors would be smaller and more correctable. I hoped to avoid saying or doing something odd and blowing it big time, which I had done before in tries at dating at college. The group did hold parties where we could get together, but not around this particular time. This was taking too long.

I was friends with Sue's friends. I'd been attending church and the group for a month, with a perfect record of doing nothing noticeably dumb. I would not be a total stranger. I got up my courage and phoned Sue at the church's Christian school where she taught third grade. She said yes and we spent our first date bicycling around my university's campus. That was early February 1970.

Much later I learned some behind-the-scenes information from Sue:

She was curious about me and planned to take time off jail to attend lunch for a better look. That was when she saw me in the one car in the entire church parking lot that I was plainly visible sitting inside. Since Beverly apparently had gotten me, she instead continued with her regularly scheduled program.

Of course, she never noticed me at the original party. She had seen me every time at church and knew I was also with the singles group. There was less communication among the girls than I assumed: she knew nothing else. The one girl most likely to tell her something was her roommate in her apartment, but also the one who did the jail services with her. She had no idea of my name or anything else except that when she first saw me from the choir, she was impressed with how well I knew how to dress (this she told me much later). She would later find I really did not, but by then it was far too late. She did take over my clothes selection. Sorry if it sounds sexist, but I always thought selecting my clothes was a woman's work and it continues so to this day. The folks at that men's store certainly did know how to dress a dummy.

Church secretary Betty Karlberg was well known as a strait-laced spinster who had married late a man in the church whose wife had died leaving a number of children to raise. No one was nicer, but she was the last word in circumspect formality. She knew everything and conveyed nothing to anyone ever by word or even expression. She picked up my call, I told her my name, that I attended church and the singles group, and would like to talk to Sue. When Sue arrived, Betty handed her the phone with a smile unlike she had before seen. Betty never had an expression of any sort when handling business in the church office.

Before she put the receiver to her ear, Sue realized something unusual was afoot.

So, my plan worked, although plans never work as expected. I performed well in the role of a nice but quiet new guy at the church. Maybe a little impressive (remember the car, its window sign, and the suit), but no sign of anything worth gossiping about. Not much, but some, filtered back to Sue. Hey, even that church secretary knew more about me than I realized. Of course, she knew more than anyone about everything at that church. She definitely approved, and if a lady like that approved, it just had to be clear sailing from there.

THE ONE DAY

Think for a moment of the long chain of iron or gold, of thorns or flowers, that would never have bound you, but for the formation of the first link on one memorable day. — **Charles Dickens**, *Great Expectations*

That first moment I saw her had expanded into a month during which my whole drive and purpose was to get together with this girl. That was a lot of time to think about this day and how it might go down. May I say I was concerned? Thinking and evaluating. I had never seen her like. This was my one chance — otherwise, I would drift along and maybe someday settle for a reasonably nice girl with a nice personality and a not-too-unpleasant appearance. I was a 6, maybe even a 7, but I would be with a 10. Going out with 6s and 7s had not worked for me before, and I was expecting what?

Saturday, I picked her up at her school classroom. Conversation flowed from the start. I was at ease with my concerns of the last month not coming to mind at all. Whatever social lack I had she must have compensated. I'd been on dates before and it didn't work like this. She was as adept at social interaction and conversation as I was at physics and math.

With hundreds of flat acres and no cars allowed, bikes were the mode of transportation at Stanford and my roommate kindly loaned his to Sue. It was an easy-riding time and could not have gone better.

I had not thought of one incident during the ride until Sue mentioned it months later. The ride was flat until we hit the recreational Lake Lag. There was a five-foot berm around the lake. You just sped up a little to get up the side to where you could ride along its wide top. I forgot to warn her about the "sped up" part. Sue ran out of gas near the top and toppled to one side. I froze and could only watch as I saw the entire thing. She fell off, leading appropriately with her backside. I recovered enough to come to her aid. Her padding for such occasions was adequate, while not at all excessive, and she was fine and laughing. I said "sorry" or some words like that, but her attitude made everything easy. There was no problem at all.

Once I helped her up, it was clear that the light brown dusty area showing prominently on her dark pants would be a problem. I pointed it out, brushed the dust off until she looked fine and we went on with the rest of a date that can only be described as the greatest. Much later, she told me how she was glad I was looking elsewhere when her countenance must have registered the shock of the moment. With people all around, she was standing after participation in a well-noticed event, with a boy she just met beating her on the butt! I hadn't thought of that. The solution to the problem was straightforward and necessary, so I had fixed it without further thought. The fabric involved did require a little arm strength to adequately remove the dust and she needed to look OK. Once done, the event dropped from my mind.

Lake Lag, when it had water in the '70s. These bikes are all up on its surrounding berm.

Our ride's last stop was the Stanford church, famous for its inside and outside scenes rendered in mosaic tile. It was her first visit to the largest and most beautiful church we both had seen. Like any girl her age would naturally think, she mentioned it was a wonderful setting for a wedding. Providing useful information without thinking, I mentioned that you had to be a student or faculty to get married there.

We ended with hamburgers and cokes at the Red Barn by the Stanford Shopping Center. This was the first time I had ever taken a girl to a restaurant. When I grew up, we never went to sit-down restaurants. We did go to a few drive-ins.

Finally, we drove back to her school and stood in the

parking lot to say goodbye … for more than two hours. Neither of us ran out of things to say, and both knew we would continue that conversation. Nothing like that had ever happened to me.

Love at first sight at that party describes this. A month before, I saw how she dressed, how she stood, her posture and hand motions while she talked, her expression moving from a smile to serious as she talked and listened, how she appeared to act around others. What I could see just made her better. For the next month, what few additional things I learned were what I expected, and I expected good or better. Now, as our first date ended, everything still was all good.

For me, having such a successful date and realizing she did like me was huge. I'd never thought past that. I had assumed I would like her, so no surprise there. For my part, I did know that a second date would happen and that chances were good this could go on for a while. If it did, she might even get serious about me.

Sue later told me she had never talked that easily with anyone before. As she drove home that evening, she decided she would marry me. Of course, she said nothing about this until after our engagement. I likewise said nothing about my previous month. For younger people reading this: people were more conservative back then and we were young Christians. The idea of kissing after a first date never crossed our minds.

So, it comes down to the most important single day of my life, with one shot for the approval of the most important person in my life, and that's where I came the closest I ever have to beating a woman! The situation had required correction, and I applied the one she needed. With apologies to modern feminists, it was both necessary and for her own good. I guess it wasn't as it appeared or sounds like here, but I did dodge a bullet there. That could have worked out differently.

As far as the 6, 7, and 10 ratings referenced above: Sue's views and understanding of things numeric or mathematical have always been different from mine, which in turn is different from most of the earth's other residents. Whatever her rating system was, it was not like mine. Her turning out to be a 10 in more than just looks (my reference system) didn't hurt either.

THE NEXT DAYS

Gravitation cannot be held responsible for people falling in love. How on earth can you explain in terms of chemistry and physics so important a biological phenomenon as first love? Put your hand on a stove for a minute and it seems like an hour. Sit with that special girl for an hour and it seems like a minute. That's relativity. — ***Albert Einstein***

In grad school, I understood the more popularly known kind of Einstein's relativity. This other kind, not so much.

After our first date, I was back to finishing up my last year of coursework in classical mechanics, quantum mechanics, etc. as well as reworking the pion channel design to optimize how it met various conflicting requirements. I also spent time in the high-energy lab's mechanical drawing department and its machine shop, working through full-size plans and prototype parts for channel components.

The first date had come off amazingly well, but I wanted to show a little restraint and not push my luck too quickly. Ron, my roommate at the time, told me about a Japanese country-style restaurant in San Francisco near Temple Emanu-el. They cooked the food at your table, you sat on the floor, and other authentic, or at least impressive, things made it interesting. It was the weekend two weeks after our first date that we went to San Francisco for a Saturday lunch at the Ming Giey Ya.

Sue and her father before their walk down the aisle.

It was certainly different, and I had told Sue how it would be, at least to the extent of my knowledge, which was not much. We were both dressed much better than before, she especially nice in a skirt and high heels. The lunch was good and enjoyable as much for the novelty as well as the food. Except for the group lunches with the church singles and the more informal Red Barn, this was my first experience in a normal (where you pay after you eat) sit-down restaurant of any kind, floor or chair. Sitting on the floor was interesting. Sue's legs went to sleep, so when it was time to go, we worked together to get her back on her feet and into those high heels. We then walked around the Jewish temple and fancy homes of Presidio Terrace.

Our third date was to the blowholes on the beach in Santa Cruz. When I went to Sue's apartment to pick her up, her roommate and her boyfriend as well as another boy and girl from the singles group piled in the back seat. I did not expect that, and I found out after we got to Santa Cruz, Sue had not expected it either. Word had gotten around the singles group that something was up between Sue and me, probably starting with Sue's roommate. I knew our friends by now too, and they just decided to get a better idea of what was going on.

We all had a great time, and Sue and I got away from them long enough that evening on the beach to have our first kiss.

More dates followed. I kept a one-line record of each, but the notebook was lost long ago in a move. The singles group had a few parties at a member's apartment where we'd play games such as "liar." Three people would have an obscure event or topic. Two would make something up about it and we had to guess which one was telling the truth. I'd seen things like that in movies or TV but had never been a part of it. Getting to know these people was a definite plus to getting to know Sue.

By spring break near the end of March, I had already met

Sue's parents and invited Sue up to north Idaho to meet mine. We made the trip each way in one shot of fifteen hours of driving with maybe two more for stops along the way. We ran out of gas on the freeway two miles to the off-ramp by my parents' house. A policeman soon showed up, helped us get some gas, and we reached the house around 2 a.m. We sneaked down to the basement rooms and sacked out on beds under my parents' portion of the duplex and under my grandmother's portion on the other side respectively.

The three families. This is not the only time Dad wore a suit. He did for graduations and my sister's wedding also. He really did not like posing for a lot of pictures, however. He wasn't used to this kind of thing.

The next morning, my grandmother did express concern at what the neighbors might think of us down there together, but after seventeen hours or more on the road, and a running-out-of-gas incident, there was not a whole lot going on down there but sleeping. Thereafter, Sue was up in my sister's room since she had stayed at her college, Seattle Pacific, to work.

Needless to say, the more Mom and Grandma learned about Sue, the happier they were. I knew Dad well enough to know he would be fine with Sue as well, but I also knew that Sue had never been around anyone like Dad, and would take some time to adapt, which she did by the end of our week there.

I introduced Sue to my hometown, the lake, and some of the surrounding forest area. Dad and Uncle Jim were then developing a new KOA campground (now called Camp Coeur d'Alene) at the northeast end of Coeur d'Alene Lake right next to a bald eagle sanctuary, so we spent some time out there as well.

On this trip, we both discussed how we were serious about each other and, barring some extraordinary event, a marriage proposal was on the near horizon. Knowing what we know now, we should have talked over many things we did not discuss, but I'm guessing we were still far more purposeful and deliberate about what we were doing than many were. She had dated many guys and remained friends with most of them afterward. In each case, often with their disagreement, she had decided they were not for her. I had essentially dated no one and had never known or even seen anyone else I considered at all, so we had each decided the other was our only possible choice. There was no one in second place for either of us then or at any other time.

When we got back, we went ring shopping. One evening, I formally asked her to marry me and she said yes. There was no surprise for either of us. If there was any decision on my part, it had been made months ago when I first saw her; no doubts or second guesses had ever come up. Long before meeting me, and unlike me, Sue had made a list of the things she hoped for in a future husband. After our first few dates, she checked it over. I did not meet one thing on the list, so she threw it away and forgot about it. I would have been curious to see that list.

This was still a busy time for me with coursework, work as a teaching assistant, and the pion channel design work whenever I could do it. Some of our together time was when Sue drove to Stanford to be with me either at the library or the medical center office I used. Sue actually "fell in love" with me in the classic sense. The symptoms were normally seen elsewhere. While on the freeway, she would miss her exit and a few more.

At a San Jose State course to maintain her teacher's credential, her professor came up and said with concern, "Has anything happened to you lately?"

"I'm engaged," she replied.

"Maybe this is not the time for you to be taking World Geography," the professor said.

Once back from Idaho, there were singles group pool parties and a beach party at Santa Cruz, and, as always, Sundays with the singles group. We announced our engagement with a party at the church after their Wednesday midweek service. Maybe it was a surprise, since Sue had gone out with a few guys in the group in the past. We looked into a June date for Stanford Church and ended up with the evening on July 11.

We had not explicitly told Mom and Dad, but I had never before taken a girl home to meet them. For that matter, I had never taken a girl anywhere as far as they knew. I knew they would have no issues at all. There were still Sue's parents, and I had a formal obligation to her father. Sue's mother had always dreamed of her staying in their church and hopefully becoming important there by marrying a pastor.

Having been in "community" churches since college, I reached back to where Mom took us to get a label. Sue's mother was not thrilled with a Baptist. In fact, she was quite solidly opposed. Sue did not tell me this immediately and was fine marrying me without her mother's approval if it came to that. Following tradition, I asked her dad for Sue's hand and he was all good with it. Sue's mother wasn't home at the time, but I wouldn't be asking her anyway. Her dad never mentioned anything about Baptists. I think he never mentioned anything to her mother either.

Sue's mother could not miss her daughter's grand wedding at Stanford Church. How would that look? Her whole church there (and it was) missing only one member: her? Seven pretty maids all in a row on one side, her own Pastor Willis there in grand formal robes for possibly the only time in his life with frock coats and top hats for all the men. You're darn right she was going to be there! Besides, Stanford had a great and surprisingly inexpensive wedding package for students: church, organist, wedding planner, and the large upper floor of Tresidder student union for the reception. They even had the people to do the cake and catering. All I had to supply were the pastor, guests, girl, and getaway car. Plans for the wedding were out of her mother's hands, but she warmed up to me a bit when it saved her a boatload of money. She became fine with me, if never warm and fuzzy, as she was never warm and fuzzy with anyone.

~

The week after Sue and I announced our engagement, her roommate and boyfriend, who had come to the group just a few months before me, announced theirs. Within a month, two more couples from the group announced theirs. Another guy became engaged to a girl from my original church in Palo Alto. Finally, the group's leader got engaged. By the time Sue and I married, ten members were out of the group. Did we throw a bomb into their midst or something? I don't know if or how the singles group rebuilt. We did keep relationships with some other married former members of the group for years after that.

SUE BEFORE ME

'That's the worst of girls,' said Edmund to Peter and the Dwarf. 'They never can carry a map in their heads.'

'That's because our heads have something inside them,' said Lucy. — **C. S. Lewis**, *The Lion, the Witch and the Wardrobe*

Even today, Sue has not adapted to using Google Maps. She and computers do not mix well. Given what she has done, however, it does appear that Lucy is correct.

Sue attended four years at her denomination's nearby Bible college to be ready for the mission field. Sue's mother was more realistic, hoping she would prepare for that most noble of any girl's aspirations, the position of pastor's wife. Sue did lack some qualities for this. She had earlier not responded well to piano lessons required for helping out in those first smaller churches as well as the typing lessons to qualify for a job to help a meager pastoral salary. I think she could have gotten a guy capable of quickly getting to a larger church, but her mother could not have known that at the time.

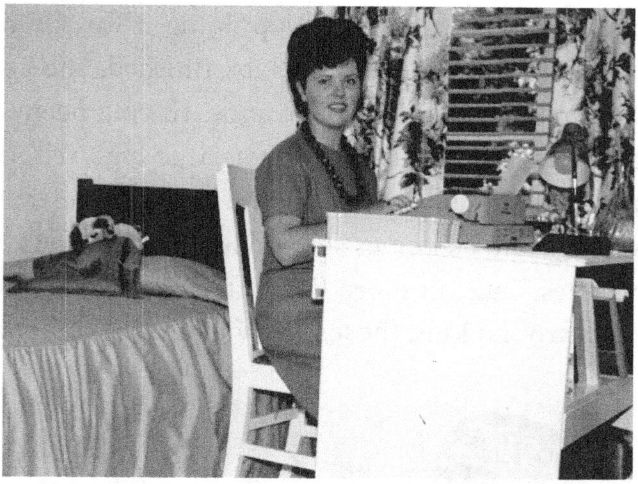

Sue in her dorm room at Bethany Bible College.

Foreign missionary work was promoted in the church where Sue grew up. By high school, she thought India was where she was needed. Right after high school, she went out for mission work in the Bahamas for three months in a group of 146 kids. This was before today's safety measures and lawsuits, and it was a real adventure. I'm especially glad Sue did not fall off the roof of the small mail boat where she and her friend held onto each other while they slept to avoid falling in somewhere between the islands. They protected my young girl's innocence by having the team's boys and girls sleep in little country schoolhouses a few miles apart. It was dark and quiet, with little lightning bugs all around them, or were they cigarettes of the surrounding Bahamian men watching these new visiting girls? Maybe they were watching the nightly cockroach herding sessions, where the girls took turns jumping off the tables onto the bunched-up herd? She doesn't know how long they watched because they all finally just went to sleep.

A lady working with Sue's college did summer kids' clubs in many Northern California churches. She retired from that and sophomore Sue somehow ended up doing it for the next two summers. Each year when kids' clubs finished, she continued doing the same in Oregon Bible camps. Having been a lead in most of the plays and musicals in her large high school drama department, she could ham it up and be in her element with puppets, signs, and costumes she brought with her. As I've seen so many times since, in more than a few places and countries, when Sue is around kids, those kids will be all around Sue.

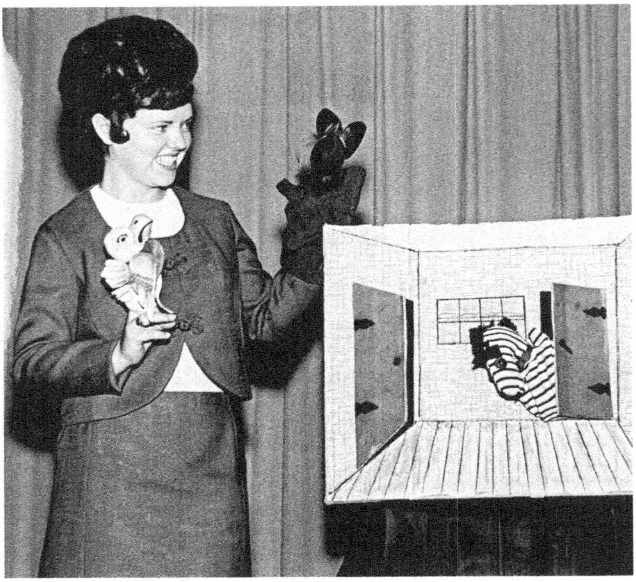

Sue with puppets and props for summer kid's clubs and camps.

On the way home and back to school from Oregon the second year, Sue was in her own nearly new Mustang from her mother. Sue was happy with the summer, out on her own on a beautiful day and singing away, when a cop pulled her over. He was obviously horrified at the sight of her. No one had thought about sending an apparently high school age, 5'2" cute, pony-tailed girl off by herself driving around in two states. The cop was nearly in tears as he told her she was doing 85. He had a daughter her age and was genuinely afraid for her. He made her promise to watch her speedometer and then just sent her on her way.

Sue with her father and mother.

She was innocent and naïve. She was in a new town, maybe asking where an address was, every few days. There were men in the world with extreme persistence who might take her smile that she always gave as a come-on. "Hey, I'm going out that way and you can follow me!" She would have. She now knows she should have been prepared for that. She was shielded from other boys in high school by the son of her mother's best friend. In college, they were all Bible school kids. She could say no to these boys, and any resistance to that, and there was some, was pleading rather than anything physical. She could not conceive of yelling, "Buzz off!" and shoving someone away. Anyway, there were other incidents, with a couple that could have gotten dangerous, but she got back OK.

To be a real missionary meant finding a future foreign missionary to marry, and her Bible college was the best place to do this. Unfortunately, that line of work had been drying up since the end of WWII as country after country began prohibiting foreign missionaries. Even so, more than one guy who actually did become a foreign missionary proposed to her, but she did not feel right about them.

Before graduation, girls expected to have a husband or at least one solidly lined up. They thought it best to get a boy from their denomination and they were in the only school for that denomination for a good distance around. One of her senior friends had run out of options until she found a freshman. Sue's mother wanted her to be a pastor's wife and often suggested she find a boy at school. Every boy she brought home from there was warmly approved. Sue had several asks. When turned down, some even went to her parents, older sister, and brother-in-law to get them on their side, but Sue eventually decided that whoever she was to marry, he was not at her college.

Sue did become a foreign missionary, of course, but that's another story.

That Sue was the "marrying kind" of girl I was not at all the first to notice. Well after we married, I learned she'd had proposals from college and afterward, within her church and outside it. She remained friends with those still in the area and some I got to know as well. All were educated, one was quite wealthy at a young age, and all I knew or knew about were great guys. Perhaps innocence and naivety were not a problem for her. She did not present herself as the kind of girl a man with any integrity would want to take advantage of. Those men she had gone out with that I knew of had plenty of integrity, so maybe things like that tended not to come up.

THE LITTLE YELLOW HOUSE

Some day you will be old enough to start reading fairy tales again. – ***C. S. Lewis***

That happened, then I got busy. Long afterward, it would happen again. I should stay old enough this time.

During my first year in grad school, someone in my church's singles group introduced me to Warren, since we were both Stanford guys. He had been an undergrad and pitcher on their baseball team. It's deceptive to say "we hit it off" because Warren hit it off with everyone. Warren liked to talk, and everyone liked to talk with Warren.

Looking from the little yellow house backyard to the water tower early in the morning. We really wanted to keep that tower.

Warren's interests were books and literature. He talked of things I dimly remembered from school and college classes, maybe with some distaste due to having to write a paper about them. He lived in one of the oldest homes in the area, tucked back on an acre in the Redwood City county area. He would talk of English authors, Arthurian and Norse legends, and even the dreaded Shakespeare.

I had the greatest times sitting in that chair in his library with him behind his desk talking about MacDonald, Lewis, Morris, Chesterton, etc. There was more to it than I realized; there really was something there. I just had to read their books! In no way did Warren resemble a teacher, at least none that I'd had. He was excited and had to talk about what he read.

Two years later, in a conversation with his landlord, Warren found he was thinking of selling the acre where Warren was living. Warren had long been friends with the landlord, so they talked about a deal and settled on fifty thousand, with seller financing for all but ten thousand. Warren called and asked me to chip in. Half of that down payment was a lot of money for Sue and me, but we had saved a thousand dollars, borrowed a thousand from my parents and three thousand from Sue's. Warren got some help from his wife's parents and we each went in for half and bought the acre.

Sue, our young son Adam, our English bulldog Ralph, and I moved into the other house on the property. We were in Redwood City just a few blocks from the upscale rich people town of Atherton. Our loans would be manageable for each of us.

Adam and Ralph in front of the little yellow house.

Both homes were well set back and hidden away from the street and surroundings in rustic going-toward-shabby splendor. A concrete pond, big enough to have an island, along with many trees and bushes, meandered between the houses and the street. Behind the houses was a no man's land of trees overgrown to the ground and bushes that might have been trimmed and part of a garden before we were born. Also back there was an old wooden water tower high enough to give vertigo if you stood on the walkway at the base of its big oakwood tank.

Mom and Dad visited us in the little yellow house. I have pictures inside, but we never took a full picture of it outside.

While not old as Warren's, our house was one of the oldest around. It had three small bedrooms. As far as we knew, the second bath was not invented until years after it was built. It was painted yellow and was nearly as small as the house where I grew up in north Idaho. We all referred to it in the only obvious way.

We started a quiet, wonderful life out in the country in the little yellow house.

Sue and Adam in front of the fishpond. It had two houses and a lighthouse. I kept a house; it was last seen in the garden at the big house when we sold that.

Before we bought it, I was concerned that fifty thousand for that acre might be too much, so I spot-checked surrounding home prices. Small ones were about twenty thousand. Twenty-two years before that time, Dad had bought our small home for ten thousand when I was in the third grade, and north Idaho prices should be cheaper. Our house on the property was equal to those twenty thousand dollar homes. I would pay five thousand more for a small house, but with far more property. The homes I checked were on recently widened San Carlos Street. Some had almost no front yard and a busy street in front. Our kids would have an acre to play on.

The property was 150 feet across at the front and back and 300 feet deep in from the street, with the two houses 100 feet back. The front was fenced with gates on both sides with neighbors' wood fences bordering all the rest of the property.

One day Sue came back with Adam, then between three and four years old, in the car. This was before child car seats and Adam was in the front seat. While Sue got out to open our south gate, Adam slipped over and pushed up the column shift to put the Buick into drive. The gate was open, and the car eased on through, tearing off the driver's door handle on the steel fence post as it went by. Amazingly there was no other body damage. Sue was inside the fence as the car slowly went by her with an unopenable door. It stopped when the front bumper hit the brick planter in front of the little yellow house, knocking a few bricks loose with no significant bumper damage.

There was a two-car garage to the front and side of our house. We parked our cars in front of it since Warren and I had a shop with tools inside. We heard loud cracking sounds, went out, and could not see any part of our Buick. A large tree had fallen across the driveway and completely covered the car, which I guessed to be a total loss. Anyone who owns a chainsaw loves to get a chance to use it, and one of our neighbors was right over. After a lot of cutting the car was finally uncovered with not one scratch. It was a hardwood tree, so no single big trunk, and the large limbs and branches missed our car but did hit the driveway and supported the rest of the tree, so the car was spared.

It was on the property that Ralph discovered his love for

basketballs. I would never have had a basketball, but Warren did. Ralph saw it bounce a few times, caught up with it, and tried to bite it. When he could not, he pushed it and kept going. Immediately, he was running full steam across the area with his nose touching the ball. He kept going in a straight line until the ball and he ran into the side of a house, a fence, or more likely, under one of our overgrown trees or bushes. There you'd hear a furious thrashing sound until the ball, immediately followed by Ralph, burst out at full speed in a different direction across a wide expanse until something else was hit. They would continue in straight-line zigs and zags until finally the ball and Ralph went into the fishpond. There was nothing Ralph loved more than chasing that basketball.

On the driveway looking out to the front of the property on the side of Warren's house.

WARREN'S IDEA

*Yet some men say in many parts of England that King Arthur is not dead, but had by the will of our Lord Jesu into another place; and men say that he shall come again, and he shall win the holy cross. — **Thomas Malory,** Le Morte d'Arthur*

Warren and I would sit in his library and talk about things like this, but then our conversations began to change.

We settled in on our acre. I made little as a Stanford research associate and Sue had quit her even lower-paying job at her church's school to become a stay-at-home mom with Adam. She joined babysitting coops, coops for bulk unpackaged foods, shopped at Goodwill and other secondhand stores, picked up things from garage sales, and raised some of our food in her garden. We even had a few luxuries from garage sales in nearby upscale Atherton. We started getting that $4,000 back to our parents. Sue did our budgets at the time and it was no nonsense allowed. But we were now property owners, I'd soon get a real job, and we would be normal people. Looking back, it seems more romantic than it actually was. We were both busy and never ran out of things to do. In a little more time, we would be settling in more comfortably.

Malory Court before paving; taken from the water tower. The little yellow house is now being remodeled to be much larger. This is about when we had to move out.

About two years after we moved into the little yellow house, the "Bay Area" was renamed "Silicon Valley" and became a different place. People flowed in for the high-paying jobs while the housing supply grew slowly if at all, forcing prices up. We had bought our acre in early 1974 when prices had been stable for a long time, with a small house costing maybe just double what my dad paid for our small house in north Idaho when I was in third grade.

I had enough work out at Stanford Linear Accelerator Center (SLAC) as a research associate to be plenty busy. Warren had enough time to get into trouble. He was visiting a builder just the next block over who had bought a little less land than us, had subdivided it into four lots, put in the Beresford Court private road, and was building the second of four homes. Like us, this builder was caught unawares by the home price rise: he would make a lot more money than he had planned.

Warren and I would talk every evening. He was getting excited. We could be real estate developers and home builders! I was less than thrilled. I planned to leave SLAC and Stanford for a "real" job out in the world and I was definitely going into computer software. Companies were hiring BSs in computer science, not PhDs in physics. All this would take my full attention. I needed this quiet place to come home to.

Sue, Adam, and Freya, Warren's dog. We lived there a few weeks after the roof was off. The old house ended just a foot to the left of the big window. The small window is for a bedroom, with one more bedroom and window off the picture.

I put off telling Sue. It hadn't taken her long to fall in love with working her large garden and living in the cutest little yellow house. She could be happy there forever.

Warren had set up a drafting board in the library over in that ramshackle house. He'd already picked up basic small subdivision ins and outs from his builder friend, along with other tips including which engineers and subcontractors to use. His friend even passed on how he would deal with taxes due to all the extra money.

I needed an idea of just how much trouble Warren could get us into. I rechecked the prices of the small homes on the same street as before: $20,000 was now $35,000. I thought this trend was sure to end[1] but looked to continue until prices possibly doubled. I was thankful we had bought when we did and could afford where we lived.

Warren worked out a private road that would access four new homes, as well as a fifth home on the street in front. It just barely met all the requirements. A home larger than anything in our neighborhood would fit on each lot, way larger than those small cracker boxes I price-checked.

I wanted to avoid all this, or at least delay it until I had a job and felt ready to take on something else. We were working on paying off the original purchase of our acre, and now this! Warren believed I would soon be making plenty in my new job so, along with construction loans, I could help finance things. Warren would be the working partner and build the homes. Of course, we'd use subcontractors for all the specialty areas like plumbing, electrical, roofing, etc. It would be the same for building the private road. We would need one more body to work with Warren. Better include with that a mind knowing more about home construction than either of us.

I still didn't like it, but with all this price rise, cost information from his builder friend, and a little high school math, we reviewed what he was saying: We build five homes, sell three, and we each get a free, large, custom-built (by us) home in this new Silicon Valley. I rechecked. "Free" was the correct word. I still didn't like it, but things were rising to the point where it was just wrong to refuse Warren. OK, we'd go over and tell Sue, but he was a coward. I had to go alone.

Around the table from left, Warren, Sue, Ruth, Steve, Ken, Eilene at our house demolishing party. Some of Warren's old house behind us.

Warren moved to a rental. Friends and neighbors came to scavenge as we tore his old house down. The largest garbage bin we could get was dropped on the property and became a common sight for the next few years. We all loved the old water tower and wanted to save it, but even with losing one of our lots, it was impractical in every way. It was dismantled and loaded into a big truck. The guy said it was really hard to find wood like those huge oak staves from the tank. Trees and bushes were cleared. Our plan kept the really big trees, most of which had been on the acre's boundary. Finally, only the little yellow house remained. It was so different out there all alone, but it was possible it might live through all of this.

The surveyor marked various spots. His office could do the whole subdivision development up to ready for building homes, all for one of our lots! It was a struggle, but we paid for the surveying. We paid for what little grading we needed since the acre was already flat.

Finally, a road contractor came in to complete the kind of narrow road ending with a turnaround that was allowed for accessing four or fewer houses. This type of road was called a court. The court Warren loved above all was that held by King Arthur at Camelot. Thomas Malory was the English author who made the good king and his most noble companions of the Round Table live on to this day as inspiration to all of us lesser men. Sue and I would someday live on Malory Court.

In March 1977, the subdivision got final approval. We had five lots: one up front on the street at our original address, and 2, 4, 6, and 8 Malory Court. It was amazing we got that far with the money we had but going further required a construction loan. The banks would only loan if a licensed general contractor was in charge, but we wanted to do the job ourselves with just a little hired help.

~

[1] The upward price trend obviously did not end. In the early '70s, I was spot checking-homes on San Carlos Avenue, where the smallest, oldest homes sat too close to the street after a road widening. I just checked and they have not been upgraded or replaced. They're still little old cracker boxes. Prices are surprisingly uniform, presumably for the lot, not the house. All close to $1.7 million.

WE BUILD HOUSES

We meet no ordinary people in our lives. – ***C. S. Lewis***

The body Warren found to "assist" him was great. The included mind even better, and better yet later on.

Warren still visited construction sites to get ideas, and at one site met Al. Al did ceramic tile work for floors, bathrooms, countertops, or anywhere else you wanted it, but planned to expand his business. He had just received his general contractor's license. Warren had found that other body, fortunately with the mind and even a license thrown in. Warren drew the plans, except for my house at 6 Malory, and both Warren and Al built our houses with help from me evenings and weekends.

Warren's partially demolished house at left. Water tower center. Little yellow house at right.

Al on the roof, Warren atop the scaffold. Roof shingle delivery guy below. We've moved out.

The banks were still skittish. They weren't sure about a new contractor doing an entire house. He should start more gradually, like a remodel job. Getting five lots into that acre allowed no leeway on the lot boundaries, but the little yellow house just happened to fit well at 2 Malory Court.

So, we'd do a remodel. Our little house's size would more than double, with just some of the old room layout, our two front bedrooms and bathroom, remaining in the old portion. We'd retain the old foundation, some of the old floor platform and the studs of some walls at the back end; any less was not a remodel by the building department's definition. There would not be much left. It would be essentially all-new, but the permits were easier, and the bank saw the permits, not what we did.

The first day, Al came to work early as I was leaving for my first day at work. I had gotten a new job at Science Applications Inc. (SAI) with typical pay for the area, which by our standards meant a lot more money than we'd ever seen before, so I would assist financially and add some labor evenings and weekends.

The guy up there paid us for the water tower. He especially wanted the oak tank.

Our 4½-year-old, Adam, was outside and saw this big man walk over and start breaking up the front planters. He immediately and ferociously attacked. No one was going to break up Adam's little yellow house! Al had a big hammer in one hand, a big crowbar in the other, protective clothing not quite up to riot police standards, and a four-year-old taking him down. He looked a little helpless standing there but was quickly rescued by Sue.

Al had been doing this sort of thing for a while. He worked fast and made quick decisions on the site; we ended up assisting him more than the other way around.

Al and Warren did things beyond a bulldog's comprehension. That Ralph was not the most intelligent or adaptive of dogs didn't help. Ralph never attacked people, but would not hesitate to attack steel wrecking bars, sledgehammers, 4 x 8 sheets of plywood, or industrial nail guns, more so if any of them made noise. He usually missed his target, but seventy-five pounds of charging bulldog proved inconvenient using tools in confined spaces or when carrying heavy objects. The guys sometimes did have a basketball they could throw at him that would keep him out of the way for a while.

We continued to live in our house during the first part of the remodeling. Warren and Al tore off the back third of the living room, floor, walls, and all, leaving the carpeting hanging out the back. After they pulled the back end of the carpet up to the ceiling and nailed its edges up the walls on both sides, Warren said, "Now you really have wall-to-wall carpet." Strong winds could blow leaves into the house, and Warren's Samoyed got in a couple of times for a snack from our kitchen, but a little more nailing low on the walls fixed that. Later, they framed a new wall across the kitchen in front of the counters. Sue stood on one side and reached through the studs to the stove and sink.

With us still living there, they got in the new foundation walls and framed up the new sections of the house that were near Malory Court. They framed up an extension onto the back of our bedroom with an additional master bath. Finally, they tore off the old roof and framed the new one. There was a week or two where rain would have not been disastrous, but certainly inconvenient for Sue and me.

Little yellow house in the background. Adam and I stand in front of the new living room.

We finally had to move out. Our back fence neighbors, whose twins often played with Adam, had a shed in their yard. It had a small bathroom and two alcoves. We moved the refrigerator over from our house into one alcove. Al and our neighbor scrounged a small sink and cooktop and made a little kitchen. Adam would sleep in the other alcove. We built a fold-down dining table at one end of the main room and put our hide-a-bed at the other. When the hide-a-bed opened out, there were about eighteen inches between the walls and sides and end of the bed. Ralph was also there but was old enough not to move around much unless there was a basketball close by.

Our stay in the shed went well. Certainly not much room for housework. Sue took cooking and baking courses at the local community college and enjoyed that. Adam was in a nice nursery school at our church and I was busy writing software to manage the data produced from all the fuel rods currently and previously in all the nuclear reactors in the United States during the day and hammering nails after I came home. Concrete pours and things benefiting from all three of us being present were on weekends if possible.

We moved out of the shed to house sit for the parents of a friend for about a month, and then into a rental on Atherwood Avenue, just a few blocks from our property, where we would live for just over a year until our new home on our property was finished. Having lived in two apartments and another converted to a condominium and sold out from under us during the three years before we landed in the little yellow house, we were getting used to moving.

I adapted quickly to homebuilding. I already knew the basics of carpentry and working with saws, hammers, screws, paint, and wood from growing up around Dad. If anything like that was being done around Dad, he would be the one doing it. Soon after moving to Coeur d'Alene, Dad provided me with scrap wood and access to his tools and workbench down in our basement. I built a whole fleet of boats with one or two saw-shaped boards for the hulls and several smaller boards attached to them for superstructures, smokestacks, gun turrets, etc.

I worked through all the phases of building a house, from the foundation up. We did all the things a general contractor would do. We contracted out only the roof covering, electrical, plumbing, heating, and sheetrock. After getting home, I would work until it was dark or even a little after and then came in for a late dinner. There were almost romantic evenings nailing skip sheathing up on the new roof, the quietness interrupted only by hammer blows to eightpenny nails, their heads shining in the reflected moonlight.

We finished and sold 2 Malory Court. This allowed us to pay off our parents, the seller-financed loan for the acre, building the road, and all other subdivision costs. We immediately started on the front house on West Selby Lane. We owned four lots and had an experienced contractor applying for a construction loan. The bank was happy to work with us. The new home would have a piling foundation needing an engineer's design. We'd use this on all our new homes. I engineered the roof trusses which we built ourselves. They turned out fine — well, more than fine with my overengineering. Truss companies were not standard and everywhere like now, but still adding their expertise would not have cost any more and their lighter trusses would have been easier to handle way up on the roof. I was learning.

2 Malory Court today. The old house started seventeen feet behind the garage and entry.

We got the occupancy permit as soon as possible on the front house and Warren moved in and finished trim and other details while he lived there. We sold the front house after owning it for a year, and thus paid lower taxes on the sale. Warren's builder friend had told him of this and of course we had hired a tax accountant to get our relationship with our senior partner, the IRS, correct. We had already sold 2 Malory Court, where Sue and I had lived more than a year. As a remodel of our "personal residence" that had also qualified for better tax treatment.

Warren finished some of the front house details in his spare time while the three of us started on Sue's and my house at 6 Malory Court. I got the corner lot with the deepest backyard and designed the largest home we would build. I made it look small and less impressive from the front, as Google Street View shows. Space at the front of pie-shaped lots at the end of a cul-de-sac is tight (so we could get in all those lots) so smaller looks more appropriate there. We weren't going to sell it anyway.

Our original plan had been to next build and sell the house at 8 Malory with perhaps another year while Warren lived there. At this point, Warren had some financial issues and sold his lot at 4 Malory. The buyer started a house there soon after we started 6 Malory.

~

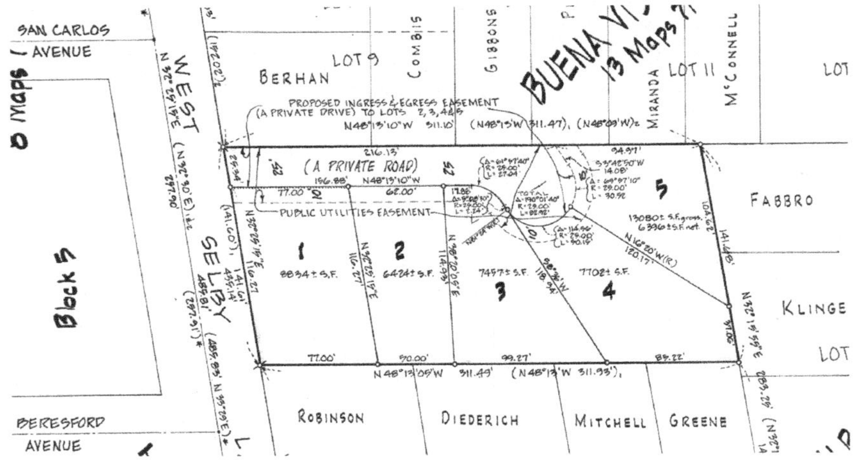

Lots 2, 3, 4 & 5 are addresses 2, 4, 6, & 8 Malory Court. Lot one is 1435 W. Selby, our second house.

My overengineering the roof trusses was a mistake, but did start my familiarity with them. Twenty years after this, many home builders would use roof and floor trusses automatically designed and modeled by software I would write, helped by this experience. I would do a better job that second time.

Our Grand Plan for Building Houses

We had a good plan. It would have worked had the world kept on going like it was for another six months, but the early '80s recession came and suddenly interest rates on our construction loan for 8 Malory more than doubled, as you see in the chart below. The house was completed. We could have sold it for double the construction loan had conditions not changed. We ended up selling it for the construction loan.

Warren also had an unrelated issue that he sold his lot to cover. He left for Oregon soon after selling 8 Malory and built a nice home on a lake up there within a few years.

In theory, the detailed framework of the grand plan was:

- Remodel & sell 2 Malory.
- This should pay the purchase of the acre, subdivision, and 2 Malory building costs. This worked. We were free of debt at this point.
- Build the front house. Warren moves in for 1 year for tax saving.
- Build my house at 6 Malory.
- My house completes and we sell the front house.
- Build 8 Malory. Warren moves in for 1 year.
- Build Warren's house.
- Warren's house completes and we sell 8 Malory.

This plan assumed some continued home price rise.
Our plan was altered by

- Warren sold his lot.
- The recession doubling the already high 10 percent rates killed our 8 Malory sale.
- Our construction loan on 8 Malory changed to over 20 percent.

We still needed to sell and did, but at a much lower price. Half the difference would have nearly paid my mortgage on 6 Malory, and the other half would have done the same for Warren had he still had his lot.

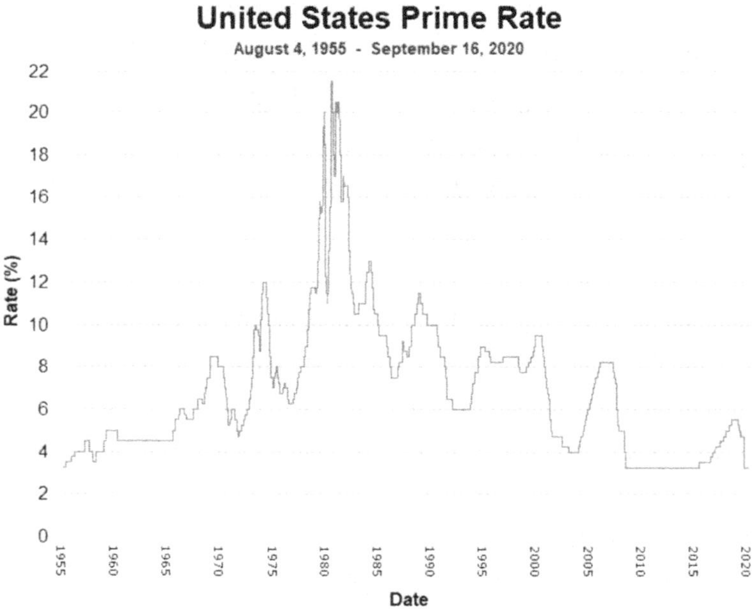

TO BUILD A HOUSE II

Dad came down a couple of times for several weeks. He had a job painting houses after high school and knew what he was doing.

I had been developing the database management system for my job at SAI and contributing much of my pay to finance the subdivision. In my spare time, I worked with Warren and Al.

I started drawing the plans for our own home when we decided to do the subdivision. I spent a lot of time and thought on them. The first time I did this was for my parents fourteen years ago and at that time I worked to make the best design possible within space and expense constraints. Now I wanted to get the best design for us, again with the same constraints, using pencil and paper on a portable drafting board, the same one I used when in high school.

I had an overall square footage limit and spent time fudging a wall this way or that, giving more space in one room and less in another, until I had the best plan I could make. Each change was time-consuming, requiring walls and their connected walls to be erased and redrawn. Then any dimensions which located the walls had to be redrawn. Other changes were more difficult. I liked traditional windows with muntins, or a grille, dividing up the glass panes. It took thirty-three carefully placed lines to draw such a window in an elevation. One plan change required moving two windows a foot to one side. That was sixty-six lines I erased and redrew. There had to be a better way.

I continually checked to keep the dimension lines consistent with the wall, window, and doorway positions in the plan as well as positions of items such as windows and doors appearing in elevations consistent with the plan. I would not make the mistake I did with my parents' house, where the dimension line said the wall was placed differently than it had been drawn in the plan.

I kept gables to the sides to make the front less imposing.

I had been drawing graphs and charts with computers at my current job, and line drawings depicting experiment apparatus and data at SLAC. In the late seventies, computers were used for big projects like moonshots, airline reservation systems, or handling data for the nation's nuclear power plants, which is what I did. I never thought of using such expensive and cumbersome equipment to help me to draw house plans. The new small home computers of that time and their monitor screens were still far from able to handle graphics like I was drawing with a pencil.

I learned and followed the rules that made plans standard and easy to read for anyone else. I was good with rules, I had to be to produce computer software, which is just writing rules for the computer to follow. These rules let me place dimension lines, framing, roof truss webbing, electrical outlet positions, and other things correctly without much thought. More than ten years later, when the home computers became powerful enough, what I learned here would come back to me, and I would put these rules into the new software I would be writing.

The large overhang kept the sun off the windows in the summer but not the winter. The rear faced south.

Ours was the second completely new home we would build, so we were getting more efficient. We reused the foundation forms we made for the house on the main road. All our foundations were pier and beam with two foot by eight inch concrete beams atop the piers. We would reuse these forms for our last house on lot 5, after which they were put together to make a large fort for our kids in our backyard.

The two story living room was the largest in the house.

We solved structural rigidity issues with the seventeen foot tall living room walls and special ordered twenty-six-foot 2x6 rafters for the long run of the roof from front to back. A large glulam beam spanned the garage side to side to support the front wall for the master bedroom above. This avoided a supporting post between the two cars that might have been knocked out.

That glulam also supported a heavily framed box that dropped down a few feet below the garage ceiling level. This would hold a large hot tub for the second-floor master bath. Early hot tubs were set into the ground or concrete for their support. We would pour concrete into that box around the hot tub to support it. The county inspector came to grant permission for us to put all this weight into the box. He was a big guy, weighing at least 250 pounds. He climbed the box, jumped up, and came down in the middle of the floor as hard as he could. "It feels like I'm jumping on concrete," he said, and passed it.

Less than eight months from breaking ground, we moved into our new home with some interior wood trim still to finish and paint.

Sue had her dream kitchen with counters wrapping around on four sides. It had four big windows giving her a full view of the back and side yards. One of our kids' favorite things to do was sailing paper airplanes in the living room. The two-story ceiling helped with that, as did using the balcony as a launching place. The cul-de-sac in front with nearly zero traffic was good for their wheeled vehicles, and they were often joined out there by Ralph the bulldog.

I put in two special places with high ceilings: two-thirds of the living room had a 17-foot, two-story ceiling as did a large upstairs hall/stairwell. The entry hall also had a high sloping ceiling.

The two-story living room had huge south-facing windows. Their 8-foot overhang outside kept out nearly all the sun in the summer and let nearly all of it in during the winter. These sun angle calculations and more would appear later in software.

We intended to live a long time in our new home but instead would move on after only seven years. We lived in the little yellow house for a little more than three years. This would become a pattern in our life; it would be rare for us to live in any one place for more than seven years.

6 Malory Dining room. Baby Nathan in the background. Dad with no shirt was working on the house. Baby Andrea, foreground, has worked at my company the last 16 years.

The people who bought 6 Malory from us in 1986 still own it to this day, thirty-four years later. I'm glad it was able to satisfy someone for so long, or was it California's Proposition 13, with its low property taxes for long-time owners, that kept them from changing homes? When we found our next house we, or initially just me, could not resist switching. Six Malory was the first house we owned by ourselves, but we have lived full time in ten residences since 6 Malory, although those included one rental and four years on a boat.

MY BUS DRIVER'S JACKET

On my first visit home from graduate school, when I flew home to visit my Coeur d'Alene draft board, Dad took me shopping for a jacket. We went to an old store when downtown Coeur d'Alene was still the town's major shopping area. Dad suggested a jacket just like the one he was wearing and had worn to work for years. It was a dark green hard wool with two large breast pockets with snap flaps. It closed with snaps as well. It would be similar to today's jeans or denim jacket, only wool. This was the only time in my life that Dad took me shopping for anything. He thought his own jacket was the greatest and told me it would probably never wear out.

The jacket was not for north Idaho winters but was otherwise good for all but the few hottest days in Coeur d'Alene. It turned out right for just about any time but the middle of summer in the San Francisco Bay area. I got many years of wear out of it, and it never showed the least wear itself.

I've already discussed how my ability to dress well helped me to catch my wife, Sue. This jacket was not a part of my dating wardrobe, however, and Sue did not notice it until we were married, but then it was too late. She said the jacket made me look like a bus driver. The only bus driver we knew was Ralph Kramden, played by Jackie Gleason, from *The Honeymooners* TV show. While similar in overall shape, his jacket zipped up the front and did not appear to be as nice as mine. I had seen jackets similar to mine on gas station attendants and maybe a real bus driver, however. Anyway, it became my "bus driver's" jacket. I would usually wear it if going to Stanford or SLAC and often wore it when building houses with Warren and Al. I could not wear it when going anywhere with Sue, however.

Wearing it while building was its downfall. I got white paint on a sleeve. Since it was water-based paint, I was able to wash it off but used hot water to do so. The sleeve shrank enough to make it hard to wear, and I used it less. I was unhappy with Sue when I found she had subsequently thrown it out, but I couldn't wear it anymore, so I had to let it go.

Sue does think I inherited many good qualities from my dad, but fondness of that type of jacket is not one of them. Still, I wish I had been able to keep that jacket. I think our marriage could have withstood it.

Had I not shrunk that sleeve, maybe I could have kept that jacket. As time went on, I worked less outdoors and also, by 1981, started working from home much of the time, so I would not have worn it so much. Perhaps I could have retired it to a closet and only worn it on occasion. But what occasion? If not for work, then for play, but play only occurred with Sue. I really loved that jacket, but Sue really did not.

The wool material of that jacket would have lasted a very long time if protected from moths. The desk chair in which I'm now sitting has a wool covering. I bought it at Price Club, now Costco, in 1981 for my home office when starting my first database business. I sat in it every day. The chair went with me when I moved from home to each of the three outside offices where I worked, the last of these being my company's current Coeur d'Alene office. You can see it in the second picture, of my Menlo Park office, in the *"New Company"* chapter. The chair now sits in my office in our Florida condominium. I still sit in it every day far more than all other chairs combined, and the brown wool covering looks like it always has. I've never found another chair this comfortable for extended sitting. Maybe my posterior has adapted to the chair, or the chair to it, after thirty-nine years? Anyway, the bottom line is, properly woven wool under hard use can wear for a very long time. How many seats of my pants do you think might have been worn out by that chair during that time?

I can't show a picture of me wearing the jacket. Sue took almost all the pictures of me and would have had me take it off before any picture.

A REAL PHYSICIST

Never confuse education with intelligence, you can have a PhD and still be an idiot. – ***Richard P. Feynman***

Maybe not an idiot, but not a physicist either.

Shortly after I returned from the Pion Channel (SMPG) meeting in Boston, a mini-scandal erupted. The government thought that universities were using government-funded graduate students as "free" labor for projects that did not further the students' educational or degree progress. I don't know if it hit the national news, but I saw several articles in the *Stanford Daily* newspaper. I could not imagine an institution like Stanford doing something like that!

The professor, a low-temperature guy, leading the SMPG project called me in for a talk shortly after the second article appeared in the *Daily*. While the SMPG would undergo a lot of tests to prove it worked as designed (it did), none of these were purposed to discover new or validate existing physics. I had finished my coursework and it was time to determine in what field I would like to do physics research. It was time for one of my rare visits with my advisor, Robert Hofstadter, a high-energy guy.

I had a conversation with my advisor but still had no particular direction or interest. I took the path of least resistance: with the original 600-foot electron accelerator in back of the Physics Department building, a new superconducting electron accelerator being built near it, a two-mile-long electron accelerator at SLAC, and an advisor who won the Nobel prize for a series of high-energy experiments using an electron accelerator, I somehow ended up in high energy physics. Perhaps I would have a thesis experiment using – you guessed it – an electron accelerator.

I say "I ended up" because I was not sure how or by whom my direction was decided then. The physics professors had their priorities for me. I was developing some different ones for me also, but mine were still unformed. Anyway, since we did have a lot of electron accelerators about, and the accelerator that had the big experiments requiring the most people to man them was the one at SLAC, I ended up hanging out at SLAC most of the time.

Stanford Linear Accelerator Center (SLAC) was an independent Department of Energy (DOE) government lab operated in close coordination with the Stanford University Physics Department. The two-mile accelerator, huge "end stations" containing equipment for experiments, and the machines at its computer center were beyond what any university could afford. Stanford professors and graduate students contributed to the large experimental teams at SLAC and so moved back and forth freely between the university and SLAC.

The SLAC linear accelerator got an electron moving at 99.5 percent light speed in its first foot. At the end of two miles it moved at 99.999999995 percent the speed of light (I checked. I counted the 9s right). Those last 9s take a lot of work. At the other end of the accelerator was the experimenter's equipment to detect those electrons and other atomic bits they slammed into. With two miles of acceleration, it took a lot of distance for those electrons and other bits to come to a stop at the other end, and physicists looked at these processes clear to the finish. That meant the detectors to look at and stop all this were large also.

Our experiments used the Stanford Positron Electron Accelerating Ring (SPEAR), located at the end of the two-mile accelerator that fed it. The ring was 260 feet across and had two "interaction regions" where the positrons and electrons collided. Our experimental group of about twenty physicists had one interaction region and Dr. Burton Richter's larger group had the other across the ring.

Our area had racks and racks of electronics that transferred data from our detectors to a "real-time" data acquisition computer which processed some of the data just enough that we could monitor the experiment. Its main job was to write the data onto large mag tapes. The stack of tape reels found their way to the SLAC Triplex computer center where the data was analyzed in detail.

I wrote the smaller, simpler software for the real-time computer. Smaller and simpler because it was all in machine language, which was difficult for people to deal with, so it was too hard to write anything large. Machine language ran much faster so it could keep up in real-time with the data coming in from the detectors. The data did not wait, the computer always had to respond – no delays, ever. As the data came in the computer stored it into memory. In its spare time between handling incoming data, the data in memory would be written to tape. If there was any time after that, the computer processed some of the data and sent it to display screens so we physicists could monitor what was happening.

Spear ring to the left foreground. Experimental apparatus was on its left and right. We worked in foreground buildings. Two mile accelerator comes in from the upper right.

Who worked on our experiments? I will leave out the Dr. in front because everyone's a Dr. at SLAC, or if not, soon would be. Robert Hofstadter was my advisor and got the Nobel in 1961 for work similar to what we were doing thirteen years later. His "henchman" was Barry, day to day as well as night-to-night overseer of the experiment. Erwin and Leo were visiting professors from Germany and Greece.

Leo was hard to forget as a big, bearded, and loud Greek who seemed more used car salesman than college professor. He was serious when it came to research and was always after me to give him new ways to analyze the data. Once I developed a new way to see interaction results in 3D on just introduced CRT screens up at the computer center. Leo had not seen the like. He messed with it for five minutes and declared he absolutely needed four additional ways. Now that he could view things from the side, he also wanted to see it from the far end of the detectors, and there were I forget how many other places. Hey, what if I could put my eye right at the interaction region and look outward? Leo loved his physics.

Larry and Richard were the other graduate students. All three of us were pretty much on the same level, average Stanford physics grad students. There were others in our group I did not interact with as much.

All of the people mentioned, and most I do not, were real physicists except for Richard and me. We were both seduced into computer software. Since my name was on eleven papers, there must have been around that number of experiments. We needed at least three to get PhD theses for the three students.

Larry did the physics calculations to check what our experiments should see. These were no joke. Larry would do one week-long complicated calculation and then find a completely different way and take another week to do the whole thing over again to check his results. That was real physics. I'd like to say if I learned a little more physics and worked as hard as Larry did, I could have done what he did, but that sounds like an alcoholic saying he could quit anytime. If in Russia and a commissar had a gun on me, I think I could have done it. Richard was certainly up to my programming ability, although different, and did other software for our experiments. I think he worked with other physicists, unnamed here, on our large team.

The "publish or perish" rule was in force at Stanford as in all the big universities. Papers published from these experiments would have a long list of names. All our physicists, including students, would be on the list, so I ended up with my name on at least eleven papers for the work done at SPEAR. The software I wrote was a crucial part of all our experiments, but I never did write a word in any of those papers, and never read more than two of them.

Early on, the real-time programming was finished and the experiment running. Running at night, that is. The technicians worked on the accelerator, SPEAR ring, and equipment during the day. They must have been union or something to get the best hours. I pulled a lot of night shifts, which were no fun for me and less for Sue. The fun happened when I moved up to the SLAC computer center to work with a wonder of the known world, the Triplex.

One night when I was gone, someone slid Sue's bedroom window open and started to climb in. He disappeared when Sue, still awake, suddenly sat up. Still, she called out and the big guy who shouted at his wife all the time next door was soon running back and forth outside yelling and waving around the biggest pistol Sue had ever seen. She locked the window after that, and intruders never came back.

To me, Barry was a sometimes pain in the you-know-what bureaucrat. He wrote the group's publications (from where I plagiarized a little thesis content, but don't tell anyone), put me on the night shift, and sometimes said I wasn't thinking about the physics side of things. I had only one real argument with him when he got after me for something around 3 a.m. It was short and most likely was my fault. I was not in the best mood at the time.

The night of November 10, 1974, Barry and I were manning the experiment. I would soon be leaving at midnight. Someone from the experiment on the other side of the ring called and told Barry they were seeing something new. Could we adjust our electronics to look in the same area? Dials were turned, cables were unplugged and plugged in somewhere else, various switches all over eight racks of equipment were checked or reset, and we sat back to watch the data come in.

We saw something: a momentous, earth-shaking, Nobel-prize-winning, big-deal discovery. You don't see this every day; in fact, even if you're a physicist, you probably don't see this in your lifetime. To a real physicist, it doesn't get better than this. Well, except maybe if you're the head real physicist on the other side who would actually end up getting that prize two years from then. Barry was thinking, "It's not our discovery, but I'll still be able to write important, decisive, corroborating papers for our group." I was thinking, "Now I'm going to have to stay here until morning and we shut all this stuff down." This was my final, conclusive realization that I was not then, nor would I ever be, any sort of a real physicist.

As the discoverer, Dr. Richter named the new particle. Everyone hated his name. When they decided to use a Greek character as most other elementary particles did, they found all the Greek characters they knew already used. I think someone in Richter's group said something like, "There's that big crazy Greek over on the other side, let's ask him," and so they did. The character "psi" (Ψ) was left, and so the particle was named. Leo would be immortalized in Wikipedia for that. Check under "The Name."

On November 20 at 3:20 a.m., the typical time for this sort

of stuff, the Richter group discovered a second particle, the psi prime. It was "here we go again." I was not there that night, but requests for software mods both for our real-time computer, as well as the data analysis up at the computer center, were through the roof. These eleven days would be the most momentous in the entire history of SLAC. I was working nights and days like crazy. Sue was not pleased.

When all this was done and our own experiments finished, all three of the students on our experiment, myself, Richard, and Larry, became "Doctor of Philosophy in Physics." One became a physicist.

Physics lesson:

Electrons, protons, and other "elementary" particles help make up atoms. Far too small to study in any ordinary way, we can get them moving very fast, run them into something in an "interaction region," and cause an "interaction." The interaction can scatter whatever the electron hits away from the interaction region or even split things up into different new kinds of elementary particles which then scatter away. The original electron, if it still exists, may scatter away also. We learn about the original electron as well as others scattered out by watching how all this happens.

We may even see a completely new particle, the kind that when combined with other new particles would make up a proton or other already known particle. In fact, we did.

We place "detectors" in as many positions as possible to detect and track whatever scatters out of the interaction region. The detector may show the direction, type, and speed of a particle passing through it. We like to have a theory that predicts how the interaction and scattering should happen. This helps us put the detectors in the best places as well as tells us what information to expect from the detectors.

Overview of our experiments at SPEAR:

Our experiment had about twenty physicists. The bigger one next door had maybe forty. A few SLAC technicians assisted us. The parts of our experiment were:

A. Conceiving the experiment and funding it,
B. Physics calculations of what to expect,
C. Overall detector design and layout,
D. Detailed detector design and specifications,
E. Detector construction and maintenance,
F. Processing data from the detectors on site,
G. Physics observations and defining calculations to interpret results,
H. Software to assist observations and to perform calculations for F and G.

The person doing A would be a real physicist, often at the Nobel level. In my experiment, it was Robert Hofstadter who had won the Nobel in 1961. Next door to us, Burton Richter's experiment resulted in his getting the Nobel two years later in 1976. Real physicists did B, C, and G. Larry a lot of B and Erwin and Leo a lot of G. Technicians did most of E with physicist supervision. This left D, F, and H for the rest of us.

On my PhD experiment, I ended up writing software controlling the real-time computer for F and writing most of the software for H. Others decided what calculations to make, what data was important, etc. I just wrote software that calculated what they wanted and showed them what they wanted to see from the data. I did not make physics decisions or myself look at physics data, but they all decided I was doing physics, and my name is on all the research papers as well as my thesis.

I did substantial work in the D area for a later device, the Crystal Ball.

This was well after the early days when reactions were captured on photographic plates. For us, it was done with large detectors that produced electrical signals to electronics. The electronics passed on what they saw to a recording real time computer. There were a lot of special crystals, exotic light detectors, and racks and racks of custom electronics with wires plugged in all over the place.

Experiments at SLAC were BIG

The average experiment at SLAC was large; after all, if you accelerate an electron for 2 miles, it usually takes more than a couple of feet for it to stop, so any equipment to look at it extended over long distances. Experiments are done in large places, which we called "end stations." Experiments like this cannot be done by a normal college or even a large university. This was the high part of high energy and was done in government labs in the US and international labs in Europe.

The equipment was complex and could take months to set up, so you used that equipment for many experiments before switching to a different series of experiments with different equipment and people.

A RETREAD PHYSICIST

The SLAC Triplex was a wonder of the world. IBM built only twenty 360/91 machines and six remained at IBM. The rest went to NASA for moon shots and a few government labs. A dozen IBM employees came with it to keep it running, and they worked nonstop. The software was buggy, and hardware failed a lot. They needed every one of those people all the years it was at SLAC. Of course, your iPhone now is much more powerful, up to 1,000 times, in every way, but at the time, it was fantastically fast, huge, complex, expensive and whatever else that made us in awe of it.

Few people in the world could access and use such a machine, and I was one of them. I did much of the computer work for experiments closely related to Nobel prize level work being done right then. These were the most important experiments in the entire history of SLAC. That fantastic computer was put there for me, and I could get all the time on it I could manage to use. My programs grew in size until they reached some basic limits.

Handoff of the new 360/91 from an IBM manager (obviously the guy in the suit) to the SLAC director of computation. All those lights on the panel could tell you what was wrong, and there was often something wrong. To check them, you first pressed a button that turned them all on, checked for and replaced the burnt out ones, and then used them to diagnose the problem.

The first limit was that each line of my program was written and stored on a punch card. We grad students had to do all our own keypunching. We stored our cards in the boxes they came in. Each box held two thousand cards. I could carry five boxes at a time, and you definitely did not want to drop a box and scatter the cards.

Possible errors from reading tens of thousands of cards also limited my programs to twenty thousand cards, or ten boxes. Each punch card averaged about a hundred holes. That's a total of two million holes for one of my programs. How often might a hole be missed by one of the small wire brushes that had to poke through it to make electrical contact with the metal plate behind as the card moved rapidly past it? That error could be hard to find since in Fortran, blanks were ignored. In other words, if a card had the number 368 and the "6" punch was missed, the number would just be 38, causing no error to be flagged, just an incorrect result.

This limit went away in a few years when SLAC installed new front-end computers where we could type in and edit our software and large disk drives where it was stored, ending the use of punch cards.

The second limit on program size was the Fortran language. Large Fortran programs grew unmanageably complex. This would later improve when the computer industry abandoned Fortran for better computer languages, but I could not wait for that.

Fortran was what everyone used at SLAC, but a new computer language called C was being developed at another university that was better for writing large programs. I wrote a program to read in a C-like language and translate it into Fortran. The programs I wrote with my new language had less than half the lines of code to produce the same amount of Fortran. Besides, the new smaller code could be better organized – it quadrupled the amount of Fortran code I could produce.

I called this translator STEP. At the SLAC Computation Research Group, I learned others had the same problems I had with Fortran and some had developed "Fortran preprocessors" to allow writing code in a better language that would then be translated into Fortran. I used ideas from them and an IBM research paper to design STEP. To my knowledge, it was the most comprehensive and powerful Fortran preprocessor in existence. My SLAC publication to describe it was CTGM No. 177, 1979, which was presented at the IBM GUIDE meeting in Montreal the following year. STEP turned out to be crucial in the job and businesses I had after I left SLAC.

My software processed experiment data in the traditional batch way used at SLAC, but also in new interactive ways using just acquired video displays to show 3D pictures of high energy reactions. Experimenters could look at pictures I produced and get insights into what was happening in our experiments. They loved the new ways. They spent hours of quality, and expensive, time in front of the IBM 2250 display looking at reaction after reaction, getting a feel for how they happened.[1]

I wrote a lot of software, learned to handle massively large programs, and discovered I enjoyed doing that. This was like the pion channel design software I fell into when I first came to Stanford. Of course, in addition to all this, I still had to get that PhD. When the experiment assigned to me for that was finished, I wrote and got approved a thesis that described it.

Just before the final oral examination, I had to show my ability to read a scientific paper in a foreign language. I chose German since I had two years of it in college, which proved you can get a good grade in a foreign language but not learn it. I was afraid I'd get tested by Felix Bloch, a seventy-year-old professor emeritus and Nobel laureate who escaped from Germany before the war. That would have been a disaster. I don't know how long I would have had to study German to read that well. Instead, I got another professor, not from Germany. I read the paper and got stuck a few lines in. He looked at it, got stuck too, and just passed me. Other than that, my PhD orals came off without a hitch.

Sue was waiting for me when I came out from my orals. She had Adam practicing standing at one end of the physics building main entry area. Professor Bloch and I came out from different hallways into the other end of the main vestibule. Sue gently released Adam, who took his first steps, crossing the hall as Sue exclaimed that fact, walking all the way to me. Professor

Bloch expressed his hearty approval of the entire process, "So, both father and son graduate today!" While Professor Bloch may not have approved me, he did approve my son.

After finishing our experiments and receiving my PhD in June 1975, I stayed on at SLAC as a research associate. Our series of experiments continued, and I continued doing the same work as before, further enhancing our ability to look at our data in better ways.

[1] I was going to say, "the 2250 display cost as much as a house," but that's wrong. At that time, I had been checking prices of small homes on San Carlos Ave in Redwood City to compare with the price of the acre we bought. They were around $20,000. This display station was $280,000. Maybe that's why SLAC got only two of them. Fortunately, they were so new to SLAC that there was little demand for them, so Leo and Erwin happily sat there by the hour, using the keyboard and light pen (like a touch screen today) to change the view.

The 2250 became usable at SLAC when the IBM 370 "front end" computers were installed in 1974 – they weren't going to take up 360/91 time with someone fooling around on a display. Stories got around SLAC about the guy who spilled his coke into the keyboard of one of the expensive terminals we used to edit our code. No rumors of the same with the 2250s. They each had their own room. Take a glass of water in there and you'd be shot.

THE CRYSTAL BALL

This chapter is a bit technical. It contains nothing that bears on future chapters.

Around the time I graduated, Caltech, Harvard, Stanford High Energy Physics Lab, and SLAC got together and submitted a proposal for the Crystal Ball detector to be built at SLAC. Being shortly after the momentous discoveries of 1974, the government said yes.[1] This was simpler for me than the medical pion channel but still called for detailed machining of hundreds of delicate and expensive parts. I would do all the detailed design and engineering specifications and drawings for the machining of 672 crystals that would fit together to form the ball.

The three drawings below came from my design program. The twenty big triangles of the top icosahedron shape each divide into four sub triangles that warp outward to make the shape more spherical. Each of these triangles divides into nine more triangles and warp outward, making 20 x 4 x 9 = 720 triangles. We took twenty-four triangles out on each side so the SPEAR storage ring beams can come in from both sides and hit each other in an "interaction region" right in the middle of the ball, leaving 672. This is the same kind of geometry used for geodesic domes.

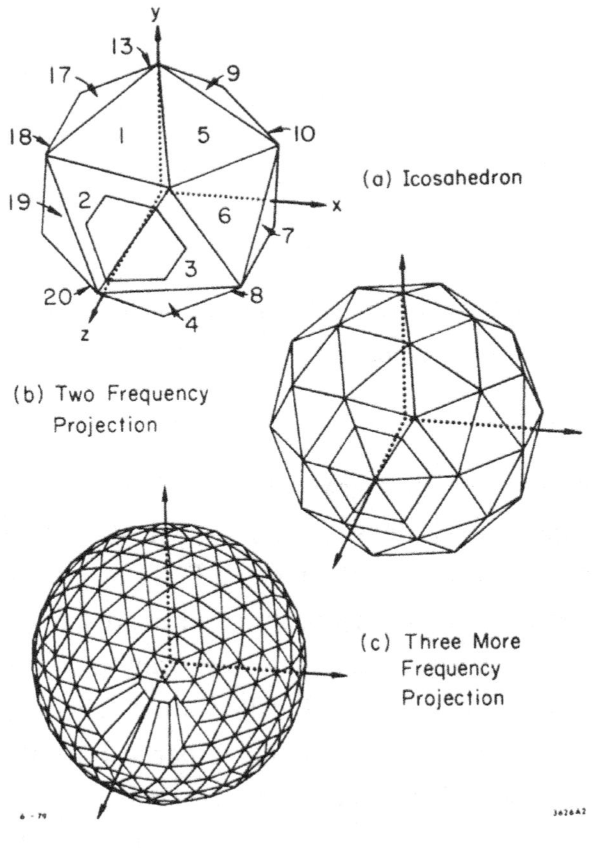

Fig. 2
Geometry of the Crystal Ball

The triangles on the outside of the ball are the large end of a crystal "prism," with the small end at the inside surface around the interaction region. You can see about six prism sides showing if you look into the hole on the third ball diagram. The warping in the above paragraph caused twelve different prism shapes which repeated and rotated formed the ball. Of course, whether the 672 prisms needed 672 different shapes or only twelve made no difference in the design difficulty since once you figure out how to do one, the computer will do all the rest. That said, the entire design process would have been difficult if not impossible without a computer.

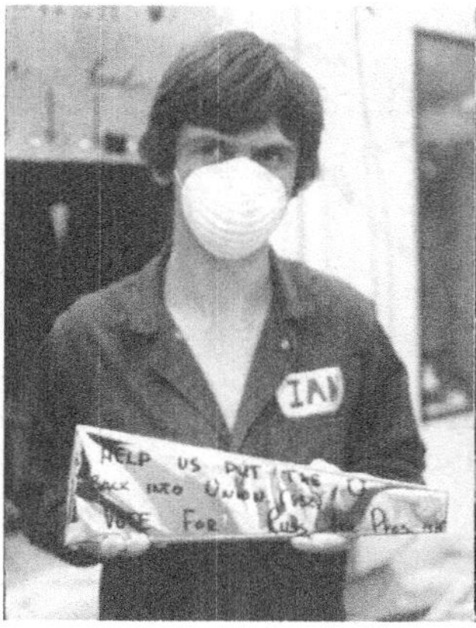

The crystals were machined from lab-grown sodium iodide crystals and a completely dry room. The material is hygroscopic, meaning it will suck any moisture out of the air and become useless in seconds. Once completed, each crystal must be sealed with a thin covering.

The Crystal Ball was not so large but was one of the most expensive devices of its type. Normally detectors — especially sodium iodide detectors with their strict temperature, shock, and moisture issues — last only the life of the experiment series. This one was different. Once finished with its experiments at SLAC, the ball was moved, along with its team of support people, to DESY, a national lab in Germany, using a special-made truck. The truck was loaded into an Air Force C5 which was refueled in the air — only one landing shock was allowed. After years at DESY, it came back to the US Brookhaven National Lab. From there it later went to the Mainz Microtron facility in Germany where it remains in use to this day.

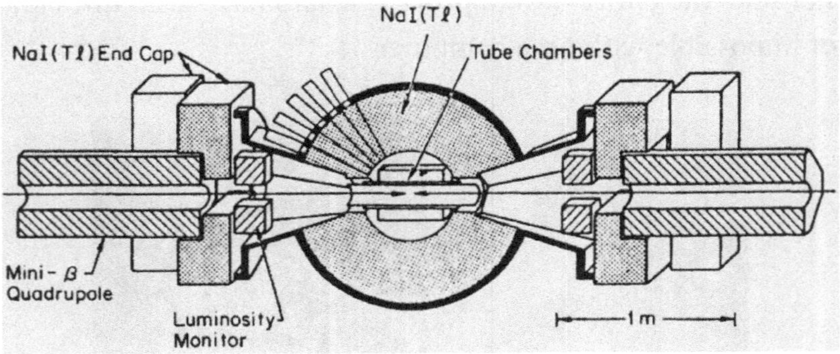

Crystal Ball layout. Crystal prisms extend radially between thin inner and thick outer circles.

[1] This was the second try for funding. The first try shows that, even with Nobel laureates from three universities and a national lab, stupid mistakes can be made. The original plan was for a larger, even more expensive, detector. Congress might have bought that, but they used an impolitic name. How do you think it would look in your home district in Mississippi if they found you voted a ton of money to some fancy intellectuals on the coast for a "Crystal Palace?"

A REAL JOB

The past is a foreign country, they do things differently there. — ***L. P. Hartley***

I had success for a limited time using methods that would not work later on. I spent endless hours solving hopeless problems that few now are aware ever existed.

I was out interviewing at various computer companies while working as a research associate at SLAC. I visited a friend of Warren's, who was a manager at HP, and several other places. I was offered a horrible-sounding job writing software to test new printers at Varian. I was to write test routine after test routine, this variation and that, for years. I'd rather do physics! The real world and its problems proved mundane and boring compared to working up some new way of doing things with large systems at SLAC.

Dad, Adam, and me in front of my office building.

A doctorate in physics meant little to these companies. Most posted offerings saying CS (Computer Science) graduates only! The new field, not in existence at my undergraduate school, was a requirement seven years later.

Science Applications, Inc. (SAI) had a large office in Palo Alto specializing in contract work for Electric Power Research Institute (EPRI), which was funded by US electric power utility companies. My new boss, Ed, was pitching EPRI a four-year contract to produce computer software to track all nuclear fuel rods, in use and spent, in all US nonmilitary reactors. A single reactor can contain 45,000 fuel rods. A nuclear power plant can have several reactors plus onsite deep water pools where spent fuel rods are kept. All are radioactive. All must be tracked.

The word "database" was his description of what EPRI wanted. Ed and I both heard of the term and figured that computer software called "database management system" (DBMS) would be needed to handle a nuclear fuel rod database. Hundreds of programmers produced other DBMS running on big IBM computers for airline reservation systems or tracking parts at big aerospace companies. Somehow Ed decided that I was the best person for the job because:

- I had built large software systems that worked for tasks not initially understood.
- EPRI wanted to use Fortran on the new Prime minicomputer. Fortran was a horrible language for this type of system, but the research types at EPRI loved it, and my STEP language processor would handle that.
- My physics PhD looked good on the contract bid to EPRI. They all were PhDs at EPRI.

In short, Ed didn't know what to do and neither did I, but it was research, and we both were familiar with starting out like that.

I started work at SAI in March 1977 but soon found myself back at Stanford. A little reading turned up articles about monster DBMS projects, some of them spectacular failures, and other scary things. I had previously read various CS books as part of my change from a physicist to a software person, but nothing about database. At the Stanford Computer Science Department, I asked if any professors worked with DBMS. I was soon talking to Gio Wiederhold. We started with an overview of DBMS types and their issues.

As you would expect for a university professor, soon the latest DBMS ideas, and the next big thing, the Relational Database Management System (RDBMS) with its new Structured

Query Language (SQL), came up. RDBMS was the most flexible and adapted easily to any type of data. It paid for this by being more difficult to efficiently implement. EPRI's attitude was "When we get all this data on the computer, then we can figure out so many different ways to use it!" No one had a handle on what any of those ways might be, so the RDBMS idea looked good to me, and Professor Wiederhold thought the same.

While the RDBMS idea was known, the only implementations I found were research projects at IBM (System R) and UC Berkeley (INGRES). Other than a few experimental test systems, RDBMSs would first be available in 1979[1], but not on Prime computers.

The whole idea of relational databases was to make them simple and logical for the user to understand, which made the whole concept easy for me. Making the database simple for people made them much more difficult and inefficient for the computer to handle, however, making the whole job difficult for me. Fortunately, UC Berkeley published papers of everything they had done so far. No idea if or when their system would ever be available for use outside, and Prime did not support the programming language they used, so the Berkeley system would not be on Prime computer anyway.

I had an RDBMS running at SAI in two years and the completed project was turned over to EPRI in four.[2] In addition to producing the lists of data expected from the system, new graphics-capable terminals appeared a few years after we started, allowing graphs and charts to be produced directly by the RDBMS. This may have been the first DBMS or RDBMS to directly produce graphical reports, but I never verified that.

This was my first "real job." Here and afterward, I continued building large software systems mostly on my own. I worked on a new frontier. The process of writing large software systems was still not well understood. Since large expensive computers were required, why not put a large number of people to work on a project? But many people caused even longer development time, huge failures, and systems which required inordinate ongoing maintenance for bugs that could never seem to be eliminated. Would fixing a bug just introduce an average of two new bugs because the fixer and the original developer did not quite understand each other?[3]

Could I, working by myself and later on with one assistant for well-defined sub-projects, produce an RDBMS to compete with those produced by development teams at large computer companies? Many software development process experts a few years later would say "Why not?"

Gradually the process would be better understood, the corporate approach would work better, and it would become harder, although never impossible, for one person "working in his bedroom" to compete. Then something new, like the personal computer or new more powerful software language, would upend the industry, making another new frontier. While the corporations tried to understand the new ways and shift personnel away from the old, that person in his bedroom might come up with something new and have it out in the market.

I had started work in a new frontier. I would, by accident, end up working in more new frontiers that would appear over the next fifteen years.[4]

[1] Oracle released the first commercial RDBMS on the DEC Vax in 1979. Two or three other systems followed in a few years. Computers became fast enough to allow wider use of RDBMS in the mid '80s, and they were widely used even for large-scale

databases by the mid-'90s. About 115 companies now specialize in RDBMSs. None were ever released on the Prime or SEL computers except for mine.

[2] SAI used only Fortran and our client specified and used only Fortran. I wanted to use my STEP translator to produce all this RDBMS code faster. When I showed my boss a sample of how the new program code would look using my invented language, it gave him a scare. I explained things and then showed him how the equivalent Fortran would look. That really gave him a scare. We used the new language. It translated into Fortran, which was what EPRI required.

[3] The Wikipedia article "*Mythical Man Month*" summarizes many of the "counter-intuitive" issues that appeared in the early days of software development. The last half of this article outlines about ten necessary sequential phases to develop a successful software program. A team must follow the sequence to avoid disaster. One person working alone can do all of them at once, at least I did.

[4] All the computers and companies I worked with in this chapter and the next had just come on the scene, in many cases replacing the old mainframes I worked with at Stanford and SLAC. They would be outmoded and disappear in fifteen years, replaced by the PC and other newer ones. Then I would use a completely different language, requiring a whole new way of writing and even thinking about software.

It's interesting and exciting. It's also hard. What you knew would no longer work; you had to learn new ways on different equipment. You become an expert, and then you're not.

A NEW COMPANY

No matter how hard you work, someone else is working harder. ***— Elon Musk***

Sometimes you lie in bed at night and you don't have a single thing to worry about. That always worries me! — ***Charlie Brown***

With my own business, I always had something to worry about. Once an issue was solved, I was immediately on to the next. Normally I went to bed with something I had to solve but had no idea how to do it. Either that, or with a bug for which I could not fathom a fix. I would have to get a fix. Any bug I could not fix would be the one that ended the company.

In November 1981, after completing the database project for Electric Power Research Institute (EPRI), I looked at the twenty other projects at SAI and found nothing I liked nearly as much as building large software systems. I asked SAI and EPRI if I could take the RDBMS technology I created with me and form a new database company. In return, I would be available for advice if any issues came up with the EPRI software and they agreed. I heard of no issues. Seung Lee, who had assisted me through most of the project, took over anything that might be left. He handled things fine and no one ever called me.

My office in the back small bedroom at Malory Court. I needed air con in the window with the prime computer, lower right.

Starting my own business for the first time seemed a natural thing to do. To start a business, I had:

- Software I spent four years writing while at SAI. I ended up using none of this except for my experience writing it, which was invaluable.

- Free use of a Prime computer in their sales office. Prime needed an RDBMS and had known about my RDBMS work for years.
- A consulting understanding with Graftek in Boulder, Colorado to integrate my RDBMS with their CAD software. Before I left, SAI sent Sue and me to an RDBMS conference in Los Angeles where I met a Graftek representative. I somehow got on the speaker list for a short presentation after Larry Ellison of Oracle. I was able to pretty much match everything that Larry said about Oracle. I said I would make my software run on the SEL computer Graftek used. Neither Oracle nor any other RDBMS software ever would.[1]
- My dad's outlook on life, that made starting a business as natural as getting a job. This I did not understand until much later in life.

My talk at the Los Angeles conference went over pretty well for an unknown, one of the few times before or since I have performed well before an audience. While I developed on the Prime, with the STEP processor, transferring my code to the SEL used by Graftek should be possible. Immediately after leaving SAI, I visited Graftek. They were willing to pay for my moving the software to the SEL machine and linking it up to their CAD software.

I worked in the small bedroom at 6 Malory or at the Prime sales office that had my development computer. I had no business expenses to pay and had living expenses from Graftek. I quickly decided that the different architecture used by the IBM System R research system was much superior to that I had followed from the Berkeley INGRES and decided to rewrite the entire code. I ended up using none of the code I developed at SAI, but the experience developing it allowed me to work much faster to build a better system in much less than two years.

Second commercial office at 1550 El Camino Real, Menlo Park. Prime on left, SEL on right with tape drive above.

Electric utilities knew of my older RDBMS through EPRI, since EPRI's job was to disseminate all its research findings to its member utilities. Prime computer also informed their customers, such as GE and MCI communications, of my system. I got business from software sales as well as general consulting about RDBMS issues from various large companies and power utilities.

The Gould SEL Computer Systems Division soon contacted me because of my Graftek work and asked for my RDBMS as part of the software they sold to various military contracts. So, I started numerous trips to their Ft. Lauderdale facility.

My contact there was Denny, a great guy that I worked with a lot. This was my first time working long-term for a large company. There were politics and other craziness that could come up in a computer company where the company attorney made considerably more than either the person in charge of the entire hardware effort or the other person in charge of the entire software effort. Denny was my guide to dealing with corporate America, mainly by telling me it did little good to worry much about it. Things just worked the way they did, you tolerated it for a while, could satisfy them with less than you would think, and they would soon go off to something else and leave us alone. Seung Lee, a little older than me, was a little like that at SAI a few times. I could play better with others if I had a little help.

I made money from software sales on the Prime. Graftek and Gould sold my software as their own RDBMS on the SEL. I also had payments for consulting. Prime could no longer grant use of their computer but had just come out with a new compact computer for $40,000. It was the size of an under-counter refrigerator rather than a standard one. My dad bought one and got a tax benefit by leasing it to me. In mid-1984, my youngest son, Jordan, was born about the time I got the new Prime and both were installed into my office. Jordan was a quiet baby and was never a problem as an office mate.

Two years in, I hired a marketer and then a secretary. We closed off our family room from the kitchen with wallboard and insulation, so no sound got through, and made it into the marketer's office. He was on the phone a lot.

I did not exactly hire a secretary. Sue's best friend Ruth visited one day, coming into some kind of pandemonium due to the new baby Jordan, the marketer needing something, or the other two kids and Ralph getting into things. I was not aware of it; I was working up in my office and Sue shielded me from it as usual. Sue was going crazy trying to keep things peaceful enough that I could work without interruption. Starting a business was as stressful or more so to Sue as it was to me, and she needed help. Ruth declared she would be my secretary and I could pay her when and if I had the funds. Ruth made things run smoothly, helping me and the marketer, but also Sue, who she correctly assessed needed the most help.

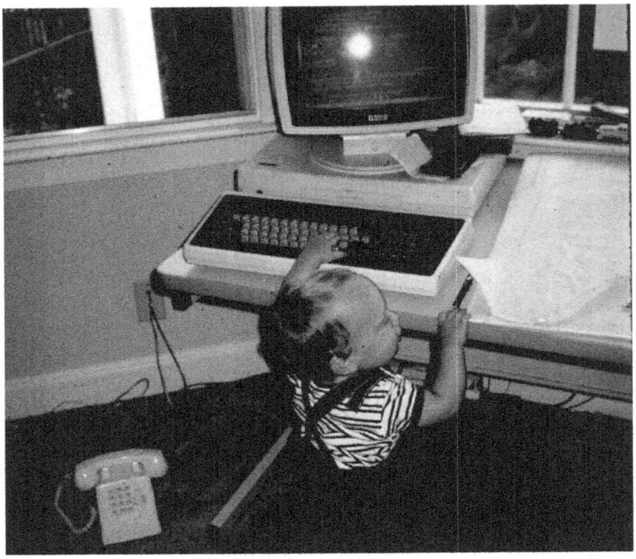

Jordan at the Prime computer's console terminal.

One year with the three of us at our home was enough, and we moved to a commercial office in Redwood City. We stayed there for two years and then moved to an office in Menlo Park.

I visited with Professor Gio Wiederhold from time to time to exchange ideas. While research into database theory was done at Stanford, I had completed one RDBMS and was now working on another one. I knew how ideas in the academic papers coming out of UC Berkeley and IBM research worked out in practice. Professor Wiederhold sent people who contacted him regarding the practical side of RDBMS my way. He sent the Koreans, who we visited in 1991, as well as others interested in RDBMS implementation or consulting.

Ideas exploded then. I saw the Xerox Alto at the Stanford computer science department, thought to be the first personal computer in all aspects but its price. It had an advanced graphics display was the first computer to use a mouse. It and its Xerox successor the Star, which I also saw, both worked much like a modern PC or Mac. Steve Jobs saw them, and they were the inspiration for the Apple Macintosh computer. It was a time of missed opportunities, first for Xerox and later for IBM.

[1] I did find out another reason why Gould had no other software like mine. Their machine had limited memory and required me to do my own memory management using "overlays." I had done this before on PDP-11's and other small machines with much simpler software and it was no fun there. Overlaying a large code like mine on their machine was truly a monumental effort. Denny and I got it working, but I still have trouble believing we were able to do that. Thankfully overlays and other crazy things we had to do have been long gone from computers since the start of the '90s, and on some computers like the Prime and the Vax were gone by the early '80s. In the early days, it was easy to write software that would be too much for a computer to run. Then the fun began when you developed more and more clever ways to make it run anyway.

MACBAIN

There is nothing like looking, if you want to find something. You certainly usually find something, if you look, but it is not always quite the something you were after. — ***J.R.R. Tolkien****, The Hobbit*

Those were the days! – ***Archie Bunker****, "All in the Family" TV Show*

At five in the afternoon in October 1989, I was in my Menlo Park office across the street from Menlo College when I felt strange. My office chair was on rollers and did not move much, but I looked down and the floor was going back and forth underneath me from the Loma Prieta earthquake. The bookcase! I had built a huge seven-and-a-half-foot-tall bookcase for the little yellow house, moved it to 6 Malory, and then moved it to Jordan's bedroom in our subsequent home in next door Atherton. I had meant to fasten that to the wall. What if it fell over on Jordan? I tore out of there, sprinted across El Camino Real, front to back through the college, through our front gate, another 60 yards to the back of the house, into the house, and into Jordan's bedroom.

60 MacBain seen from the driveway.

The bookcase stood. Where was Jordan? Sue and Nathan had been in the back enclosed porch. They ran out of the house, whereupon they both said, "Where is Jordan?" They ran back into the porch but from its side windows saw an upset five-year-old running down the driveway. "That front porch is jumping up and down and making me draw out of the lines!" It was not only the porch that was jumping. Days later I learned that our house had been inches away from collapsing completely.

We had lived in our custom-designed home at 6 Malory

Court for seven years and had completely finished some of its details just a year before. That house was perfect for us, just how we had dreamed it.

View out the living room windows to the front. The swing was in the large tree center-left.

Our house was just two blocks from the town of Atherton with its minimum-acre lots and large estates. Our Sunday recreation was often to drive around and look at Atherton open houses. Prices were out of sight, but the homes, furnishing, and gardens were out of the pages of the finest House Beautiful, Colonial Homes, and other magazines of the time. Sue got many new ideas both for interior decoration and outdoor gardening.

One Sunday, we had visited a few homes and had time for one more. Signs were out for the end of the MacBain cul-de-sac, so we drove through the gate and a long 150 feet onward back to the house. The yard needed major work and they'd lost track of any gardens that must have been there in the past. The house was not ready to fall down but clearly needed work.

Sue wasn't getting out of the car, but I thought a quick look wouldn't hurt. I walked into a large living room containing ordinary furnishings and a real estate agent. I was honest with him about only looking because Atherton was entirely out of our price range, but we got to talking. He was at the end of a slow day and told me his troubles. The owners had divorced, were still fighting tooth and nail, and the court had ordered the house sold. The husband was for the sale and the wife, still living there, was decidedly opposed. She had messed up I forget how many of his sales and he was not the first realtor affected. The listing had been on the market forever and was getting stale, etc. The house and yard were a mess, which I already knew, but the garbage piles and far greater mess out back I didn't. The price had dropped over the months and other realtors, even from his own office, had stopped bringing clients by.

Living room viewed toward front entry. Yes, a crack runs up just left of the clock. No leak, so no problem.

Designing and building a house or two and planning out a subdivision and a previous yard helps you visualize possibilities, so I may have been above average in that regard. Sue's desire to visit Atherton open homes also gave me a feel for home prices there. I made a full-price offer. I also told him that he could sell our house on Malory Court. I signed up right there.

I came back to the car and told Sue we had bought a house. I'll withhold an accurate description of her reaction, but it was definitely a "You did what?!" moment. I have since learned to bring her in earlier on decisions. Some fast talking did not convince her it was a great idea, but at least she was not completely opposed. There was already one person completely opposed, who turned out to be enough.

Dad and I working in the entry hall. The Front door is on the left.

One of Dad's companies in California had been real estate.

He'd told me if he had a listing and got a full price offer with no contingencies, the seller must carry through with the contract and sell the house, or if not, pay the full sale commission to the agent. Could I make a deal out from which they could not back? I didn't think this was the kind of "fast dealing" Dad would disapprove of. They had to sell sooner or later, and every time they messed things up, they were hurting themselves when the price dropped, so it might as well be this time and to me. I had to get to that "no contingency" status quickly, so there would be no time for our house to sell. I would get a "bridge" loan.

The database company was doing well in 1986 and I had a good equity position in our current house, so getting the bridge loan was fast and all contingencies disappeared. Our realtor soon found a buyer for our current home. Not only that, this new buyer listed their old home with our realtor. He was looking at five commissions: purchase and sale of both MacBain and 6 Malory and sale of his new client's home (technically five half commissions). We were both motivated.

Our seller delayed and then balked. She dug in her heels and would not sign off the deal. Our realtor went to his broker. The broker went to his attorney. All three met with the lady and talked about how she had messed up X previous sales and the expenses they had sunk into these. They discussed the court order to sell. If this sale did not go through, she would pay the commission anyway and would still eventually have to sell the house. Then, there were those four other commissions …

We were hanging out there a little with that bridge loan, but our former house did not take long to sell, and getting a normal home loan for MacBain was easier than getting that bridge loan. It was great that our Malory Court house sale closed two and a half months after MacBain did. It was about two months before MacBain was livable.

Adventure is the best word for moving into MacBain. The house was as large as our previous home. Both had four bedrooms, but MacBain was two baths instead of two and a half. It was painfully obvious that the one-acre yard had to come first. After signing the offer, it had taken me close to an hour hacking bushes and moving things, just to have a straight path to pull a measuring tape 150 feet across the yard in back of the house.

The main garbage pile back of the house was immense. As we transferred that into several large dumpster bins, we discovered an intact, if not operational, three-wheeled meter maid vehicle, a washer and dryer, and much else of worthless interest. Head-high weeds and bushes were thick everywhere and, with other stuff, filled other bins. We got it cleaned up and partially trimmed. The house was painted. Dad visited and we fixed the interior. It became a laid-back, comfortable place.

The property was almost identical in size and shape to the acre we turned into the five lot Malory Court subdivision, twice as deep as it was wide. Its back, sides, and front were completely shielded by bushes and trees. We never did see the house on the property in the back. To one side was the Menlo College soccer field, which we seemed to use more than they did. No house had yet been built on the other side, but if it had, we would not have seen it anyway. Pass through our gate and you were in the country.

How can a home you blundered into be so much better than the one where you carefully planned every detail? Being on a whole acre with great Bay Area weather helped. A San Francisco banker built MacBain as a summer vacation home in 1910. The special inlay in the living room's hardwood floors and so much multipaned glass area was unusual for that time. Given the land value in Atherton, my original thought was to tear it down and build an elegant new home like others in the area. Loss of a contract two months after we closed the house brought those thoughts to a close as well. By then, we had both fallen in love with the house. It was perfect. We learned that we didn't want elegant, we needed easy and comfortable. We had a country home, not a city estate. Later, in another place, we had the city estate and it had its own interest and advantages, but we never lived better than at MacBain.

The vaulted ceiling living room spanned the front of the house with glass French doors all the way across. The many plants and even trees in large pots from our seventeen-foot ceiling Malory Court living room fit in easily. The entry hall was at one end and the fireplace at the other.

View out the dining room box window. The Menlo College soccer field is beyond the fence.

Sue loved the large dining room whose box window hung out from the house providing a long, deep built-in sideboard that held any amount of food. Larger than what I designed for Malory Court, the breakfast room that hung out from the kitchen into the yard with three of its sides completely covered with old multipaned windows was inelegantly wonderful; it seems magical in our memories now.

When visitors came and sat down in the living room, or especially in the breakfast room for coffee, it was a long time before they wanted to get back up. We kept a child of an upper-class Atherton lady from our church who had another child in the hospital. Nathan was eight and reading a story to Jordan, age three. It was evening and both were in their jammies sitting on a loveseat by the fire. The lady came in the entry, turned, and froze. Sue went over to greet her, and she just kept staring at the fireplace. Finally, she said, "This is like Currier and Ives."

Left to right, a friend, Nathan, and Jordan by the redwood tree in the side yard.

The property came with chickens and their enclosure which we kept for a while. Sue noticed the ruckus when they had a pecking attack on one chicken and always put a stop to it, but one night when she was in her underclothes, that ruckus started up in the chicken enclosure. She had to rescue that chicken, so she ran out barefoot into the enclosure, slipped on the chicken manure, and went down for complete coverage.

When she returned to the house, she was in no mood to be trifled with, said those chickens would be gone tomorrow, and I said a variation of "anything you say, dear." The chickens were some rare type that laid bluish eggs, making someone happy to come out to get all but one of them. The escapee avoided detection until she appeared several days later in a small tree outside Jordan's bedroom window. We named her Henrietta, and she eventually took up crowing like a rooster. Henrietta lasted for about a month until Sue decided she was one part of country living we did not need, and people came out and got her too.

The kids played a lot in our front yard beyond Sue's garden, which itself was a distance from the house. I made a round seat with a center hole for a rope hanging down from one of our oak trees there. The kids made good use of that. Our younger two liked that swing more than anything else on the property. Once we were talking to a visitor in the living room when we all noticed five-year-old Jordan a long way off the ground as Adam and Nathan hoisted him up into that oak tree. That stopped us for a minute, then we decided that's just what kids do in a place like this. Besides, I never did get around to clearing all the leaves and other stuff in that front area, so the ground was not so hard.

Our oldest son would take Meg, our border collie, out on the college soccer field, hit a tennis ball as far as he could, and Meg would get it on the first bounce. One morning, I found Meg out running back and forth around thirty students bunched between her and the front of the business school building. I didn't know border collies could do that with no training.

A foreign student from Taiwan stayed a few months with us. When we first drove in with her, we passed through the large gate and 150 feet to the front of the house. Sue noticed her eyes got big as we kept going past the house and then kept going on to the garage 300 feet at the back of the property. She said, "Is this all your house?"

We had a good relationship with our across-the-fence neighbor Menlo College. Sue checked the students at the college dining hall for months and we often ate there. I even tried teaching a short course there, but that just confirmed that I really was not a teacher. Nathan's best friend was the athletic coach's son. They had the campus as well as our yard to run all over. We also used their two swimming pools whenever we wanted. The college had other across-the-fence neighbors who complained about things from time to time. When bad letters were sent to the city council, I often countered them with letters about how a small college in the neighborhood was good for our community.

Sue loved gardening outdoors. Meg loved it too.

When the Loma Prieta earthquake hit, Jordan was drawing on our front porch when it started jumping. Back in the house dozens of glass jars of jam Sue had just put up (I told you we lived country style) had danced clear across to the other side the peninsula kitchen counter. None fell.

A few days later, a crack in our brick fireplace and chimney was inspected. The whole thing had to come down and we lost our fireplace. Most amazing was that the house had a concrete foundation wall that came only halfway from the basement floor to the house floor, the rest was a three-foot-high wall, called a "pony wall." This was not braced and was the number-one reason that homes collapsed in that earthquake. It must have shaken just right, in the right direction with the right frequency. It was a miracle that the house did come off the foundation. It is unlikely anyone would be hurt, but the house would have been lost. I fixed both the pony wall and the bookcase, but we had no more earthquakes.

All three boys and I in our MacBain breakfast room.
Looks like an Easter breakfast.

Adam, busy extracting himself from a stuck elevator where he worked at the Menlo Park public library, missed the fun at MacBain, but had a bookcase experience different from mine.

He said the domino effect took every bookshelf in the place down.

MacBain remained rustic, not up to normal manicured Atherton standards. It was an ideal place for the kids to grow up and for Sue to have a huge front garden with a dog, cat, bunnies, and even a chicken or two. We all agree it was the best home we ever had. I don't think we were the Beverly Hillbillies of Atherton, but we probably didn't qualify as normal residents either.

Our MacBain house is gone now. A Microsoft executive bought it after we left for North Idaho and decided he needed a more elegant Atherton home. Sue and I drove by about ten years ago and could see the new house built closer to the front. Little was left but the trees from when we were there. Nathan drove by a year or so after that. He got out and looked through the front fence. The old rope swing was still in the same place.

While at MacBain we rode Bay Area Rapid Transit (BART) for Saturday or Sunday trips into San Francisco. All the men had matching trench coats. Destinations were Steinhart Aquarium, Fisherman's Warf, or the fancy stores around Christmas time.

SUE SAVES

Adapted from 10 years ago at
http://www.opportunityfoundation.org/ofblog/?p=454

Sue has always been economical. When we were first married, this was a necessity. I was a poor graduate student, and she taught at a small private school, making half the salary of a public-school teacher. When I finally got a "real job," much of that money went to our subdivision development with Warren and Al.

Sue shopped garage sales and thrift stores. Our circumstances are better these days, and she buys designer clothes, only the top labels, from Goodwill. She claims the Goodwill stores in the wealthier metropolitan areas, in our case Austin, Texas and after that Sarasota, Florida, have the greatest clothes that are in great shape. When the opportunity arises, she shops at Second Debut. For those unaccustomed to high-end shopping, this is Goodwill's outlet for their better stuff and is found in select larger cities. Now she frequents Exchange, the best of the secondhand stores in Sarasota. Its goods and their quality are certainly above the more ordinary secondhand stores in our area. I've never seen her drape a sweater or coat over a chair back, so the designer label shows, but she often could. In fact, in 2013, she picked out the thirty-five-year-old boat[1] we lived on for four years while doing the Great Loop at a tenth of the price of a new one. Nothing but the best for us.

When describing his mother, my forty-year-old son, Nathan, often tells of an incident that occurred in a department store twenty-eight years ago. Sue asked me to return a defective item. I was told that store policy prohibited returns, and no refund could be issued. As Nathan watched, I went back and forth with the man to no result. When all other options had failed, I finally told the man that the only thing left for me was to take the item back to my wife and let her handle it.

I told him that he had indeed exhausted me, and it was just not worth my while to continue. My wife, however, was different. "Sue will be here to see you a number of times. She will talk to your supervisor, his supervisor, and so on. She will call and write to the company president. She will do other things that don't come to mind right now. She won't stop. When this is over, you are going to give her the refund."

At this, the man changed his mind and gave me the refund on the spot.

I do wonder sometimes, though. While Sue makes her own coffee in the United States, we do sometimes stop at Starbucks in Bangkok. Normally, Sue and I will get a large latté and share it. The problem with this is that Sue likes an artificial sweetener while I prefer hazelnut syrup. Sue decided we could easily fix things by having the barista split the large Venti size into two mugs (don't try this at home, kids). I tried to explain to her how the coffee shop expected to make money. That was ridiculous on my part. If there is one thing Sue knows about, from making the best coffee you will ever get, to where in the world the beans are grown, etc., it is coffee. She was, however, not ready to hear me explain Starbucks' business model.

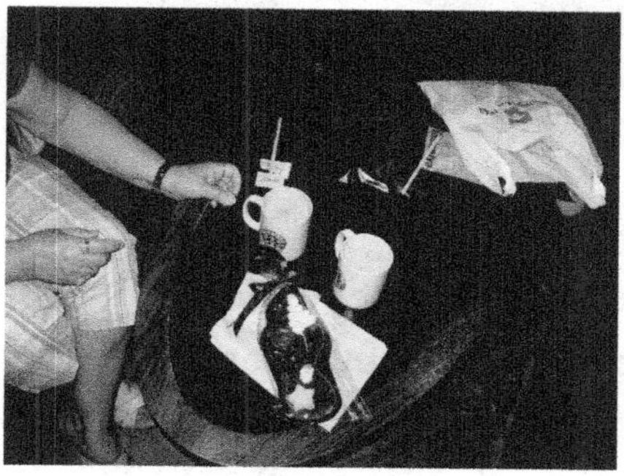

I really did not want to see this and found that I needed to use the restroom, which was upstairs.

They did go for it. Thais do like to be agreeable and to help you out when they can. When I got back, she had two big mugs with mine fixed just as I like it. We had some of our imported German chocolate-covered gingerbread with it. It was great. Sue definitely does know more about coffee than I do.

[1] Sue was uncertain about living on a boat for the year required for the Great Loop. She did fall in love with that boat. It was certainly on the large side but could still squeak by the tight spots on the Great Loop. The price was right. More important, her choosing the boat obligated her to the project. She came to love the nomad life, and we lived on the boat continuously for four years.

Sue's Cadillac at our MacBain home.

There is one time when Sue did not live up to her bargain hunting / price haggling reputation. We were impressed with the '84 Cadillac Deville Dad had bought used and decided to get one like it to replace the Brown Bomb. This had to be in 1987 or '88. We were both looking at cars in the dealer lot and got separated. The salesman, being smarter than me, stayed with Sue and was right there when she fell in love with a lilac '84 Deville. It was just what she wanted, but the color so overwhelmed her that she called clear across the lot to me, "Jack, look at this! I just have to have this car!" This put me into the perfect negotiation position. I had to buy it. I paid the sticker price. She did love that car until we moved to North Idaho, where Sue, icy roads, and that rear-wheel-drive Cadillac did not mix well at all.

DATABASE END

I haven't failed. I've just found 10,000 ways that won't work. — ***Thomas Edison***

I did find one way.

Eight years into my database company, it was 1990 and change was on the horizon. Large well-funded companies with huge development teams had moved into the database market. I had developed great relational database algorithms, but the theory behind them was known by all from the same IBM research papers I had used. My self- and Dad-funded company had focused on the basics and done well, but to sell a full system to a big company, I needed more.

Other database companies with far more manpower implemented many separate projects for support functions and communication gateways to other systems that I did not have the time to do. I was a mouse among elephants. My relational database system was still the only one available on the Prime and the Gould SEL computers, but those computer companies, along with all other minicomputer companies, were on the way out, being replaced by the new PC. My special areas, like military contracts and some public power utilities, could survive just a few more years. Eventually I would have to get a regular job.

I had released my two employees and was by myself. The one who had bought a small share of the company I paid back. Soon my lease on the office space across the street from Menlo College came up and I moved the Prime and Gould computers, along with the large disk and tape drives, to the enclosed back porch of our MacBain house. I was almost back to working out of a bedroom. I was in the room next to it. In fact, my PC did move into our bedroom.

I knew a lot about the new C language to which everyone was switching but had not had a chance to substantially use it. I had instead used the old Fortran, which was required at SLAC and my previous job at SAI. Starting the database company, I had free access to computers that only had Fortran and so had to continue using it. It still worked and all computers still supported it, but it was considered ancient history.

I started reading computer science books. Seung Lee, my assistant before he took over my database project when I left SAI, had visited in 1988 and said I was getting behind the times. I needed to get a PC. He was right. The third major PC version, the 386, was out and I got one. My computer usage started drifting to the new PC I bought for a fortieth the price of the Prime. All my software could soon run on that PC, using its Fortran compilers.

In 1988 a Japanese company bought US-based Gould Inc.

Gould had five business areas. The Japanese wanted the most important business. Fourth down the line was the SEL Computer Systems Division that had the classified military contracts that used my database system. Around the end of 1990 — with big reorganizations and foreign owners — Gould's classified contracts evaporated. I shipped the SEL equipment back to Florida and contemplated continuing with less than half my income, and that to vanish soon. I was going to be out of work.

What's Worse than Losing Your Job?

This was the first time I seriously thought about being out of work. Working satisfied my interest and ability. Pay was down the list until I faced no pay at all. Our society and my upbringing told me that supporting his family was the most important part of a man's worth. Up to then, had anyone looked, I had an upscale career, provided my family a great home, and was an "upstanding" member of the community. Without that income, I was not that person. My path had seemed upward since high school. Was it time to go in the other direction? How far?

This was one of the worst times of my life.

Would I find a job I could tolerate? Could I fit in at another company? My only "real" job was at SAI. My boss Ed did the meetings and other business there, I just wrote software. Over four years, infrequent reports to Ed were handing him a new version of the database system and its updated manual. He would check it out, ask questions, suggest a few changes or a new feature, and that was it. Seung Lee assisted for the last few years but was directed entirely by me, not the company. At SAI,

I was starting my own company, with Ed and sometimes the guys at EPRI as customers.

SLAC was like that as well. I had no coworkers. They were physicists, not software people. Software systems, especially interactive ones, were new to everyone. No one knew enough to give me direction in a meeting. There were no meetings, at least not for me. I worked on my own. Coworkers learned what I was doing when they tried out my first version. They gave feedback and I improved things, the same as when I later got customer feedback in my database company. That was not like working for a normal company. Could I handle a real job with real coworkers for a real company?

Saved by the Bell

Sue and I went west over the hills to walk the Half Moon Bay beach and see if we could think of something. Borrowing from Dad was out. I still needed to pay back what he loaned for the database company. I might borrow for a new company, but not just to live on. We had enough to go for a few months, so I had that long to find employment. I really needed to modernize some skills before anyone would look at me.

We drove back home and heard the phone ringing in the house. I ran from the garage in the back of the property up to the house. The ringing phone had flustered me, and I left the house keys in the car. I ran back for the keys and back to the house. Still ringing! It was Stanford Professor Gio Wiederhold. He had recommended me to DataSafe, a well-funded startup company with a contract to develop a software system for IBM. They needed a database component. I visited them and started a consulting arrangement that lasted about a year. A little income from my company's other projects still came in, and with it this new job paid the bills nicely.

While working with DataSafe, I continued working with my electric utility customers using the Prime computer, but it was not long before they also moved on. I was able to sell my Prime computer back to the company for half original price. One of their customers wanted the one I had, and they were no longer making them. With this and what came in from the new consulting job, I paid Dad back.

My only client left was DataSafe, but they could end up easily supporting me if everything worked out. On the other hand, I could hardly say I had my own business if that business was working for one client.

DataSafe would use my database software on their IBM machine, but to no surprise wanted it in C, not Fortran. At SLAC, I had developed the STEP computer language translator. I had subsequently used it in all my software: I could write in my own custom language much like C, and then translate it into Fortran that the computers I used could understand. I used that translator at SAI and for my database company, so I really was not at such a disadvantage using the old Fortran language.

DataSafe wanted C, so with two days' worth of modification, the STEP translator read in nearly 100,000 lines of the old database code and out came C. I put the recently released "Turbo" C compiler on my PC. The new compiler read everything in and predictably complained. Another two days of slight translation changes and fixing odd bugs and it all ran. Additional changes to get the software to run on DataSafe's IBM 370 with its C compiler were more the same but easier for being the second time. Within a week, my software ran on their IBM machine.

DataSafe would not be forever. I needed to update my skills.

I learned about new languages, especially C++. I learned about the most often seen requirements in job listings. If I did not have a lot of experience with them, I still could easily talk about them and explain why they weren't so important in my case. Some things, like C++, were so new that taking a week to write a practice program would give me as much experience as most other applicants — one advantage of working in a field were new things are constantly popping up.

By day, I worked the consulting job and in the evening, I read computer science books. I started to write some practice programs using all the newest languages and systems.

KOREA CALLS

Adventures are never fun while you're having them. – ***C. S. Lewis***

In May 1991, a visitor from Korea called inquiring about database technology. He was referred by Professor Gio Wiederhold. His group in Korea wanted to build a specialized computer, a database machine, which was a new idea. It was a computer custom designed to run database software much more efficiently. A few US companies were already working on it, and later some got products into the market.

Specialized computer hardware, like the graphics cards used in PCs, tremendously increased efficiency for certain tasks, so doing the same for database tasks sounded like a good idea. We arranged to meet at my place of business. I had recently closed my Menlo Park office, so that was our house on MacBain, where my setup was not specialized to impress possible business associates.

There was a lot Sue did not know about the computer business, but dealing with and giving visiting folks a great impression was something she could do. Our bedroom was quite large and already had a beautiful oriental rug. Our bed went into Jordan's room. His room was large, and Jordan required little space. My desk and PC were already in our bedroom. A few large plants from the living room filled things out.

My new spacious office was entered from the back door through the enclosed back porch "machine room" holding the larger Prime and Gould computers, disk drives, and even a tape machine with those big reels still seen in movies from the '60s to '80s. Keeping one door closed made the bedroom and machine room a completely separate office area. This was not the last time we would use a "home-office" arrangement like this.

This guy would be from crowded Seoul, traveling in a built-up area running from San Jose to San Francisco. He would drive into our gate and enter the country. It would be different from anything he expected.

The meeting's upshot: Sue and I would travel to Seoul as their guests, spending five days there to see if we might put something together.

We arrived at Gimpo Airport in Seoul and came down the stairs to the tarmac.

"Do you golf?" was the first thing our three friends said when they met us at the bottom. A lot flashed through my mind. Those huge rectangular structures around the city that I puzzled over from the air were nets over practice driving ranges! I'd heard Japanese were so golf crazy that they flew to Hawaii for a game and right back afterward. Any room here? Those driving ranges were pretty closed in. Do they have to fly to Hawaii too? Was I expected to participate in extreme Korean business entertainment I'd read about? I'd heard about five-figure costs for a typical night out. Binocular vision was not needed to hit the ball or judge the larger distances of golf, but I could never develop an interest in those kinds of sports. I'd go crazy walking around a golf course for hours on end or sitting watching dancing Geisha girls, or whatever equivalent they had here.

I wanted to talk about database software, computers, and things I could handle; I'd thought the social aspects of all this would not be so important. They were just friendly, but those first words, "Do you golf?" did send my mind off to places better not visited.

They took us to the upscale Intercontinental to rest up for the next day. Instead, we went out and hopped the subway to downtown. I think we went downtown. There was a lot of downtown here and there, but where we went was fine.

In a large department store, all the help were young girls dressed in the same color, type, and I think size of dress. Maybe they were going for a certain look or some marketing standardization I was unaware of. We walked wide aisles with sale items in glass counters arranged in large squares with the girls inside. When Sue and I approached a counter, about twenty of them glided into position across from us, smiled, and were ready to help.

None of the girls spoke English at all, but Sue was happy to talk with them while they showed her things.

The smell of kimchi knocked Sue back at the entrance of another large food hall / shopping center, but she recovered and powered in. We walked a long aisle with colorful vegetables and maybe fruits on both sides. Sue and I puzzled over them but recognized nothing.

Communicating had been difficult as few knew English. We knew from discussions with our hosts that all children from first to twelfth grade received English instruction every day in school, which contradicted what we saw. We did run into a few men from time to time who spoke well, but all had been in the United States for extended times. Many years later, I ran into the same situation in Thailand, where everyone is supposed to learn English, and no one does. The gap between English and Asian languages must be much larger than between those of Europe or even Africa.

The guy at the counter in Carl's Junior at the International center had to have at least twelve years of English. The burgers and Sue's Coke were fine, but we could point at the menu for that. My water was not on the menu, so I said "water," then I wrote it out for him, then wrote it all uppercase, and then got another Coke. OK, English is not spoken here. How well could we learn Korean?

One of the wives whisked Sue away to fancy shopping centers and the best restaurants in the city. Our hosts' parents were right at the top of Korean society in wealth and influence — big people in the chaebols with as much influence with the government possible without being in the government. Sue, who does shop in the very best of secondhand stores, was fine and her host, traveled and educated unlike ordinary people there, spoke English well.

"Unlike ordinary people" was the heart of our problem. They were horrified to learn we had ridden the subway. They, that would mean we, never did that. We would be driven in our car. We did go this way thereafter, and it only took a bit more than twice the time. There turned out to be many social restrictions, I mean privileges, for those of our high status.

There were meetings, though fewer than I expected. I had read that Koreans, like the Japanese, like to begin with the social end of things and leave technical details to the end. For me, the technical part is not "details." Some other details at the final business meeting involved the stock ownership of the company-to-be. I would receive special stock different from theirs. They claimed this would give me several advantages over them, while any disadvantages would not be important to me. Really? Why should I be different? Dad had told me about situations he knew of where stock had been manipulated in new companies and what had resulted. I did not smell a rat but maybe did get a whiff of a small mouse.

We had two meetings where they asked all kinds of questions about the ideas behind my software, which was fine with me. I stole it all from IBM research papers. I didn't hear much about any kind of related technical capability at their end. They wanted to start a database machine company. The machine part of that required a hardware expert or three that I never met. It didn't add up.

Finally, how could I leave out the last night's tens of thousands of dollars (rough estimate) of entertainment? We went down a beautiful parklike walkway with many historical Korean homes from the previous generation back to ancient at the far end. There we went in, were greeted, sat down to a small meal course and saw dance and entertainment, all from that time in Korean history. We then passed on to the next house and so on. We saw Korean history as few Americans did, unless they had two or three extra vacations' worth of money to blow.

What can I say? We felt like crass, ignorant, ugly Americans. I'm sure we were missing something. Their whole history, culture development, dress, and song seemed all the same to Sue and me as a group of department store girls.

The trip was not a high point in our life. I'm not saying Korea is an uninteresting place, but it might be if you only go where we did. Not one thing about this looked good. If this was a decision, it certainly was an easy one for Sue as well as me.

I had the core technology. Additional software pieces were needed but could be straightforward separate projects done in parallel by reasonably smart hires. They had money with government and chaebol connections. One of their wives was the daughter of the chairman of Samsung, and all were from the "best" families. I had seen several pictures on walls with their parents and various dignitaries, including former President (dictator?) Park Chung-hee, who even I was familiar with from various US news reports. The one thing neither they nor I had was hardware knowledge needed for the "machine" part of a database machine project. Maybe they were not serious and just fishing for ideas?

A few US companies that were already working on database machines would later get products into the market but found them unsatisfactory. They worked fine but not so much better than a normal computer running database software. If any of those companies survived, it was by adapting their software to normal computers.

Much later, I learned that our kids were excited by the idea of living in Korea, but they were always up for adventure at that stage. They were hot on Japanese culture. Two of them would learn Japanese, the oldest really well. They thought Korea would be like that. Later, my oldest spent time in Korea with some young Korean people and decided they were so group-oriented that he would go bananas in a few weeks.

Sue was terrified. Starting and maintaining a business was

already more familiar to her than she liked. She had been hanging in there for a long time. Starting a business in Korea was getting toward over the top for her. If I had been saying, "I think we might make this work," she might have had something to say about the meaning of "we."

I never do get to make decisions. When you're in a strange place and in every direction you look, nothing appears right, you don't "decide" to get out. You just get out.

TO BUILD A HOUSE III

Coincidence is God's way of remaining anonymous. — ***Albert Einstein***

The secret to creativity is knowing how to hide your sources. — ***Albert Einstein***

The only support for my database company in its last year came from my DataSafe consulting, with the coming licensing of my software hopefully adding to that as well. DataSafe's own survival was in question since their entire support was from the contract they had with a larger company. DataSafe had to accept my product, and their client had to accept their product for this whole thing to keep going, so my continued working there was not certain.

I might need to get a job somewhere else, and for that I needed up-to-date skills. Most important was experience with the new C language and then with the even newer C++ object-oriented language. My Fortran experience meant little now. The just-out Windows 3 was proving wildly popular. Some experience with that would certainly not hurt.

Even though I did not write it in C, my STEP translator had converted my database software to C. Now I could say I had implemented a large relational database system in the C language, that ran on both the PC and IBM 370. This was a definite step up on my resume. This left C++, which was so new that any experience with it would be great. Many companies were looking at it, but at best could only be starting to use it.

The Borland C++ compiler and Windows 3 were both released just after I started with DataSafe. I put both on my computer. I got a book and read about object-oriented programming. The book used an example of a simple CAD program where a line, a square, a circle, etc. could all be objects, so I decided to write such a program using the new C++ language. I made it complex enough to use and get practice with every aspect of the new language and how it implemented objects. Since I was running everything with Windows 3, I learned its graphics and other parts of it as well.

If I did go job hunting, telling them I worked on a test program in C++ at home, rather than on a big system for a company, would not be impressive. Large-scale software systems were something I had done several times before, so I decided to do something more impressive that I could demonstrate to anyone. Everyone would understand a house plan. I had always liked messing with house plans, so I would write a program to make one quickly appear before their eyes. That would interest them and show them what I could do!

I had some ideas, heavily influenced by the new object-oriented programming, that would help me build this new software. I did not look at any existing CAD programs. Though a few of them ran on the PC, they all cost money, and how what I did might relate to them meant nothing to me anyway. I was just trying to get some experience writing something that looked good. That it might someday compete with other CAD systems never crossed my mind. I knew how to draw house plans by hand, wanted to duplicate that process in a computer and that was enough.

Drawing pictures on a computer with the new graphics tools was a kick, much more fun than my database programming.

Database had grown tiresome. I was relieved when the Korea deal went south; I would not spend years working on database software there. At DataSafe, I faced more years of working with code to organize, sort, find, fetch, store, and otherwise move data around, a task picked for me by my first job at SAI. Still, the company paid well, and once my software worked well with theirs, licensing payments would add a lot more money. The licensing deal also required that I stay on three more years. It was not a completely unpleasant thought that DataSafe's troubles might lose me both job and licensing payments but would also relieve me of a longer-term database programming obligation.

Meanwhile, back home at MacBain in the evening, my house planning program grew. As I drew a plan, my program did not just draw lines like other CAD programs, but instead constructed models of walls, windows, and doors inside the computer as the plan was drawn. American house design is so standard that wall heights, window and door sizes, vertical dimensions, and other things could be assumed. I was building a model of the whole house in the computer. The computer knew where the walls met the floor, so it added baseboard moldings. It knew where the windows and doors were, so it added their casing and trim. Framing is standard, so all the floor, wall, and other framing was also added to the model, all automatically.

The computer could then produce elevations, perspective views, framing details, dimensions, and even a list of materials from that model. All were from one model. All were consistent, unlike that plan I drew for Dad long ago.[1]

Finally, in late 1991, DataSafe faltered. It was out of money and everything stopped. I went home with no licensing agreement and missing my last two weeks of pay. It was a small shock, but soon I was glad to be done with database. I never looked at that database software into which I had put ten years of work again. I was going forward with the C++ language, so I never looked at the STEP language translator again either.

These were the early days of computer software. Programming standards, languages, and techniques kept changing. Many new ideas popped up promising to change the world, and a few of them actually did. A software project could start in your bedroom or, if you formed a small team that dressed better and talked well, a new venture-funded company. Most projects disappeared in a year or two. DataSafe was like this. They had an interesting vision for a new product, but it took longer than they hoped, the market had changed, and their funders' interests turned elsewhere.

I still had a little money and could put off the job search a little longer. The floor planner had gone together amazingly fast. Roofs were complicated; I'd do them later. No roof let me look inside the house. I located a guy who produced a few hundred 3D computer models of various furniture and fixture items like tables, couches, toilets, and sinks for a few hundred bucks.

I learned how to turn a 3D model into a 2D picture on the screen. As with all of the math involved in this project, it wasn't beyond what I learned in high school. That's one good thing about getting a doctorate in math and physics: you know your grad school material well enough to look things up and relearn them. You know college math well enough to teach it with a day or two prep, but you know your high school math cold. I was building my new program faster and doing more than I ever had.

Working days and evenings, by September everything worked and could be used. Sue's friend's husband, who was an architect, had come over for a demonstration and was impressed. He thought it should be sold, not just put into "shareware." I had not worked with an architect before, but I had worked with a homebuilder. I called Al.

I had not seen Al for a few years and found that, in addition to building homes, he had been drawing plans for himself and other builders using AutoCAD, the PC world's most used CAD system. He was interested in what I had and took a copy home to play with. A week later, he came back and said, "I've been using AutoCAD for a while now. This is better. I like using it. Sell it." Al was not the kind of person to say what he didn't mean or to "improve" his speech to make you feel better. He told you what he thought.

I had not thought to start another company, but to get a decent job. At that time, I had recently interviewed at a few companies but could not seem to find a match. I had issues with the restrictions and narrow scope of the jobs offered. I think they may have had issues about how I might fit in with their work environment. I had always worked alone, but software development in these companies was a team effort, even as it is in my software company today. I suspected then, and know now, that I'm not at my best in a team.

Al's approval was a big deal. Architects are fine, but most homes were designed and had their final plans produced by builders. When Warren, Al, and I did our Malory Court subdivision, Warren and I drew all the plans ourselves. Later, Al drew all the plans he needed, and now he used a computer. "Design-Build" was a common term describing most home designers who also built what they designed. Most were not architects. I could sell a lot more house design software to builders than I could to architects. There were a whole lot more builders than there were architects. Al wanted to graduate from drawing lines on a computer to building a house in his computer. The only way he could do that was by helping out.

Now starting a company to "sell it" made sense. I reborrowed that money from Dad to live on another year while I turned the program into a product. Al reviewed new versions and showed me what a professional designer wanted instead of just a house plan hobbyist. This was August 1992. In the next four months, an unbelievable number of things happened. How I still spent most of my time writing software then I'll never know.

A friend recommended me to Kleiner Perkins, one of the first venture capital firms and just across the road from SLAC. A tall and noticeably well-dressed guy came out and we talked over my plans. He took everything in and told me their firm could not work with my company. He said it could grow and have good success, but its growth would be slower than what he financed. Kleiner Perkins put significant money in at the start and wanted a number of employees and a management team in place. They took a large ownership share, often a majority share, of the new company as well. They expected the company to grow fast and become public in no more than three years, hopefully two. Then they would cash out and go on to the next deal.

That would be no deal from my viewpoint as well. I could use a little money and a few employees, but I could not soon use the number of people he normally dealt with. I still had a lot of ideas and a lot of areas to develop and was not far enough along to put more people on the programming end of the business. I would be wasting their money. Besides, Dad told me never to give up majority ownership, along with a few stories of people he knew of that did.

The venture guy was right. Our business would grow just as he said.

I hired a CEO who came to work for stock options and started planning marketing, sales, advertising, trade shows, etc. At that time, software was sold in a box that had to be designed. The box had to show a name. I called it "Chief Architect." The software was easy to use but did so many things, with so many more planned, that a user manual had to be written. That took a while. I didn't finish it by the end of the year but did get a good start. The manual had to look professional, which meant graphic design for its cover, but we just used the box design there. Then I got a call about Dad and everything moved north.

Everything happened fast. The C++ compiler I used was released in November 1991. I had built my test CAD program and the house plan program and had them both usable by September 1992. Deciding to sell the software, starting a consumer version, and all these other preparations happened before we left California at the beginning of the new year.

It turned out a huge advantage was given to our company by the designers of the new systems and especially that C++ language. Competitors were stuck with old software programs bound to old languages and systems. The new methods were a lot better but were so different that to best use them, existing software had to be rewritten. It took a company quite a while to decide to throw away an investment of hundreds and sometimes thousands of man-years developing and start over. Some never did and disappeared.

To qualify for employment, I had adopted the latest software tools and techniques. Instead I got a company based on the latest tools and techniques. My software was built in a new way and naturally designed houses in a new way. Customers liked that new way, and as I write this they still do. Who would have guessed?

[1] Learn more about how this new way of building a house in a computer works in the Appendix B: Home Design.

BRODERBUND'S CONSUMER VERSION

When I started working with house plans, I noticed the magazines whenever I checked out at the supermarket. Half of them were for house plans, home design, interior decoration, or planning your yard or deck. The do-it-yourself house design market for consumers had to be much larger than the building contractor market! Could I sell to that, too? I would have to sell something for a lot less money, like the price of a computer game. I didn't know how to sell in the stores like consumer software did in the early 1990s. I'd need help with that.

Broderbund was one of the largest computer game companies and located just north of San Francisco. I called them about selling a consumer version of the software. That led to a visit with Harry and a demonstration. He liked it, but he and his group decided it was not for them; they wanted to concentrate more on games, not "productivity" software. Two weeks later, Harry called back. Doug, the chairman of Broderbund, had been designing a large new home in Colorado Springs and decided to try out the test program I left there. Apparently, he liked it and told everyone something like Al had said to me: "Sell it!"

I visited Broderbund again, and now they liked the virtues of an "evergreen" product. Games are popular for a while and then must be replaced by a newer version or something else entirely. A great many people will always want to design their own home, however. It was an amazing change in attitude by everyone there.

We started talking contract. There were two ways: they could pay advance licensing fees starting right then or wait and pay the fees as the product sold. Of course, I would get less money long-term with the first option. I also suspected I would have more control of things with the second option. I voted for long-term. With Dad's help, I had enough to get through until it should start selling. If I had to be beholden to someone, Dad was by far the best bet. It was also easier for him this time since he and my uncle had recently sold property bought for one of their "failed" businesses to a large development company for enough to have a more comfortable retirement.

I hired a contract lawyer familiar with consumer software licensing, and we squared everything up. One unusual feature of the contract was non-exclusivity on Broderbund's part. Normally if they were going to spend their money to make a product popular, they wanted all the resulting sales. That was certainly fair, but I was looking at two separate products based on the same software: the consumer product that they would sell for $60 and a professional version with additional features turned on that we would sell for no less than five times as much — $300. Ours would be called "Chief Architect," and theirs could be called whatever they chose, which turned out to be "3D Home Architect."

I made sure the contract preserved my ability to also sell the software as long as I priced it well above the cost to consumers. Their consumer product took off so well that a year later, they looked longingly at our professional market and tried to widen their exclusivity. That cost me a trip to their California offices to sound things out and then went no further. I had an issue like this before in the database days when Burroughs-Unisys bought Graftek, the CAD company that had licensed my software. My contract was with Graftek only. Burroughs reinterpreted that contract to claim they had full rights to all sales of my software, even to companies outside of Burroughs. That one took a few lawyer visits before it went away. Big companies do like to try things like that. I suppose it must work sometimes.

Once the consumer product started selling in mid-1994, it really took off. Broderbund took a lot of the money, but our licensing fees were still great, almost half our total income, and we didn't do so much for them. Our CEO called it our "welfare check."

~

Chief Architect for professional building contractors, and 3D Home Architect for amateur home designers, were both successful. My second company worked while my first one did not. The first company was doomed from the start because I could not grow it fast enough. DBMS sold to large corporations and the government. Large entities wanted to deal with other large entities. One customer could have 1,000 or more users of my product. It took me a while to realize that the big companies would eventually win over me. I had better technology and performance when I started, but they had the money and manpower to eventually catch up, which they did. They could also produce the many different special systems and adaptations a large customer would need. One person did not look right walking into a big company; a sales team did. The first company was a great example of needing a larger team and venture capitalists for a good start.

The second company sold primarily to home building contractors. Many of these worked on their own or with one or two assistants, hiring subcontractors as needed. When a contractor became larger, he would often hire a smaller design-build shop, maybe just one person that used our software, to produce his plans. Al did this type of work for other contractors before he joined Chief Architect. Our size company was a good match for our customers, and really big companies did not do well when they tried to enter our market. As the venture capitalist I talked to when starting the second time told me, I did not need or want his help.

STARTING COMPANIES WITH DAD

It is indeed a desirable thing to be well descended, but the glory belongs to our ancestors. – ***Plutarch****, On the Training of Children.*

I now understand that what I did and why I did it, things I avoided and what success I had, would not have happened without Dad.

Near year-end of 1992, I got phone call from cousin Dianna in Coeur d'Alene, Idaho. Dad had lung cancer. I was in the San Francisco Bay area, the middle of Silicon Valley. I was also in the middle of starting a new software company specializing in home design, the sort of software you now often see displaying designs on HGTV. I had three employees, a new CEO (I just build software, don't ask me to run things), an expert on home building and design (Al – you met him in earlier chapters), and an office assistant.

Dad walking in front of our Military Drive house two months before he died.

We had gotten an unusually great deal on a great property on an acre in Atherton with great weather where Sue had enjoyed seven years making the garden and house, well, great. Dad had come down a few times to help me repair and remodel several areas of the house (Or was I helping him? I forget). It was and always will be the greatest home for our family that we ever had.

Most major decisions in my life have been obvious, at least to me. There were various risks and rewards along the way but always one way appeared the most sensible, with Sue agreeing, except for the few times when nothing was said but I later learned she was terrified. This time, I had to be with Dad. I told Sue the diagnosis and would wait to ask her about leaving, but she immediately said, "We need to go."

In about a week, we moved all our furniture into the cottage out back and arranged with a realtor friend to lease our house. Meg, our border collie, could go, but our travel in midwinter was too uncertain for a cat. Buddy had to stay behind, hopefully to be cared for by our future renters. That did work, and later I was able to fetch him up to Idaho. We left in our '73 Toyota and '84 Cadillac and drove north toward mid-winter. In good weather, we might have driven the one-thousand-mile distance in one go, as Sue and I did during our first spring break from school in 1970. This time we'd be in sketchy weather before we left California.

We decided to take the longer route through Salem, Oregon, where Warren, my partner in the Malory Court subdivision, had moved and built himself a house on a small lake. We'd stay one or more nights there. We started to hit some weather on the way but made it over the main pass in California. Once I got concerned when, leading in the Toyota, I went under a bridge on a straight stretch and felt the car lose all traction. Not a problem for me since I started driving up north, but I watched in my mirror as Sue went through in the Cadillac with a noticeable swerve, but came out fine.

It was great to have a few days' visit with Warren, since the weather had closed in. The lake in front of his house was frozen over except for a hole someone had broken through near shore. Meg loved to swim and jumped right in. Sue claims her eyes bugged right out, but anyway she exited the water faster than she went in. Warren had enlarged his library, and we had a few days talking like we used to. Warren and I were out on Interstate 5 once in his car in the evening when he noticed freezing rain starting. Warren slowed down and drove close to the edge. He said it was common there, invisible on the road and many just driving through didn't know about it. It instantly made the road completely slick. "Just watch what happens. We'll be OK if we can avoid anyone coming too fast behind us." We had a few more miles to go and started seeing trucks and cars off to the side and off in the center between the roadways. Nothing bad, but most of the cars I saw were not on the road.

After three days, the weather neither let up nor got worse. We decided to go, but the Toyota would not start. We finally got it jumped and I did not turn that engine off, whether pumping gas or not, until we reached our destination.

About a week from when we started out, around New Year's Day 1993, we — our two boys (Adam was at school in Japan), dog, and both cars — arrived in Coeur d'Alene, Idaho to more snow than they had had in many years. It was just after New Year's and the plows had shoved the snow into the middle of the streets in long mounds you could not see over. Immense snow piles took up whole parking lots. It was a real change from our Bay Area weather.

We got a place to live across the street and spent the next fourteen months with Dad and Mom before he died. Not only did I get to be with Dad, but he saw his greatest wish come true before his eyes – that his son would be successful in business.

"You're going to be in charge of a big company, and I'll walk with you and carry your briefcase," my dad would tell me several times in college, well before I had started anything.

My CEO and Al decided that north Idaho would be a good place to live, so they moved up, spent many years there, and the company grew. Before Dad died, he attended our breakout appearance at the National Builder Show in Las Vegas. The area around our booth was so crowded with customers that the photo to advertise the next year's builder show, taken from high in the convention hall, had our booth dead center. Idaho turned out to be a better place for our company than California, and it successfully continues there today.

At our first trade show in 1994. Dad was still feeling good on this trip. My son Adam demos the product.

People have commented to Sue that it must take courage to start a company by yourself as I did. That hadn't occurred to me. There was really no decision. I just did what made sense at the time. My dad had started several companies, along with his identical twin brother Jim. They were: TV repair; metal plating; Vactron, which was a company to make large vacuum tubes for army radar; selling insurance; selling real estate; selling uranium detection equipment; uranium mining; Convac, a company to make vacuum switches; a KOA campground; and they ended with another TV repair company. That last finally went out when TVs were no longer repaired. Along the way, Dad also bought and sold some items for profit and bought, repaired, repainted, and resold a house. Some businesses went for years and others never got off the ground.

Dad and his brother bought some cheap land out away from town for the vacuum switch factory, which did not go any further. Some years later, they still had the land, the state decided to run a new highway right by it, a development company wanted it for some major stores, and the twins could retire decently with minor investments.

I was not old enough to work in any of these enterprises. I did have a couple of paper routes and a brief job at a supermarket. I was fired from that last one. My touch of autism was just enough to make relating to customers not go so well. I did not so much watch or specifically try to learn from what Dad did, and fathers in those days did not have the concept of "quality time" with their kids. Even so, Dad formed the background of my life, more like the water in which a fish swims than any particular thing it would see in the ocean. I did not realize this so much when he was alive, but later it was as if I was still getting advice he was not there to give.

Somehow, Dad made enough for us to get by. We had adequate clothes and shoes and ate well enough. At that time, Coeur d'Alene was a logging town so we did not stand out by being barely middle class. I have not since noticed houses smaller than we had, and I have a house design company.

I can't remember a single time I ever knew or heard of Dad breaking a promise to anyone about anything. I have to guess that had he promised to pay back money, he would have done so, but I don't remember him ever borrowing. I may be missing a mortgage for his purchase of our homes. If the companies he started with his brother ever did borrow money, they must have paid it back appropriately. I think I would have heard or suspected a debt of any size or duration from someone. Dad did talk to me of people who had borrowed a lot to start a business and then spent years paying it back when the business failed. I also remember Dad talking about "deadbeats" who did not pay their debts and I grew determined that would never be me.

I did not realize how little Dad made until Mom told me after I was out of college. It's still a little puzzling how things in our family had stayed together so well. There was no money for extras, but the lack had seldom registered. For example, not once had we ever eaten in a restaurant, so I had not thought whether that might be a desirable thing to do. Things that I did know about were few. I desperately wanted a boat to water ski. One day we were looking at a modest boat that would just be able to pull a skier. As Dad looked at that boat, I realized that he wanted it more than I did. He loved to fish. Later, he sat me down for a rare bit of "quality time" to talk over why we could not get that boat. We learned to be careful with money growing up with Dad.

Later on, when I could not find a job I liked, I just started a company, like my dad. I needed minimal investment and that was a loan from Dad. His past lessons made me careful along the way, however, so when I shut that company down, I was able to pay him back. I should add that Dad had decided to trust me completely back in college, a long time before I ever started a business. He never once asked or hinted about repayment from me.

Then I started another company. With a good reason, I borrowed that money back from Dad. That company worked out. I was unable to pay him back before he died, but he certainly was pleased with his shares in the company.

Dad's last instructions to me were, "Take care of your mother," just as he had always done. With my sister Sharon, Mom's niece Dianna, and Mom's (also our) housekeeper Shirley, someone was there in a few minutes if she needed anything. We didn't have to take care of her financially. Dad did. His last investment in my company made her wealthier than she had ever been for the last twenty years of her life.

I'm fortunate that having a PhD did not go to my head enough to cause me to ignore my high-school-educated dad. His advice regarding business setup saved our family a lot of dislocation and grief in our Korean episode two years earlier. I followed his advice when I set up both of my companies and that headed off other potential trouble.

There was one thing about stock buy-sell agreements Dad told me on several occasions that I definitely meant to do but had not yet got around to. The unexpected happened and that omission cost us a lot of money and much time with lawyers when we should have been focusing on growing the company. We came out alive and OK, but I was kicking myself over that for a while.

Dad was gone. I didn't use a briefcase that he could have carried, and was never in charge of anything either. I just wrote software. However, I do wish he could have been around longer to walk with me.

THE BIG HOUSE

The Big House at 1321 E Lakeshore Dr. in Coeur d'Alene. The sunroom is on the right (east) behind the greenhouse. The next two windows left are the living room, the two windows beyond the porch are the dining room, the bay window beyond is the kitchen. Beyond that is the family room (not visible) and the west side yard.

We returned from our success at the Las Vegas National Builders' Show in January 1994. We'd been living in Coeur d'Alene, Idaho a little more than a year. Dad started to decline a little but still looked to be with us for more months.

Al and the CEO had come up to Coeur d'Alene. We didn't know how long Dad would be with us, but it was full speed ahead for the company, so we hired a few people to help with sales and the phones. Hiring more software people still did not make sense. We all had just come to think in terms of staying in North Idaho. We called our program Chief Architect, and in both California and North Idaho, I worked on Chief all I could. It was coming together.

When we first arrived in Idaho, Uncle Jim, Dad's identical twin, had just bought a house and had not sold his downtown condominium next door to Dad's apartment building. He let us move in there. After eight months, we moved to a rental at 312 Military Dr. just on the other side of the city park from Dad. Dad easily walked to either place.

Back of the house looking west. I designed and Gene built the fence and gates after we moved in.

Sue and I had not thought beyond our day-to-day being with Dad and working on Chief. We had not been back from the trade show more than a few days when Sue got us into trouble. It was only fair, I suppose, after I bought a house on MacBain before I told her. She was driving along East Lakeshore Drive, on the other side of town, when she saw cars parked across from the Easton house. Cars would park there because of the lake in the summer, but not in February. A realtor was showing the house to some clients! It had been for sale for more than a year for close to 2 million.

It was the largest, grandest home in town, the one you could see when you were miles out on the lake and looked north. It was built in 1922 by mining magnate Stanley Easton, chairman of the Bunker Hill mines to the east in Kellogg, the richest man from the Montana border clear to Spokane. When Dad and Uncle Jim were little boys, their father, famous in the mining districts as "Steamshovel Bill," and who worked for Bunker Hill, came there once to see his boss's boss and brought the twins with him. Uncle Jim remembered Mr. Easton taking them both by the hand and leading them into that house. Shortly before graduation, I attended the unauthorized "senior sneak" my senior class put on in that house. Most of our class of two hundred students were there, but the vice-principal never did find us even though the police were called in to help. Why the owners at that time, two back from the current seller, gave permission for that I'll never know.

Sue and I were always interested in houses, especially traditional houses, like say, a huge 12,000-square-foot Georgian Colonial on the lake. We'd been by many times and were curious about what was inside. Sue went up and knocked on the door. The agent came and told her the house was being shown and she could not come in. Sue persisted and said she would stay well away from her clients and just quietly look around.

The sunroom at the east end was the prettiest – full of windows on three sides. We installed the benches underneath them.

"Do you know how much this house costs?" the realtor asked. "You can't possibly afford it!"

This, of course, was absolutely correct, but Sue kept insisting, and the realtor had to get back to her clients. Sue can be a little hard to deal with this way at times.

Sue kept out of sight and looked around until she came across a phone in the kitchen. Surely one phone call would not bother anyone. This was back before people had cell phones, but they could actually remember phone numbers, so Sue called me up and told me if I got over there right now I could see the Easton house. I did and we went through much of it. Finally, the realtor walked her clients out and then came back to find Sue entertaining a man behind her back and threw us both out.

The house had been on the market for some time at two million and had recently had a minor price reduction. Sue insisted it was at least worth talking about, so I visited John, the listing agent. Since buying MacBain, the only house I'd ever bought, I preferred buying through the listing agent, who would be that much more motivated to see the deal through if he got both sides of the commission. Anyone in business for more than a few years is going to be carefully honest to both sides. John filled me in on the history of his listing, and as expected gave little information on what the seller might take other than the current listing price.

My office off the first floor entry hall. I started on the third floor but needed it quieter. The door on the right opens to a large copper humidor for Mr. Easton's cigars. On the left, out of the picture, was his gun cabinet. My desk was on the opposite wall.

I had a business taking off, but with no history. I still owed on MacBain, but its price had gone up along with everything in Silicon Valley. Lockheed, a major employer in the area, had just lost some big contracts and were laying off a lot of people, enough to depress the Bay Area market. That would cut into MacBain's price rise. I could afford half the current asking price. John said he would try it out with the seller. I knew a decent realtor would always take an offer to the seller, no matter how nutty. It was all I had.

The seller agreed. Maybe he was just tired of the whole thing and wanted to end it? I don't know. I never met him face to face. We wrote it up and I called our Atherton realtor friend. The renters, who were great to take care of Buddy our cat and knew how things could go if MacBain had to be sold, made ready.

2001 Chief Architect Christmas party in the living room. This shows about half the people. Most worked in our commercial office.

I still needed a loan, and my employment situation was at least a bit unusual. Fortunately, the seller had just started a bank in town and was still on the board. Why don't I apply for a loan there? That sounded like a great suggestion! My CEO wrote a nice letter to the bank. I got the chairman of Broderbund software, which was getting ready to sell our lower-cost consumer version, to write a letter to the bank also.

We got the loan, MacBain sold at the end of March, and the

Big House, as we started calling it, closed at the start of April. I flew down to California to deal with the movers and fetch our cat, Buddy. Adam had not been with us since he left for Westmont College in Southern California in the fall of 1992. He spent his summer in China and was finishing up his last year in Japan. He would be home soon.

Meanwhile, back at the Big House, Sue, Nathan, and Jordan moved in. Sue slept in the master bedroom at the west end of the house on the second floor. The two boys each got their own bedroom suite with most of the bedrooms and the majority of the house still left unused.

With me still in California, Sue bedded down alone in her new master bedroom. Once things got quiet at night, various wind noises and the old hardwood floors adjusting to the night temperature were heard. The scary clanking sound was the worst. It would go away for a while but then come back. She was quickly joined by the two boys. All three went to sleep in the same bed in a huge, empty house.

Nathan started exploring the next morning. In the basement, he found a large room with a still-lower floor and an old furnace like you'd expect to find in the basement of an old, multistory, big-city school building. It was huge with pipes and flues all over. One of the flues had a swinging damper that was randomly moved by winds that found their way down the pipe. The furnace was no longer in use and would need removing, one of the many projects we would have in this house.

I got back from Idaho with the cat. We brought Meg, our collie, back from the small farm where we boarded her.[1] The movers came a week later. Nathan and Jordan moved into their bedrooms, one was reserved for Adam, and Sue became friends with the owner of a secondhand furniture store.

So how did it feel, moving into the biggest house in town,

easily three times any home we'd had before? It happened so fast that we could not savor the acquisition. We'd known about the house before; most of the town knew about the house, but our coming to own it was never a thought. Still, it happened.

Our cat Buddy went to live with Adam when he got a home. We found Josephine on one of our St Joe river trips.

It was traditional Georgian Colonial, our favorite style of home. Now we could furnish it. I liked looking at Sue's shelf full of Colonial Homes magazines almost as much as she did. What was it about arranging some chairs, tables, and other items around a fireplace that looked so pleasing? I can't explain it. It affected Sue as it did many homemakers, but it affected me as well, influencing me to make a product that could render 3D pictures of that fireplace and surrounding furniture items. Now we had five fireplaces. With furnishing and gardening on this home's acre, Sue would be kept busy for years. As if the new company was not enough, I would be busy as well. A home like this was a project for us both, just as it had been for the previous owner as well as those who would buy it from us ten years later.

Did we know all this when we bought it? No, we didn't have time to think about where this home would take us, or how we might best use it. We thought the deal was good enough for us to jump quickly in, and jump we did. The details, and there were plenty of them, just had to be sorted out later.

[1] When we came to Coeur d'Alene we first stayed at Uncle Jim's condo and then in the Military Drive rental. Both places did not allow dogs and Meg needed more exercise than she could get there, so we boarded her out at a small farm. She got along well there and became a heroine when the family lost their pet ferret. They were looking everywhere with no results until they noticed that Meg would not move away from an indoor floor heating grate. They opened the grate and there was the ferret. Had Meg not located it quickly, the ferret probably would not have survived long in the hot air when the heat was on.

When we came to get her, her new family let her out of the house and Meg ran to the cows, the horse, and other animals, touched noses with each, and then came to us.

Meg loved life at the Big House. She had always liked the water and swimming, so she especially loved the beach. She would find someone sitting in the sand and drop a stick in front of them. The stick got thrown out into the water and Meg went and got it. She did a lot of that.

CHIEF ARCHITECT MOVES IN

Handoff for our second version on the third floor
when I was still up there. Al on the far left.

With our company growing fast and us unable to use even a third of our new home, we soon had a new housemate. Chief Architect moved in. On the second floor, the CEO and Al took bedrooms as well as another for an office down the long hall from us. This still left a craft room for storage and additional bedrooms for guests who would not be long in coming.

The western room on the third floor became sales, marketing, and tech support, and the east room was software development. Both of these rooms were large, each just under a thousand square feet. I started working up there but eventually moved to the first-floor office when the noise and pandemonium from added software engineers and other employees became too much.

We used a large basement room for shipping. Stack of user's manuals to the right.

The large central room in the basement became shipping. Boxes, manuals, and other supplies were in adjacent storerooms. Within a year, we were the largest FedEx shipper in the area, with semitrucks backing into our driveway to load software boxes. A separate stairway leading to the second and third floors and another separate stairway to the basement allowed for separate work and home entrances.

A crew of Mennonite carpenters came to work on the house. One of their first jobs was the removal of the old furnace and a lot of asbestos. We kept them busy for a few years with many improvements. The largest of these was rebuilding the old two-car garage into a five-car garage with a nice apartment for Mom overhead. One of the crew, Gene, asked if he could finish off a small three-bedroom apartment in the basement for himself, his wife, and three children. With plenty of room, we would hardly notice it was there. He did that and continued doing light construction and remodeling work for a number of years. His wife and two older girls cleaned, did some cooking, and helped Sue a lot with various special events at the house.

The outside basement stairs were used for delivery. We slid product boxes and manuals from the trucks down a board.

The director of the Culinary Arts Department at North Idaho College became a great friend. Richard was over twice a week on his days off to cook four or five huge dishes. Each was placed on a large round platter and stored in the commercial refrigerator in the back of the kitchen, then brought out as needed to feed the troops. He also produced a lot of different soups. Depending on your point of view, it was a home, business, or asylum.

Al and Richard in the kitchen.

We did get a lot done. Sue looked out the dining room window one night as cars slowly drove by to gaze at the grandest house in town with lights rimming all the windows and glimpses of the Christmas tree lights in the living room. "They must be thinking how wonderful it is to spend Christmas in this house! I'd like to get up, beat on the windows, and scream to get out!" she thought as she loaded more 3½ inch floppy disks into the duplicator. Every hour someone would come up from shipping in the basement to get Sue's production and deliver a new bin of blanks. Everyone who could was pressed into service, producing product for the upcoming January National Builders' show in Las Vegas. After our surprise performance last year, we had to be ready to sell boxes of software as fast as possible.

We tried to release a new version just before the big trade show, which usually was late January. That gave Sue and me some downtime in February before starting the next version and fielding its problems. This travel time with Sue made up for my immersion in developing Chief at all other times. Normally I could not get away from the latest bug or otherwise seemingly unsolvable problem. When one problem finally was solved, the next would be there waiting for me. I seldom went to bed without a serious issue on my mind. Some were tough enough, and took long enough, that the possibility of the ultimately unsolvable problem appearing, the one that could stop our business cold, occurred to me. Like other times with the database software or times developing Chief in California, I never lacked for difficulties and a fair amount of stress. The winter travel time was when I could get away from it for a while. It was a huge thing for both Sue and me.

We bought this former bank building and doubled its size.

The company grew fast. Within a year the CEO bought a home and moved some support staff there. In early 1997 we bought a bank building surplused from a recent merger. We moved the CEO, sales, marketing, and tech support in while we remodeled to double it in size. The company cleared out of the second floor of the Big House while engineering took over the entire third floor with my office on the first floor and storage in the basement.

After ten years engineering outgrew the third floor and the rest of the company outgrew our bank building. In 2003 we leased the main and lower floors at 6500 N. Mineral Dr. and I moved there along with everyone else. I sold the bank building. With the company gone and our kids all married or in college, the Big House seemed awfully big for just Sue and me. In another year it was sold.

Finally, a place bigger than the Big House. We all moved here in 2003, ten years after our move to Idaho.

We had not planned to have a house like this. We had not planned on anything. Dad was at the end of his life, we were busy with our company, and our rental house on Military Drive was adequate for our family including son Adam when he returned. We had plenty to do without a house, big or otherwise.

Certainly, the company could have started up without the Big House. Starting the company in the Big House gave us three years to see how the company would grow and then to get and remodel a place that would be right for us for seven years, which is almost forever for a software company.

Sue loved gardening, entertaining, and fixing up the house. With my part of the company there, I could enjoy our house when I was at work as well as those few hours I was not. It was a great place to be, with things happening all the time.

LIFE AT THE BIG HOUSE

1321 E. Lakeshore Drive from our beach.

Once we had enough employees that Sue was not pressed into work continually, she started hosting events at the house for our church, various community groups, and NGOs. Among these were fundraisers for the Coeur d'Alene Police Department and the Spokane area youth symphony where Gene's two girls, Becky and Sarah, from downstairs played viola and violin. We hosted the Coeur d'Alene symphony fundraiser which I hope helped them to get better. There were breakfasts and warmups after the New Year's Day Polar Plunge on the beach across from our home. The Christmas boutique with many long folding tables around the living room, dining room, and sunroom raised money for aid in India. We hosted the public library which in turn hosted the American Girl Mother-Daughter Tea at the Big House.

The sunroom, at the east end of the house, adjoined the living room and greenhouse. These three rooms and our dining room often held tables for luncheons and dinners.

Our church held its Easter sunrise service on our beach in

front of the house. One hundred twenty-five came to breakfast afterward. That was maybe a limit. Normally we'd have one hundred inside for a sit-down dinner and two hundred outside for weddings. Missionaries visiting to speak at local churches often stayed with us. We often sat down with a husband and wife who barely escaped Saddam's Iraq, another couple who worked behind the Iron Curtain before its fall, a man who broadcast Bible studies throughout northern India, or someone who worked with untouchables in southern India. Our guests made an impression on all of us, including our three sons.

Sue once took a phone call from a group of young people going on a mission trip. They were delayed due to a breakdown and needed a place to stay the night. That night, we hosted over thirty young people along with their adult leaders. That did exceed our available beds, but they had sleeping bags for which we had plenty of space at the west end of the main floor.

One guest was a tall, elderly, Minnesota Lutheran of Swedish descent. Orv was going to lead an overseas tour leaving Valentine's Day in February 1995. Sue, Adam, and I joined with six others for a week in Thailand and two weeks in India. This started relationships and projects that continue to this day, as well as the marriage of oldest son Adam to a girl from south-central India and middle son Nathan to the daughter of a Thai rice farmer. We continued the tradition of traveling to India and Thailand, usually in February when we completed a release, finished the big trade show, and when the weather was best there and worst in north Idaho.

Our west side yard was especially large, with its surrounding trees and plantings giving privacy on three sides. We set up a green and white striped canvas pavilion at the west end that turned out perfect for a wedding party with up to two hundred seats set on the grass facing it. Sue, Gene's two girls,

Gene's wife, and Shirley, our housekeeper, hosted weddings there. They also had weddings, but with fewer guests, hosted inside in the winter. Wedding party photos on the main staircase were standard. We were lucky for the large outdoor weddings: a sudden rain drove the guests inside only once. One dinner for a wedding party and family was in the side yard just as the sun was going down one August evening. It was still warm but windless, with candles burning in glass shields on many round tables. As close to magical as it gets.

Our nephew John married Mara in the west side yard.
Below left they are on our beach.

The weddings were for friends, people in our church, and then friends of friends. We never charged, although they paid for catering, with Gene's family making a bit. As word got out, it got to be too much, and I limited us to two weddings per year except for special cases. Two of those were Sue's nephew and my mom's second marriage years after Dad died. Sue and the girls catered those, including the wedding cake.

Sue's exercise group had always rotated their luncheons to various members' homes, but soon all decided, "Let's just have them at Sue's place."

How elegant could it get? There was a five-member delegation from Japan. They were interested in marketing our software, helped us produce a Japanese version, and sold it there to a so-so market for two years. This was in the formal dining room and came off more than perfect. Our chef Richard came over that evening to produce a dinner for ten to remember. Of especial note was Richard's Fuzzy Navels. Our guests had not had anything like that before and got seconds, thirds, and... Finally, all were in the kitchen for a lesson on how to make them.

Dessert potluck New Year's Eve party throughout the house with illegal fireworks from the Indian reservation spewing out the third-floor dormers toward the lake, dinners for raising money for Russian ministries when the situation was fluid and in doubt there, famous conference speakers and concert pianist houseguests, Christmas parties for our company, beach parties for our company, and many other people and events came through the house. Sue had a crew of five from our downstairs family plus Shirley, a continuing friend who worked for us, and Richard the chef for help as she had fun in the Big House, its beautiful side yard, and out on the beach.

Sue's older brother Jerry was diagnosed with terminal

cancer in California and came up to spend his last months with us. His son John and John's fiancée also came. Jerry felt pretty good for all but the last few days and was able to spend his final months in a good place close to his son and future daughter-in-law.

Sue's brother Jerry, with his son John, lived his last months. Shirley working on John & Mara's wedding.

End of the Big House

After six years with us, Gene and his family moved out to a home he built. Finally, in 2003, the company and our kids were gone. Sue and I thought, "What do we do with this place now?" We put the Big House up for sale. A house that size is always something of a white elephant and takes a while to sell, but in a little more than a year it closed in October 2004.

When I think of the ideal family home, MacBain wins hands down. For ten years the Big House was still a great place for us all to live, but it was more than that. Where else could our kids watch and learn from a professor of culinary arts as he worked? Nathan, our middle son, became special friends with Richard, who later visited him when Nathan lived in Thailand. Where else could kids sit down to breakfast and learn how the other half of the world lives? Where else would they talk with a missionary and his wife about how they sweated border crossings in Eastern Europe in the 1970s or another about the best ways to improve the lives of the poorest of the poor in India? Where else could they watch a business grow from three people to fifty right in front of them?

FAMILY

The most extraordinary thing in the world is an ordinary man and an ordinary woman and their ordinary children. – ***G. K. Chesterton***

Sue and I have had three sons, and they have given us four grandsons. Sue and our two daughters-in-law are the only girls in the family. Each of our three sons has had extensive foreign travel and experience, which may account for marriages to girls from Hyderabad, India, and the Isaan area of north-eastern Thailand. When I've called some of my grandkids "wild Indians" in the past, I did not mean what you might think. My youngest son has yet to marry. Should that happen, I'll predict that the girl he finds will not originate from North America.

I'll defer most topics, such as just how great their life growing up in our family was and what kind of jobs Sue and I did as mother and father, to stories they will tell and maybe even write down someday, just as these stories are primarily about how I grew up. Yet, I can summarize a few incidents.

We got Ralph, an English bulldog puppy, when Sue was pregnant with Adam. We may not have been thinking clearly at the time. We brought our new son into our apartment with a cordoned-off kitchen having several fragrant bulldog deposits scattered about, which was not the homecoming Sue had in mind. Our apartment was on the ground floor and came with a good-sized backyard for a dog, but Ralph still got a lot of his puppy exercise indoors. He was compact and heavy, would run as fast as he could, but never did learn how to stop except by running into something. Any light furniture or other items would simply fly out of his way, and Sue had to take care not to be knocked down. Ralph was fine with kids, and our first two enjoyed growing up with him. Unfortunately he was not long-lived, and Jordan, our third son, never met him.

The day after Adam was born, my friend Warren gave our offer to buy, as partners, the acre that contained Warren's house as well as the little yellow house into which we moved. Adam spent his first three years on that acre with all the room he needed to explore without ever going outside the gate, except when he played with the twins. Marcus and Tony were close to Adam's age and lived on the other side of one of the many fences that bordered our acre. Their parents, Marsha and Claus, were people of the highest quality and quickly became our friends. We fixed one of the fence boards to slide up so our kids could easily move between yards. After our subdivision forced us out of the little yellow house, we spent a year in a very small cottage behind Marsha and Claus's home before moving on to our Atherwood Avenue rental.

Later in 1979, after we moved back to 6 Malory, Marcus and Tony were early adopters of the Apple II computer. One of the twins became a software engineer, as did Adam. I don't know how much influence their computer may have had. Of course, computers became common around our house later on when in 1983 I moved the Prime computer into our house at 6 Malory for my first business. These, however, were larger, expensive, and not attractive for kids to play on.

The twins had a cat named Roosevelt Franklin, after one of the Muppet characters on *Sesame Street*. Roosevelt was a large orange cat who could stand up to any dog in the neighborhood. Ralph, however, was different. Ralph loved to push our cat down and nuzzle into his fur, so he was excited when he first saw Roosevelt visiting our acre and ran straight for him. Roosevelt bravely stood his ground as usual, and Ralph ran right over him before he could stop several feet later. I was there for that event. The cat seemed to bounce up from the ground after his compression from Ralph's passage and was quickly gone. Roosevelt soon learned that stepping out of Ralph's way was easy and could be done with dignity and that once he came to a stop, Ralph was no problem at all.

Ralph could be a problem with other dogs. We took down our northeast gate when we built the Malory Court road into our new subdivision. Ralph rarely wandered out, but another dog might occasionally wander in. Once I came out to find Ralph had grabbed a German shepherd by the neck and was just holding on. I managed to grab Ralph's collar and pull him off. The other dog's thick leather collar, which was chewed through and came off with Ralph, had protected him from damage, and he was out of there immediately. When we were in our Atherwood rental, Sue saw a Doberman jump our back fence, presumably to investigate Ralph. She didn't know what his intentions were, but Ralph's were clear and immediate. She said she never saw a dog jump like that as he immediately went back over the fence.

Another Ralph incident happened when Warren and Al were working on our house at 6 Malory. A man with his big dog on a leash walked down Malory Court. We normally kept Ralph behind a fence, but somehow he had gotten out and went after the dog. Warren said that if the man had just let go of the leash, the dog could have easily avoided Ralph. Anyway, the man was pretty upset, as was Sue when she finally got out to corral Ralph. No damage was done, but the man threatened to sue. Nothing came of it. During the whole fracas, Warren and Al were at pains to take a "we just work here, don't look at us" attitude about the whole thing.

Adam and Ralph lived in the little yellow house for three years. We then moved to a few temporary houses and finally moved into our new home at 6 Malory Court when Adam was almost six years, and Nathan was six months old.

Nathan's first few years in a large two-story home proved that self-esteem, so popular these days for children, is not as desirable as you might think. Nathan had plenty of esteem and confidence, which far exceeded his maturity and good sense. He could and would do anything. There were several times when I weighed putting bolt locks keyed from the inside on all our exterior doors to prevent Nathan's periodic escapes. Early on in his second-floor bedroom, he had moved some furniture, climbed up, opened his window, removed the screen, and was climbing out headfirst. Sue caught him by the shoes and pulled him back in.

I was in my upstairs office when I heard Nathan running in the hall. I could see the top flight of the stairs and Nathan flying down it upside down with feet high in the air. He came out of that one, and several more that I did not see, OK. That was one thing I thought of when I designed a three-flight, two-landing stairway, onto which we put a thick carpet.

When grocery shopping, Sue turned back after getting something off a shelf to find Nathan had climbed out of the seat in the cart and into the adjacent open chest freezer. He had half the cans of frozen orange juice on the floor before she could get him back into the cart.

Nathan learned to ride his Honda Kick 'N' Go scooter quite early. Once, Sue informed me, not for the first time, that Nathan was nowhere to be found in the house. I ran around the outside looking for our seventeen-month-old. Ralph was gone too. He couldn't have gotten out of the fence at this point; someone opened the front door for him. The Kick 'N' Go was not in any of the paved areas appropriate for it. I finally ran him down more than a block up San Carlos Street on the sidewalk, halfway to Woodside shopping center. He was wearing just a diaper, and Ralph was walking close behind him.

Sue had a group of ladies over for a Bible study and tea in the dining room. They all paused as two-year-old Nathan came down the stairs with a big pair of scissors and a lot of cloth material slung over his shoulder. "You know those curtains that were always in the way? Well, I fixed that!" Sue had made the curtains for Nathan's room from expensive material. They hung just above the floor and were perfect, but after that could not even hang to the windowsill. Nathan had not informed her about any problem with his curtains. Why bother when you can easily fix it yourself?

I was present for Adam's and Nathan's births. At that time, they had started letting the husband in the room during the birth. Lamaze was popular; we both went to several classes and I was Sue's coach when Adam came. He took a long time. Nathan, on the other hand, came within minutes of getting to the hospital. No time for coaching there. Jordan came early. I had started my database business and was in Washington, DC with a client, so my marketer got Sue to the hospital and everything went quickly and easily; so my third son, Jordan, got home just before I did.

Jordan was an easy baby. He would sleep when you put him down and not fuss when he was awake. When Jordan came, the Prime computer was installed in our fourth bedroom, which was my office. Jordan moved in with me along with his crib and change table and proved to be a good office mate. There were any number of things that disturbed me more than Jordan.

Jordan was always pretty quiet. He started talking very early and in multiple full sentences at eighteen months, which we thought amazing. After around four years, we noticed that his memory was unusual. We could ask him anything about a trip or other activity we had had together, and he could tell us the details. He might not know what people had said, but he probably wasn't listening at the time. He could tell you where we went, how we went, what we saw, buildings, parks, animals, etc. on a trip we took a year ago. As the years went by, his memory seemed to change; he didn't retain quite the wealth of details he used to, but I think he started noticing things differently from before, when everything he saw was something new. Today his memory remains well above average. He easily retains what he needs from schooling or whatever he reads.

The Tough Question

Have I been as good with my sons as Dad was with me? I could not have bettered him. He was a hundred percent behind me always. He still had to work a lot. He just barely, but adequately, kept our family with food, clothing, transportation, education, and housing. We needed those things, and he knew it. It took nearly all the time he had to give those to us, with not a lot left for "quality time."

I should have spent more time with my family. I spent about as much time with them as Dad did with me, which was not so much. We both worked hard and long, though differently. He had to do it to keep from going under. Could I have worked a little less, had more family time, and still have been adequately successful? A software company that sells a product nationwide must be very competitive. There is room for only a few to be really successful. If my company could have been halfway successful and made half as much, it would have supported my family just fine, but another company that was all the way successful would have been the end of us. It was like baseball great Satchel Paige said, "Don't look back — something might be gaining on you." I could not aim at halfway.

But the amount of quality time was not what ended up being the most important. It was Dad's attitude and feelings toward me. How many boys long for their dad's approval? I've read about people who excel in school, and then again in their early career, hoping to finally receive their father's approval. I never wanted my dad's approval. You can't want what you've always had. I'm not sure I noticed it so much when younger, but I eventually started to notice how he referred to me with others, whether I was around or not. I was the greatest, smartest, best boy in the world. He was certain, if not realistic.

Dad knew a lot of people in town. He had lived there since the mid-thirties except for his time in the war and a five-year stay in southern California. When we returned to be with Dad, people would come up to me and mention something Dad had said, and that if I was a fraction of any of it, I must really be something.

But back to the original question. I think the answer is no. I can't match Dad' being a dad. I've made more money than he did, but he made enough. I might have bested him on time spent with my sons. Time spent per each son could still be argued, but I don't think that was as important as many seem to say. Just like Clarence's personality made him friendly and likable in a way few, including me, could match, so my dad could back and advocate for me like few fathers were able. Dad was unusual in this way. Few in the world could match him, and I was not one of them.

I've done OK. I do approve of my sons. They all do well. None are rich, famous, or perfect, but all live good lives and are responsible people. None have remotely disreputable occupations. None will ever be president, but that would require them being a politician, and I already told you about their occupations.

OUR KIDS' SCHOOL

Our kids went to public schools as they were growing up. We could not afford a private school, especially the expensive ones in our area of California. This worked OK at first, but sometimes problems surfaced. Sue supervised the kids' schooling because she knew education, especially primary level, much better than me. She was a private school teacher when I met her, and had taught first grade in Santa Cruz, California public schools the year before. Things worked OK for our first two kids, if not great. We had only one school change to get Adam away from a bad teacher, and that was only for a year.

Adam was our first into high school, going to the tenth grade at Menlo-Atherton High School. Today this school functions well as a multiethnic school, sending many students on to college. When Adam entered in the late 1980s, things were different. The school had been integrated when a neighboring school in a poorer area of another town had been closed. The various issues that plagued the old school did not change when all its students were moved to Menlo-Atherton. We noticed problems when we learned Adam and other students could not use the bathrooms for the entire day, even before and after school. Some students occupied the boys' bathrooms. They would threaten and otherwise intimidate selected other students, keeping them out. I was the one who called the administration about that one. The response was unbelievable, but I did hear it. The person I spoke with would only say, "It's not our job to monitor the restrooms." Adam also had tried to find a teacher that could read some of his writing and give some pointers. No one would do that.

Adam had previously taken summer courses in Japanese at the local community college, which worked out well for him. It also gave Sue an idea. She checked a few things out with the school superintendent's office and then in a conference with the principal. Sue wanted Adam to leave the high school and see how attending classes at nearby Cañada Community College worked out. The principal told her that once he left, he could not return to the school

Adam did well at Cañada and was assuming to get high school credits for his work. He ended up with two years of college credits instead. This proved handy when Sue's mother later offered to pay for his first year at the private Westmont College in Southern California. They accepted all but a few of his credits, and he entered as a second-semester sophomore.

Adam was always interested in Japan and had already taken several language courses, so toward the end of his first year, he pitched the idea of Westmont students studying abroad in Japan. Westmont already had several study-abroad programs, but nothing in that part of the world. They liked the idea. Adam could be a trailblazer and help get the program started. In return, they would cover most of the fees for his year abroad.

Adam packed a year and a half of study into two semesters at his Japanese university plus a three-month study program in China, graduating from Westmont College before he returned home.

Our cost for that entire year overseas did not exceed a couple of thousand dollars. These savings came at a good time since the database business was getting a little tight right when Adam first left for Westmont.

Adam came back to us from overseas. We were in the big house at that point, our new company taking up as many of its rooms as we did. Adam was immediately pressed into sales. As the Internet came online, Adam developed our company's Web presence as he moved from sales into Internet software development, which was a new field of work at that time.

Nathan attended school in California and finished the last half of the eighth grade after we moved up to north Idaho. There he attended Lakes Junior High, in the same building that was my high school years earlier. For ninth grade, he went to my former high school, which had moved to a new building. He attended there only half a year and dropped out. He continued studying at home for about a year with Sue's help and then passed the GED. For college, he took courses at two different area community colleges, then a year at Whitworth, a private college in nearby Spokane. He then spent several years in Thailand, married his Thai wife, and eventually returned to Idaho and finished up college, graduating from the University of Idaho. It was a roundabout way of doing things, but nearly all his credits from the various colleges transferred OK, and it worked for him.

Jordan attended third and the first half of the fourth grade after we moved to north Idaho. It wasn't long before Sue was called in for a disciplinary problem. Jordan was reading during class and not paying attention when he should be listening. Sue asked to have him tested and met with his teacher to discuss the results. The test results were unexpected, and Jordan was exhibiting other issues that we would learn more about later. The teacher admitted to not knowing how best to teach Jordan. Sue was expecting something like that and said, "Why don't I take him out and home school him?" to which the teacher responded, "That would be great! Wait! Please don't tell anyone I said that!"

Jordan studied for several years in the Big House with minimal supervision. He was as easy as a student as he was as a baby. He plowed through the lessons and assignments pretty much on his own. We sent him to an area private high school for a few years, more for socialization than academics. He made several good friends but left a year early. He took placement exams, spent two years in our local community college, and then worked as a software development intern at my company. He was reasonably competent and liked computer programming but decided a steady diet of it was not for him. He ended up graduating from Baylor University with a BS in neuroscience.

So dropping out of school became a Simpson family tradition for at least that generation. So far, my four grandchildren have not followed in their dads' footsteps. It appears the oldest will enter his senior year of high school next year and graduate like a normal person. Who would have thought?

WHAT'S WRONG WITH DAD

You could be a fool and not know it, unless you're married. — **H. L. Mencken**

It is better to keep your mouth closed and let people think you are a fool than to open it and remove all doubt. — **Mark Twain**

I was above average when it came to math, science, and computers. I don't think I was too far below for the rest of my life except for an occasional social disaster due to following the second part of Mr. Twain's quote. There are times even now when Sue tells me, "Don't do that in public. Only children do that." When out sitting around a restaurant table with friends, she's ready to deliver a kick, which says either "don't go further into that" or "you're talking too much" or the dreaded "they've already heard this story, and it's been way too many times for me." This is usually enough for me to stop, think of what I'm doing, and apply the appropriate correction. For more specific information on corrections normally required, refer to Mr. Twain above.

It's not all bad. Later, the rise of people like Bill Gates and movies like *Revenge of the Nerds* made nerds cool. We weren't cool in high school. Some of us really did wear those white plastic shirt pocket protectors to carry our pens and pencils. No computers, of course, but there were the big slide rules with the leather case clipped on our belts.

As I got into writing software, there were situations best handled with long sessions of concentration while holding many possibilities in my mind that ordered and reordered. I'm not sure about doing all that if you just took my normal intelligence into account. It's like I was specialized for that kind of work. I'd shut down everything else, shut out the world, and go at it. It worked for the software. Sue was puzzled how I changed into a different person for periods, especially the first months of a project when I had to make mental order out of chaos, sort out how the new software would work, and rush to type in things before they fell off the edge of whatever was in my head. There is something to the expression "software nerd." To paraphrase what I've seen in business shops: I didn't have to be crazy to do that job, but it did turn out to help quite a lot.

I was never diagnosed by a real shrink, but my youngest son majored in neuroscience in college. Years back, he was home from school for one of those times when Sue was at wit's end from my behavior. Jordan took her aside and started, "Do you know what's wrong with Dad?"

My autism is high functioning, and much of the time, it may be less noticeable out in public and with those who don't know me well. Sue says I'm getting better with age. It's been a relief to her that I don't mean it and am not trying to hurt her when I say some of the things that can come out when I'm not thinking. She's always believed in me and says I should be almost normal by maybe the age of 120.

Jordan now contracts to public schools in the Seattle area to work with autistic children, from violent cases to high functioning ones, that just need some advice to round off rough edges of the type I'm familiar with. My dad inspired me to start businesses; why shouldn't I inspire my kids in their careers? But I'm not sure about that. Jordan is the one son who is more autistic than I am.

Autism Details, If You're Interested

I have an input rate limitation. I can process things, but not too much or too fast. Exceeding the limit causes a meltdown or shutdown. In a young autistic child, this can cause violent behavior: they just want to shut the input out. I'm a mild case, but I'll momentarily stop thinking and could say the wrong, "unfeeling" thing. I'll watch, uncaring, as an unfortunate event hits you when a normal person instinctively rushes to your aid. You're right that I don't care, not right away. The flood of information from a sudden unexpected event causes a partial shutdown. I will care about you; I might even show it once I've had time to process things and consciously think up an appropriate response. It doesn't take so long, really, but it's a whole lot longer than instant. Again, I'm getting better and often handle these situations OK, depending on how severe they are.

I cannot multitask. Some of my company's software engineers listen to music as they work, which I can't. The sound would just pound away at me while I'm trying to concentrate. I can enjoy a TV show or video. Otherwise, if the TV is on and

I'm talking or doing anything else, I can usually function unless you say something with any amount of complexity. I still feel such relief, like the lifting of a weight, if we can just turn the TV off. I love classical music and wish I could listen to it more but must allocate time away from everything else. I normally have too many things to do, so not much music. The old way of going to a concert where that is all you do works best.

A dishonest person "can't look you in the eye," right? Allow me to introduce myself. Again, I'm a mild case. I can look you in the eye. In the last twenty years, I do if I'm alert and thinking. But often, I don't. Eyes and facial expressions convey more information. Our speech together is plenty, thanks. I'll naturally look elsewhere and tend to lower my eyes. This can cause a problem with women, especially if their neckline is low. They think I'm looking at something when the point for me is to look at nothing. It's better to look off to either side. Is that what they mean by "shifty-eyed?"

I've never caught on to body language. You won't "bother" me with that. Not long after we married, Sue came back to me in a small grocery store and said, "Did you notice how those two girls were flirting with you?" Notice what?

This doesn't contradict what I said in "At First Sight" about Sue's expression, hand motions, poise, etc., when I first saw her. I was at least fifteen feet away, without having to process her presence, conversation, or my reaction to that. I'm not entirely blind to these things, and there I could look for and concentrate on them. I certainly wasn't concentrating on anything else. There was no effect on Sue. On that occasion, one more boy looking at her would have been no surprise.

VISIT TO KOLKATA

At the Taj Mahal on our first trip outside of North America.

Our first visit to India was with our oldest son, Adam, in early 1995. We visited a number of major cities all over the country. In each one, we saw the sights and also met with people working with various disadvantaged groups, which at that time were not hard to find. We saw people helping religious ministries, street kids, slums, microloan projects, etc. We became accustomed to wading through throngs of people on the way in and out of old airports and train stations. We had local guides in each city and needed them just to find where we should go in the crush and avoid legions of people who were there to help us in various ways, each for a small fee. Beggars were in the streets and everywhere else. Seeing a five-year-old beggar with her three-year-old sister working out in the traffic on a major city street was new to us.

Toward the end of this trip, our group of seven landed in Kolkata (previously Calcutta) and stayed in the Fairlawn Hotel. By this time, we'd had some up-and-down experiences with the various hotels as we hopped between all of the Indian cities we'd ever heard of as well as a number we had not. At first, we didn't know what to think of this latest one. It was certainly old, constructed in 1783, with green cast-iron pillars holding it up. By the time we had put our luggage in our room and Adam and I had checked out the kitchen (you would be amazed at the condition of these in some hotels), we realized that while different from anything we could imagine, it was clean and would be an interesting place to stay.

"Mother Teresa's house is just a couple of blocks away," one of our group commented to our local guide. "Could we see any of that?"

"Oh, I know Mother Teresa," the guide responded. "She is a friend of mine. Would you like to meet her?"

We could not quite believe him but told him we would love to meet her.

It was 10:30 in the evening when we had everything settled in our room and got back down to the lobby. Adam was already at the desk talking to the old British lady who ran the hotel. She had come to Kolkata in the 1930s when her mother bought the hotel; the daughter had run it since the early 1960s. She knew everyone and everything about the city and told Adam stories. Sue and I had heard so much about old Kolkata and wanted to walk around. It was long after dark, but the lady said we'd be perfectly safe. She just said, "Watch where you step, dearie, and don't eat anything! If you're hungry, come back to me. I've got food for you in the kitchen."

March in Kolkata was warm on into the night, providing us with a comfortable time to walk around the city. We quickly learned to watch where we stepped. Everywhere, people were sleeping on the sidewalks. Often, we could not get around them, but they always seemed to leave room between them, so Sue and I might gingerly step over a family of five, one person at a time, from the smallest to the largest. Not one of the many sleepers we stepped over woke up. We saw a different world out in Kolkata at midnight.

We got back just after midnight and Adam was still listening to stories. She had indicated a British embassy employee sitting at a table with a young Indian woman who was the diplomat's secretary. They were traveling together. She had a witty way of hinting that the two had more than a working relationship. She told how she volunteered to work at Mother Teresa's place when she returned to India in the 1960s.

"Those poor dying men were spitting curses out one end and diarrhea out the other," she said. "It got to be too much for me."

She did come away with admiration for the work of Mother Teresa's nuns. She seemed to know everything that happened in the city and everyone who made it happen and was more than willing to tell you all of it.

We found out later that her hotel was famous, although you would not guess that by looking around. Many famous people had stayed there, including Patrick Swayze while filming *City of Joy* four years before our visit. Dominique Lapierre, the author of the book on which the movie was based, had stayed there before that.

The lady was indeed a character, and everyone in Kolkata knew it. Her death at age ninety-three in 2014 was noted in big articles with pictures in the British as well as Indian news. The *Times of India* stated:

> "The morning durbars under the portico of the delightfully eccentric Fairlawn Hotel on Sudder Street have just become history. The 'Duchess of Sudder Street', as Vi (Violet) Smith was popularly called, will not be holding 'court' there anymore. And legions of her fans, as well as the galaxy of loyal customers of her hotel, will no longer be regaled by her stories about the Kolkata of yore."

Our guide was on time the next morning; we were ready, and we were soon at Mother Teresa's home. She greeted guests in her courtyard each day from eight to nine in the morning. There was a short line with just a few people ahead of us. She would kiss a small medal of her namesake Saint Thérèse of Lisieux and give one to each guest, then she held her hand above them and blessed them. When our turn came, she knew that Orv, the leader of our group of seven, worked for an organization that had often supported her work.

Mother signaled for those behind her to be sent away. We

were invited into her home where she had chairs placed in a circle. She knew where we were from and spoke of her visit to the National Prayer Breakfast in America a year earlier.

"I told them you do not have to kill your babies. Please give them to me. We will take care of every one of them! After I said that, everyone stood and clapped; only the president and vice president and their wives, they did not stand."

Sue was sitting at her left side as Mother told how she trained her sisters. "When walking from one place to another it is time to be in prayer for the needy."

"Mother led by example," Sue says:

> Her sisters owned one sari and a bucket in which to wash it. Her own sari was paper-thin with tears stitched every few inches. We were thanked for the help and support she received over the years. She took my hand and held up two of my fingers. She reminded us of Jesus's words. If we had two coats (then she put down one of my fingers), we were told to find someone with none.
>
> I felt goosebumps all over as I realized I was in the presence of holiness. Every time I shared this visit with someone they began to tear up with emotion. It was a powerful experience!

Life in India has improved a great deal in the last twenty-five years. It has been a long time since child beggars have been out on the street. The life expectancy for people in the slums is past sixty now largely due to simple things like immunization programs, cheap blood pressure medicines, and a free government hospital system that might scare the average American but is far better than no medical care at all, and it's getting better all the time. This is normal and part of worldwide progress toward the elimination of extreme poverty.

Adam returned to India seven years later and married a niece of the people we met in Hyderabad where we had visited just before our last stop in Kolkata. Today, they and three of our grandchildren live in Austin, Texas.

Sue did not realize it at the time, but her visit with Mother Teresa would resurrect something in her that had lain dormant since we married.

THE WILD WILD EAST

Slum can be defined as 'A residential area where dwellings are unfit for human habitation by reasons of dilapidation, overcrowding, lack of ventilation or sanitation facility and having drinking water facilities in unhygienic conditions.' – Times of India, August 17, 2016

The long fence wall was only twenty feet from the road's edge, which was ragged asphalt meeting the dirt. There was not enough room for the huts up against the wall. They were A-frame structures like large pup tents supported by lashed-together tree branches and covered by plastic from old garbage bags and tarps. The plastic, and occasional pieces of corrugated roofing sheets, formed roofs that mostly went down to the ground. The "community area" was just a few feet of dirt from the huts to the road edge. Traffic was slow and space was tight on the road in Hyderabad, India, so that the people in front of their long row of slum dwellings were easy to see.

Gabilalapeta slum, near the main garbage dump at the northeast edge of Hyderabad city, was first settled in 2005.

They came to a woman in a ragged sari at the road edge. She was screaming, holding up a baby by one arm and shaking it while she threw a cup of water at it. The water was not even a start at cleaning up the diarrhea all over. It was obvious the lady had lost any ability to cope, and then Sue's car had passed by.

In the slums, pushcarts are for selling items outside.

How do you handle a mess like that in a place like that? No place to lay the baby; no tables or clean cloth. Any sheet of material was already used for your roof, which still leaks, and if still on the ground would have a layer of dirt on it anyway. Lay it on some clothes? Then how will you wash them with little clean water? Lay it on the dirt? How does that mix with diarrhea? How well would Sue have handled it if she was that lady?

A dump for a city of ten million is filling up this valley.
We notice if the wind blows the wrong way.

It had been ten years since Sue had met with Mother Teresa. With the Big House sold, our sons out of the house, and a husband still busy with a software company, Sue had run out of things to do. With no Big House, there were no more events or weddings, no huge side yard and garden down by the beach to care for, so she started working more with various ministries in India, often going there with me, but sometimes alone. Sue and I had worked with others in Indian slums since seeing them along the roadways in Hyderabad, and Sue kept thinking about how she could work there more effectively.

A family stands in front of their hut in the slum. It is one of the better places; it has walls.

Neither of us dared to drive a car in crazy Indian traffic, and most middle-class Indians we knew at that time hired a driver. A private car was still a pretty new thing. Most drivers spoke only the local language, but Sue's had worked in Dubai and spoke English. When Ignatius told her of a really bad slum he knew about, she had to go see it.

Hundreds of families had left their villages to come to the big city to find work as construction laborers, as maids, or as drivers for three-wheel auto rickshaw cabs. They squatted without permission, forming slums all over Hyderabad wherever they found space. This slum was a large piece of vacant government land at the northeast edge of the city next to its main garbage dump, not just a strip along the road.

The slum was home to a group of stonecutters from Tamil Nadu state to the south. They lived in typical stick-framed, garbage-bag-covered A-frame huts. There was one small concrete building with maybe six children in it playing school. Someone had just fed them a little rice, and a lady came by with a cup asking if there was any left. Sue asked her how they might help and learned about the children's skin diseases. Beyond this most-noticeable problem, she soon learned of others. The government came once a year before winter with some medicine and big jugs of cough syrup, pouring out a cupful for each family. They could certainly use more medicine.

A foreign lady in the slum was news, and soon Sue and Ignatius were talking to Subramanyam, the leader of the stonecutters. He thought medicine and a little medical help were great ideas. Sue talked of a small clinic and Subramanyam said he could get a place for that.

The Clinic in Shanti Nagar

Sue and her clinic staff. Mother Tersa behind.

In a few days, Sue returned with an examination table, a washbowl with stand, bandages, various medicines, a stethoscope, and other instruments and supplies. The people in the slum had arranged a ribbon-cutting ceremony, which Sue learned is essential in India. As people gathered, Sue saw several young men sitting together on the rug placed in front of the small stage. She chatted with them while Ignatius interpreted. "What do you do in your spare time?" she asked. They looked at each other as if she should know. "We drink," they said sheepishly. This was only the first time she would encounter this issue. A large garland of marigolds, complete with many little black bugs, was hung about around Sue's neck. Tradition is to bow, take it off, and lay it down, but not knowing this, she had bugs crawling on her all afternoon.

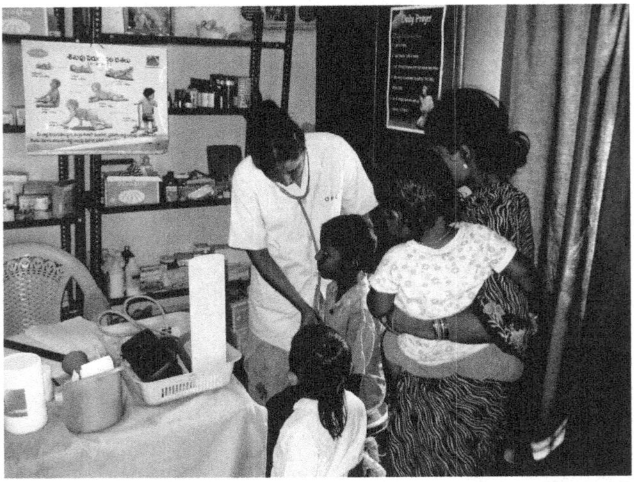

The ribbon was across a new bamboo-framed hut with hand-woven palm leaf screens for walls. It was open in front with a back, two sides, and a roof. Looking at the obvious mismatch between the equipment and building, the people of Shanti Nagar slum first realized that "Sue Ma'am," as she came to be called, would not be leaving them anytime soon.

Subramanyam located a just constructed ten-by-ten-foot

concrete house that people could rent when able to afford more than an A-frame hut. It was the third permanent building in the slum and Sue agreed to $12 per month to rent it for the clinic. Sue found a nurse who had worked in slums and hired her to staff the clinic and the people started lining up every morning.

Not enough people lining up it seemed to Sue as she looked out and saw hundreds of huts in every direction. She learned that many separate slums occupied the area, each with a leader that jealously guarded his power over his people and wanted them to stay away from others. Sue had been fortunate to run into Subramanyam, the leader most given to actually helping his people, as her first one. The next leader would require a little more effort.

The closest government school. Teachers usually were not there.

Sue grabbed Ignatius and off they went to the large next door Gabilalapeta slum. Why didn't anyone come to the clinic? "Because Ravi told us it's only for Shanti Nagar." They soon found Ravi, who explained how he was the "doctor" for his people. In his youth, he volunteered to help the nurse who visited his tiny village once a week — a 3½-hour drive from Hyderabad. He had saved many lives, stitched wounds, and delivered babies. He bought drugs in the city to resell for a small profit. He had worked only with his people in Gabilalapeta. This was how he fed his family and Sue's clinic could put him out of business.

The first rule of helping people: never get between anyone and their income. Since he was already trained, Sue hired him to be our nurse's assistant. He was to help people from all the slums, and would work and make a bit more. Sue didn't know what Ravi told everyone; maybe he said he had negotiated a deal with Sue to allow the people of Gabilalapeta to use her clinic. It didn't matter, soon the number of people using the clinic was as expected.

With Ignatius as a translator, Sue would talk with mothers who brought their children into the clinic. The nearest school was too far for the children to walk, and they could not afford transportation, so no one went to school. Sue was not aware at first, but slums were not recognized by the government and could be, and sometimes were, bulldozed at any time. Since they were not (officially) there, the government did not provide school or other services. Sue visited the nearest government school, found it was indeed too far away, and anyway was only a concrete shell, usually without a teacher present. Sue wasn't sure how good a school she could put together but bettering something like that should not be hard.

Sue Ma'am decided to build a school.

SUE MA'AM AND THE INDIAN SLUMS

There should be less talk ... What do you do then? Take a broom and clean someone's house. That says enough. – ***Mother Teresa of Kolkata***

This perfectly describes my grandmother, whose name is on Sue's school.

There was no room for a school building in Shanti Nagar, but the next door Gabilalapeta slum was much bigger and had undeveloped areas. The Gabilalapeta leader seemed not interested in meeting a foreigner, but Ignatius and Sue managed to catch him at someone's hut and ask for a meeting in front of others. He agreed and the drum was beaten at the community hall.

Original meeting at Gabilalapeta community center.

Ramana was a different kind of leader, more like an organized crime boss.[1] We found out later he had a deal with a political party to deliver the votes from his slum. He also delivered people for political demonstrations. If the government did not need the slum land for anything, Ramana would control its subdivision and get money from the sale of each plot.

Children play in front of the first Maggi School. The four-classroom building lasted four years.

About thirty women and a few men and children came to a ragged, falling-apart bamboo shed. Ramana did not care about a school, just passing the question off to the others in the meeting, whose response was entirely different. Sue asked for a large enough plot of land for a school. She would pay for the building, teachers, and other costs. Ramana granted land with a six-foot granite cliff running through it and a wide, deep hole at its front. No one else had wanted it for building anything. There was a spot where she could start with four classrooms.

Sue was scheduled to leave, so she left some funds with Ignatius. Sue now planned six months in India and six months home. She scheduled the India time so that she either went over or back with me or at least she would be there when I was traveling, usually in February or March in order for it to be after the National Builders' Show.

The first class was young. Within a year they sorted into grades nursery, K1, K2, and 1st. New buildings on either side were added as grades went up.

When she returned six months later, it was to a sixty-foot-long blue building built from "wet wood" with four 15 x 15 classrooms each opening to a long six-foot-deep porch in front. Ignatius was principal/supervisor for several years with his wife as one of our teachers. Three others came to Sue and were hired. The initial teachers did not have college degrees but did speak English. Sue trained and supervised them. She turned them into good teachers for the initial school with grades nursery, K1, K2, and first grade in the four rooms.

They ate well so they could learn well. They would not become stunted "slum people." Sue Ma'am sits in the doorway in the red blouse. She ate the same lunch as the kids.

Sue had decided her school would be "English Medium," where English was the only language spoken by teachers and students. Upper and upper-middle-class Indians sent their children to English medium schools. Government and most other schools were all in the local language, which was Telegu or sometimes Tamil in Hyderabad. In India, English was the ticket to the middle class and employment by international and high-tech companies and call centers opening up offices in Hyderabad. Not too many miles from her slum was the new "High

Tech City" being built up by the government with cooperation with Microsoft, Dell Computer, Hewlett-Packard, and other companies. The other obvious advantage of English was that Sue could train her teachers and supervise easily without interpreters.

Sue stands with local leaders. Ignatius is to the left, Ramana to the right in the white shirt. Politicians wear white shirts. There are three in this picture, all right of Sue.

Jobs were tight in Hyderabad and Sue had no problem finding young people with decent English skills and at least a solid high school education. She trained them differently from the Indian way. At that time, curriculum and methods came from the British occupation before the world war. Teachers had a four-foot rod with them, and classrooms were small enough that any student could be reached with it. Inattentiveness or a little one dozing off led to a quick whack. One of Sue's new rules horrified the parents, who were certain their children would not learn if they were not beaten.

Indian Independence Day celebration at Maggi School in 2011

Sue immediately started feeding the children at school. Tough stainless steel plates and cups were bought. Cooks and cleanup people were hired. The kids ate much better than they had before. Sue and the teachers ate the same food. When I was in town, that's where I ate as well. The only difference between us and the kids is we got chairs to sit in.

With the help of the clinic, the children were dewormed and the original skin issues, as well as other not-so-apparent issues, were dealt with. Healthy, well-fed children learned better anyway, so soon the school was running well; word got out and Sue was quickly presented with more children than she could handle. She looked for more teachers and would need more classrooms.

The granite cliff through the property was a definite obstacle, but just next door was a slum full of stonecutters. They came over and cut the cliff into proper-sized foundation blocks for the new classroom buildings. Most things we'd do with machinery were done by hand, but they got the land prepared and soon Sue and Ignatius supervised a new long concrete block building first across one end and then across the other end of the wooden building.

When the school had grown past 200 students, Ramana, the slum leader, who was used to distributing favors to constituents, "gave" out ten teaching jobs in Sue's school. Just saying "NO" to Ramana was not a good idea, so Sue told him the new teachers were not in the current budget. The only way to hire them would be to cut the feeding program. Ramana saw no problem with this, so Sue had an announcement printed up for each student. Their illiterate parents could not read it, but it would look official. Their children would tell them what it said.

That evening, 400 angry parents surrounded Ramana's house screaming at him for shutting down their children's main food source. Of course, Ramana never did that; there was a mistake. Sue found out the next day that Ramana never said any of the other things he said, and things were back to normal. Ramana adjusted to the new political realities. He could hand out land in the slum. Sue could give education. Both were important.[2] He needed to get Sue land on occasion for a separate preschool, kindergarten, baby care center, and other activities she wanted. On the other hand, she could give him money for these things, and he could claim credit to the higher-up politicians for "his school" and all the great things he was promoting in his slum. One other thing he noticed was that he could get more money for the small land plots in the slum because he had a good school there.

In 2011, Keith and Gayle, our Australian friends, started working with Sue. Gayle was a master teacher in the Australian school system, teaching math, English, drama, and other courses from primary through senior high school. There was no course in the Australian school system she was not qualified to teach and teach well. She also trained teachers and developed the school curriculum. Earlier, Keith and Gayle spent ten years living and working with aboriginal and islander people in outback Australia and on Great Palm Island, just off the north-east coast of Australia. Great Palm Island was named "the most violent place on earth outside of a combat zone" by the 1999 edition of the *Guinness Book of Records*. The Indian slums were no problem at all for people like that. Gayle made a lot of improvements and took over teacher training and curriculum from Sue. Keith, a hands-on civil engineer, did job training with the young men in the slum.

In fifteen years, Maggi High School has since grown even more and is now housed in a new building serving 550 students. With government approval, that building will soon double in size.

[1] Naxalite Terrorists

The slum leader Ramana was associated with the Naxalites, a terrorist group similar to the Maoists in Nepal, who wanted to violently overthrow the government. When Sue first got to Gabilalapeta, they were still having group training in how to fight when the revolution came using the standard four-foot staff, the same that teachers whacked their students with, as weapons. It seemed pathetic, but next door, the even larger communist slum did the same thing.

Once, the group was having an evening rally and asked Sue if they might borrow the school's PA system. Sue did not connect them with the word "terrorist," although she knew they wanted to violently overthrow the government. She told them it was "against school policy," as if she was appealing to some higher authority,[3] and they accepted that. This was the same as when she would tell Ramana, more than once, that the school budget simply did not allow her to do as he wanted her to.

The slum leader sells the slum's vote. These men voted Congress party.

The women vote too, but go in separate trucks.

During Sue's first few years, the police never came into the slum, no matter what happened. Ramana had four beefy thugs who applied discipline as needed, so they got along without the police, who were not so different from the thugs when it came to discipline.

I later learned that a truce between the Naxalites and police had been declared a year or two before Sue came to the slums. Naxalites thought police, politicians, and rich people (Indian rich people, not foreigners) should be shot, and did so as they could. The police were the easiest targets and received the most bullets. The police shot Naxalites as often as they could as well. Things deteriorated to where the police shot a Naxalite, causing them to make the effort and shoot a policeman, whose buddies would then shoot a Naxalite to the point that both sides tired of the game; a truce was called, and the Naxalites stopped shooting people. Ramana and others preached revolution for a few more years, but other than an occasional rally, not much happened.

The Naxalites still retained some political power in villages and slums and soon allied themselves with a major political party that they helped by supplying their people's votes as well as their bodies when needed for demonstrations. On several occasions, a number of large flatbed trucks with stake railings would come into the slums, get loaded, standing room only, with men and women for voting, or just men supplied with appropriate signs for a demonstration. They would all get half again a normal day's wage for their participation, the slum leader got some money, and the political party got their support. It was the Indian equivalent of "get out the vote."

Finally, the Naxalite movement just withered away as people like Ramana simply joined a mainstream party, showing that money corrupts bad politics, like terrorism, taking it away from the path of "true revolution," just as it does good politics, assuming that exists. Some of the Naxalites went into more straightforward organized crime without any politics, but Sue seldom ran into them. Either way, they did not mess with foreigners, since doing so would raise their game onto the international stage, and no one wanted that.

Sue with Subramaniam. His stone cutters made these foundation blocks.

With the Naxalites gone for the last few years, and the slum turning into a "municipality" with a more normal local government structure, the police have been enforcing the law and people have been voting as they wish.

[2] Indian Attitude about Education

On our first trip to India in 1995, we spent some time in Hyderabad, where I read a few of the English language newspapers. Most interesting were the advertisements. At least 75 percent of them were for schools, from nursery school to nursing to high tech training in some computer language. If you had any money, the first thing you did was get your kids, at any age, into the best school you could afford. Send them to a government school or a lesser private school and they would not learn in English and be unlikely to successfully enter India's growing middle class. In an English language newspaper, these ads appeared directed toward the middle and upper-classes. Class attitudes always filter down in any society, so ten years later Sue would find out just how important schooling was to her kids' parents, even though they were illiterate slum people.

[3] Sue Ma'am's Ultimate Authority?

I did visit the slums often, and in that male-centered society, may have been viewed as some sort of authority beyond the feared Sue Ma'am. I was "Jack Sir," if you must know. Chief Architect was doing great and produced sufficient funds for Sue's activities. Sue was used to being frugal and so naturally kept her spending in reasonable check. The ability to hire thirty teachers and pay them the local going rate for less than a couple of programmers at Chief made building up a whole school not such a financially formidable project. In both cases, at Chief and Maggi School, we paid good prevailing wages and had good employee retention. Obviously, the Chief employees were the engine that drove all that Sue was able to do in the slums.

So, was I viewed as that ultimate authority that prevented Sue from feeding the children when Ramana wanted to hand out school-supported jobs to some of his constituents? That and denial of the school PA system for a Naxalite "bring down the government" rally were details I was never aware of until long after they happened. In a very male-dominated society, I was a useful authority to trot out as needed, always when I was not there. When I was there, I just walked around, smiled, and kept my mouth shut.

Slum People

"Slum People" was a common expression fifteen years ago. These people were recognized as different, as if they were a different race. Sue's school became an institution to convert slum children into middle-class children. The definition of a middle class person in India was:

- they do not appear stunted or malnourished, like slum people,
- they speak English, and
- they have on a clean shirt.

At that time, even I could easily pick out slum people among others in the city. Their faces appeared sunken; they were "miniature people." I have pictures I took with my three sons, all 5'10", standing behind some families in the slum. You'd swear my kids are all standing on a box. Remember the old stories where "the fair knights were mighty warriors, standing head and shoulders above lesser men?" You could say the same about middle-class and slum people, probably for the same reasons. So the first of these three conditions was met by the feeding program, the second by English medium education. Our students and their families have figured out how to handle the third condition.

Adam, who is my height at 5'10", stands by a driver from the slums.

Today conditions are better. It's common to hear how the rich are getting richer, but I have personally seen that the poor are getting significantly richer in just the fifteen years since we've been in that slum and in Hyderabad. Finding the miniature people we used to see all over in Hyderabad is difficult unless they are old. I've seen this everywhere I've been. Hans Rosling, who has seen many more places, agrees with me in his book *Factfulness.*

Sue Ma'am Takes on Wife Beating

It was normal at that time for a man to "discipline" his wife with a beating, and it was not unusual for a drunken husband to hit his wife, but there were limits. Once, when a husband had clearly gone over the line, he had to be dealt with. Ramana's men were joined by a number of other slum men who beat the guilty party, who then broke away and ran – directly to the large hole in front of the school and fell in. Everyone else jumped in — it was a big hole — and brought the discipline to a satisfactory conclusion.

Normal or not, when one of Sue's teachers came to school after a beating, Sue took her right back to her hut, confronted the husband, and threatened to fire his wife if he did it again. She maybe didn't think that through. She didn't want to fire the wife, but the bluff worked. Whether he thought beating his wife was the right thing to do, her losing the pay from that job was clearly wrong. This was extended to fathers with a child in the school. That child needed education because he was their social safety net when they got older — no Social Security in India. They all decided it wasn't necessary to beat their wives after all, or at least not enough for Sue Ma'am to find out, and Sue fortunately was not put in the awkward position of having to back up her threats.

Sue fit well into Indian society. It can be pushy at the street level. She just pushes back.

There are many more stories of Sue Ma'am's early adventures in the slums. I have told you only a few of them.

MY BEST INVESTMENT

An investment in knowledge always pays the best interest. – ***Benjamin Franklin***

Well, it did this time.

In starting my companies, I have invested more of my time and effort than my own money. Yet, I still had to live while doing this, so Dad was the one who invested the money needed. Fortunately, the amounts were within his ability since he had sold some property and had a small retirement from it. I had my investment in my home, again more from working our subdivision than any initial money on my part. That would have been my backup if worst came to worst, so I could still pay Dad back.

After my Chief Architect company was started, it comprised most of my assets, the rest being whatever house we lived in.

Beyond that, I did not have much in anything else. I had a little in the stock market with no big losses or gains.

Adam, my oldest son, had decided to marry the niece of people we met in Hyderabad just before that visit to Kolkata in a previous chapter. She was working to support her brother's and sister's further schooling but would soon need to leave that job. I got the pleasant surprise I often got when an expense came up in developing countries. "Is that all we're talking about?" In this case, it was just a few thousand dollars for the complete education of each. So I contributed that as part of the wedding.

In a few years, the brother died in an unfortunate motorbike accident, an all-too-common occurrence in India. The sister got her nursing degree and went on to work in a pediatric hospital. She had graduated at the top level in her education, and within six years, she was in charge of nursing at that hospital. Before that, she had completely paid back my "investment" in her education. I had not expected or asked for that, but she felt she needed to do it anyway.

When her sister, Adam's wife, gave birth to their third son, Sravani had come to Austin, Texas, on one of her rare visits to the US. We were all in the room when the baby was brought in and placed on a changing table. Two nurses were getting it cleaned up. Sravani was standing there and went in for a closer look.

"He looks dull and is not accepting feeds. He has not passed meconium after this long!" she said to the nurses.

They assured her it was no problem. Sravani insisted, and they insisted back. Who was this small Indian girl? She looked like a foreign student at the time, in a plain dress and certainly with no look of authority at all.

Sravani still insisted, and finally, the nurses got the doctor.

He took a look and said, "I think this is OK, but if you feel strongly, you should take him over to Dell Children's Hospital to check him out." Some of us were undecided, but Adam voted with Sravani, and we went to Dell Children's.

My new grandson was found to have Hirschsprung's disease. It was in a form that might not have been caught for a while but could unexpectedly flare up months or years later. If it did this away from fast emergency medical care, it could be life-threatening. Fortunately, none of the other problems that can accompany Hirschsprung's were present; that was good for my grandson, but it made a Hirschsprung's diagnosis that much less likely.

Sravani's experience as head nurse in a large pediatric specialty hospital in an Indian city of ten million was different from those two nurses at a midsized hospital in Austin. What they saw once every few years, Sravani saw every week or two.

Months earlier, the software company where Adam worked had an "insurance fair," where he could change his coverage. Since his wife was already pregnant with their third, he decided, "Why not?" and loaded up to the top tier of coverage. The final bill from Dell's Children's for a full repair job did take our breath away, around a hundred times what I had invested in Sravani, but Adam's insurance coverage took it all.

Now, would you agree that that investment of a few thousand dollars, which was paid back, was the best investment I ever made?

STILL BUILDING HOMES

Our move to Coeur d'Alene, Idaho had gone well, and before we left the Big House, a new CEO joined us in 2001 to manage the change of the eight-year-old Chief Architect company from a startup to a midsized company. Greg soon hired Scott to take over the sales and marketing side of the company. Greg hired more staff and, in two years, moved everyone to a larger building. A year after that, the Big House was sold. Sue and I moved to a three-bedroom, two-bath home in a new subdivision near the company. We later moved to a two-bedroom condominium not much further away on the Spokane River.

I had read many books on the subject, but had never had formal computer science (CS) training. Now we hired engineers with CS degrees, some of whom had experience with larger companies. Our software development had to change from one person with a few other programmers assisting with subprojects to a team effort by a larger number. Marketing, sales, tech support, and other departments professionalized and grew. New software systems and rules were put in place to prevent our developers and me from interfering with each other as we all worked together on an increasingly complex system. I turned to create some of the last features and capabilities I had envisioned for the product. Now I was working on a subproject, and the team had taken over the core. The company was growing up.

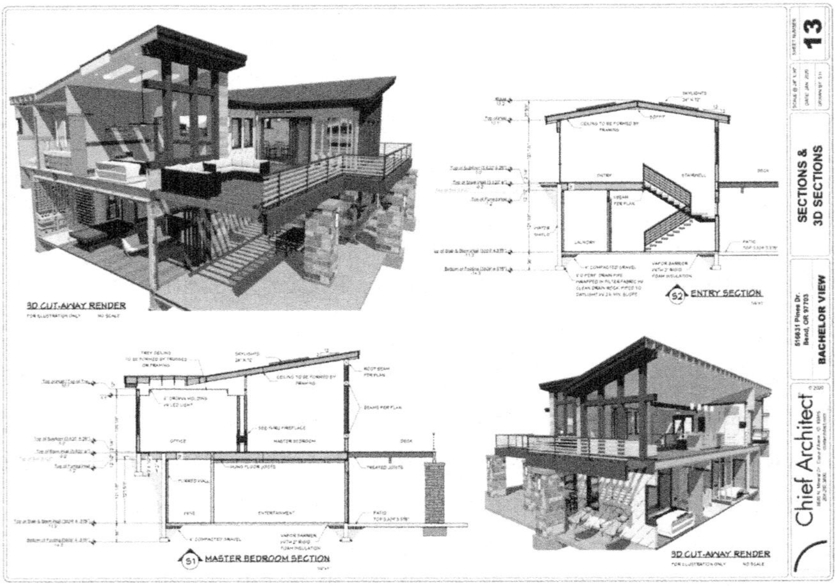

Page from a new home plan set.

Sue and I lived in a normal suburban home from where I went to work for a company with a manager, and me, one of the coworkers. While standard for everyone else, it was odd for me.

Greg was a manager, a coordinator, and a coach. He worked with our people so they could do their job well. I built a product. Greg built a company around that product. Neither one of us was the boss. Our product had already been out in the field for several years and had developed a devoted and sometimes vocal group of building contractor and architect customers. We continued going to the big National Builders' Show every year. Greg rotated our staff so that everyone, whether in programming, sales, tech support, shipping, or support would work the show, sell our software, and, especially, talk with our customers about once every four years. Everyone got to know the boss.

This and the next picture are renderings produced by the software.

I ran into Scott in the hallway once and told him about something in his area I wanted the software to do.

"I have seven things on my list that I hope to do this year," he said, and then told me what they were. "Where on this list should I put what you want?"

With a moment's thought, I answered, "I guess number eight."

"I'll get to it if I can," he said.

It did happen, but not that year.

I had discussions with programmers who disagreed with me about how parts of our software were implemented. Sometimes they were right. Other times I felt my way was good, but theirs would work as well. Others took something I had written and made it run many times faster or handle much larger and more complex designs. Could I be approaching a "your services are no longer required" moment?

I started spending half the year on the other side of the world as Sue had begun doing the previous year. I was in India with Sue some of the time, but the rest of my time was in Bangkok. There, I could get a good Internet connection and work remotely for the company while I learned the Thai language. I worked with friends that my youngest son, Jordan, had met while visiting the Isaan area a few years before. It was a short flight from India, and Sue would come over to spend a few weeks to rest up on occasion.

Around 2011, I stopped working regularly at Chief Architect. I've stayed on as chairman, but Greg, our CEO; Scott, our sales and marketing VP; and others manage things well so that the chairman has little to do. I needed to find something else.

OPPORTUNITY SOCIAL WELFARE FOUNDATION

Morning assembly at the new high school in 2019. Sue is in the red dress and sun hat.

Sue Ma'am's school operates under OSWF, an Indian social welfare foundation, and now extends from nursery school, K1, K2, and first through tenth grade. School ends at tenth in India, with the next two years called "junior college." We provide scholarships for junior college as well as for university. Recent changes in Indian education standards will bring the junior college grades into the high schools, and we are making ready for that.

We remain English medium and Telangana state recently adopted a standard English curriculum, so we use it. Our use of this curriculum is not standard: our kids take the Telangana state tests and come out at the top in our area year after year.

We are on our third main building, this one a permanent reinforced concrete structure. This U-shaped building is easily seen in Google Maps satellite view. Just enter "Maggi High School, India" and pick our most recent site to the north.

Since 2017 our management of OSWF changed to Dr. Naveen, a young pediatrician who is head physician and director at a pediatric specialty hospital and on the board for a network of fifteen additional pediatric hospitals. He has improved our relationships with the government and in the community. Given his other jobs, Naveen works a surprising amount for our school but needs the help of his wife, who does a lot for our school. I could tell you more about her, but having met her in an earlier chapter, you already know Sravani.[1]

There are perks to having two pediatric experts in charge of our school. Naveen and Sravani have a lot of friends. At the end of 2019, Naveen organized a medical camp for our school. Six doctors in various specialties, two dentists, and twenty-six nurses, technicians, and other assistants, all volunteers, processed 550 children, finding many issues that were followed up. Recently India had Cancer Awareness Week. I can now report that none of our fifty teachers and staff had any sign of cancer. A couple of those tests I hadn't heard of.

Early on, we learned the mistakes NGOs made when trying to help others. They can foster dependency instead of empowering people to work for themselves and solve their own problems. We've kept our focus, in India as well as other countries, on child education. Children are dependent anyway, and we educate them towards competence and independence as well or better than any other school around us, so I'm not worried about this issue.

Sue and Dr. Naveen, our OFSW chairman, in front of Maggi High School. We're awaiting permission to finish its second floor.

We're careful not to provide goods and services in place of local entrepreneurs and businesses. A few years after Sue started her clinic in the slums, we noticed other drug sellers and small clinics starting to open up in our area. We closed our clinic when sufficient local competition appeared, but what about our subsidized school competing with (and bettering) other private schools in our area? The less well-off people, like those in our slum, won't be going to those private schools; they use the government schools. While government schools are getting better, most still have a way to go, and there is still no other reasonably competent school in our area, convenient to our people, except ours.

Finally, people resent elites, who feel they know best, making decisions for "their own good" and otherwise pushing them around. Sue was guilty of some of that, especially when it came to stopping the beating of kids and wives, but no one is perfect. Other than that, again, we're working with kids, not adults. At a good school, the teachers and staff are expected to know best and make decisions for the kids' own good.

~

[1] Since Naveen is a pediatrician and head physician at a pediatric specialty hospital, and Sravani has been head nurse at a pediatric specialty hospital, it should be obvious how they met, but it wasn't that way. They worked in different hospitals in different parts of a city of ten million. Naveen was sure he had the phone number of the friend he was trying to reach but still ended up getting Sravani. They finally got together, never did sort out how Naveen got her number, but stayed together anyway.

OPPORTUNITY FOUNDATION THAILAND

It is useful to know something of the manners of different nations, that we may be enabled to form a more correct judgment regarding our own, and be prevented from thinking that everything contrary to our customs is ridiculous and irrational, a conclusion usually come to by those whose experience has been limited to their own country. — ***René Descartes***

My youngest son Jordan, along with several other junior-high-age kids, visited Thailand to work with a local mission effort for two weeks. While there, he hit it off and became good friends with Anita, an American expat, and Rot, a village mayor, who were working together on an agricultural project to help local farmers. Jordan liked it so much that he went back the next year to spend more time in that village.

Our staff and kids and showing two of our four child homes in 2013.

In 2006, I learned that Anita was thinking about ways to help girls who had been abused or abandoned in the area around Rot's village. There were various charities in larger cities and more famous Thai towns to help kids like this, but none were in the poorer northeastern Isaan area of Thailand, even though that seemed to me to be the area that needed them the most. Many of these kids really had no place to go. Of course, they would end up somewhere, but those places were far from ideal.

In April 2007, we formed a foundation to make a place for these kids in Nang Rong city, a six-hour bus ride northeast of Bangkok and the nearest city to Rot's village.

Where would we put this foundation? I was thinking of the acre where Warren and I had built five homes in Redwood City. If we could get an acre of land in or near the city, we could build several homes for these children. One big building containing many children seemed too institutional.

News traveled fast in a Thai town, and soon a lady appeared in Anita's front yard. She was one of ten farmers who wanted to sell us their land. Earlier, some politically connected developers had convinced these farmers to sell their adjacent properties, which together formed a rough square of twenty-eight acres. They planned to put almost five hundred small homes there. Meanwhile, their enemies on the other side of the political fence convinced the city to designate this property as the site for a future sewage plant. They were never going to build a plant there, but the designation prohibited any structures from ever being built. If that was not enough, there was a coup and Thailand came under a military government.

Life does get complicated. Suddenly the developers were on the wrong side of the political fence, were going to be charged with corruption, and quickly abandoned their project. Meanwhile, our ten farmers had already spent some of their coming money on things like buying a nice home or a pickup truck for their son. They offered us a killer price for twenty-eight acres in the city, less than a mile from the center of town. It was a great property, except we could not build anything on it.

Anita had previously made friends with the state governor's wife and paid her a visit. For various reasons, they did not want to remove that restriction, but since we were a charitable foundation, it need not apply to us.

The property was still landlocked with the nearest road 350 feet away, so the farmers prevailed upon another man on the road to sell us a forty-five-foot wide strip off the side of his land that reached the canal separating our proposed property from his. All we had to do was build a bridge, which we eventually did. I never found out what kind of trouble the farmers were in if they did not get the money from that sale, but they certainly proved motivated.

Left to right, two employees, our two co-directors, a board member, me, our chairman Gayle, and more board members and employees.

So instead of an acre, we ended up with twenty-eight of them plus a long access corridor.

The foundation started well with Anita as the managing director, but after two years, she had to step down due to health reasons. Anita had come to Thailand as a young woman and spoke Thai fluently. I did not, and since no one else on our staff, or even in town, spoke English, I could not take over day-to-day management. This was unlike Sue's school in India, where there were always many other English speakers around. The foundation limped along with temporary management. It took several years, but good management was found, and it finally got back on track.

We raise children who have been abused, abandoned, or whose parents have long prison terms. We also support other children in place, usually cared for by grandparents, providing food and support for school attendance. We have a professional staff of educators, psychologists, social workers, and house mothers with four large children's homes and a meeting center on twenty-eight acres.

High school age kids at one of our summer camps we run with the Thai special forces.

Whatever you've heard about horrible circumstances that children can be in or unbelievable abuse some have suffered, we have representatives in our homes. Nearly all of these have recovered as much as could be expected and often a great deal more. We remain in contact, as any parent would, once they leave us and assist with higher education in many cases. They live good lives and do well in school. Our director's and social workers' first job is direct care for our children, but they are also involved with court cases involving those who abused some of our kids before they came to us.

We have various community outreach programs to what has traditionally been one of the poorer areas of Thailand. Among these are camps for area high school students in conjunction with the Thai military, where we emphasize the importance of staying in school and continuing their education afterward. With a hundred high school kids there at one time, you'd think we might have a few discipline problems, but remarkably, there are none. Could that be because our camp instructors are all from the Thai special forces, some of them drill sergeants?

By now you're probably wondering who pays for all this NGO work. There are some missing, but these are most of our 82 Chief employees.

MYANMAR

You can always count on Americans to do the right thing—after they've tried everything else. — ***Winston S. Churchill***

We've seen this year after year in Myanmar. I don't think our government policy toward Myanmar has gotten to the "right thing" yet.

In December 2007, Sue and I took a river cruise vacation tour of Myanmar, which we unknowingly scheduled two months after the final crackdown for the Saffron Revolution, a popular rebellion that had continued through all of October. We just arrived back home when a mutual friend introduced us to John, a retired Cornell University librarian. He had organized another tour of Myanmar for retired university professors and ambassadors leaving in less than a month. They invited us to join the five of them on what remains the most interesting tour we have ever taken.

Gayle, standing on the right, at a teacher workshop. Linlin, our interpreter and in country trainer standing on the left.

One of our travel companions was the former British ambassador to Vietnam, Cambodia, and then Thailand. I was a little jealous because he spoke Thai, among his other eight languages, so much better than I. He had since advised governments and businesses regarding Myanmar. The professors specialized in philosophy and similar subjects and were different from people we had known up to that time. We saw more things and places strange and new to us in two weeks than we'd have thought possible.

Three months after we returned from that second tour, Cyclone Nargis made landfall in southern Myanmar and killed 150,000 people. If the Saffron Revolution did not alert the rest of the world to Myanmar, the cyclone certainly did. Western countries, including the United States, had strict counterproductive trade sanctions on Myanmar due to dissatisfaction with its military government, but at that time decided to bring relief aid to the country. They did it in such a way that it was amazing that any of it was ever allowed into the country, but finally, some did get through.

Chin State is 95% Christian and 80% Baptist. I'm in the home of the superintendent of Sunday schools for the Baptist denomination in the state. Access is normally restricted to foreigners in this area, but with the Baptists behind us, we can go where we are needed.

John had lived many years in Myanmar and knew people all over the country. He got together with the CEO of the world's largest online used bookseller, Thrift Books, and formed a plan to rebuild libraries destroyed by the cyclone. They also planned to import one million English-language books from Thrift Books warehouses for those and other Myanmar libraries. Myanmar was formerly known as Burma, a British colony before World War II, and many there spoke or were learning English but had few if any English books to read. John and friends also planned to produce and distribute local language books for schools. John got together a few others, including me, to form the board for the Nargis Library Recovery nonprofit.

The State Department granted an exception from the trade sanctions and John made a deal with American President shipping lines to move containers with our books for free. Thrift Books employees donated time to select books and load shipping containers at their various warehouses around the United States. They were able to give a lot of good children's books for the schools we supplied.

All homes in Chin State are perched on hillsides, even in the capital city, Hakka, which recently had a major mudslide a block from downtown.

Once in Myanmar, two-thirds of our books were delivered to Buddhist monasteries in the larger towns and cities, and from there distributed to monasteries in the smaller towns. The monasteries housed the libraries and were the community centers in Myanmar. World Vision, one of the few NGOs still operating in Myanmar at that time, distributed the other third to libraries in its "jungle schools" in the south of Myanmar. We were delivering books from the United States to shelves of Myanmar libraries for under ten cents a copy.

By 2015, the one million books, about twenty-five large container loads, had been delivered and distributed to 900 schools and libraries.

As Sue and I traveled in Myanmar over several years, visiting libraries working with Nargis Library, Sue thought about the different teachers who had received our books for their classrooms. We had visited their classrooms out in the World Vision jungle schools, monastery schools run by monks and nuns, and a few other private and public schools. Could the teachers use these books more effectively? Our Australian friend and education expert, Gayle, came with us on a trip to look into this further with Sue. The result was a several-day teacher training course given in several schools, reworked by Gayle, and then given in more Myanmar schools. This resulted in our current teacher training program, which has trained thousands of teachers and concentrates today in Chin and Kachin states in northern Myanmar, mountainous states where it is most needed.

We had worked in Myanmar from well before the 2015 elections, when it made some movement toward a more open society. We hope to continue there after the recent 2021 transition back to a military government.

THE GOOD SHIP STAR GAZER

Star Gazer behind with me, Sue, Cheryl, Marty (Paul's brother), my sister Sharon, and Paul at the Baltimore Inner Harbor docks, 71 years after Dad's ship landed here from Algeria.

We waited in our northbound boat as the Surf City swing bridge started to open. Just then, a southbound boat jumped on the radio and asked to go through first. If it was that important to him, why not? I said OK without thinking. As the bridge fully opened, we saw that he was a lot further from the bridge than us, and the following current was pushing us slowly toward the bridge.

As he was coming through, I was turning the boat to move back to the passage. We were waiting off to the side to let him pass. I had used reverse to stay back but the current was swifter than I thought, and I had gotten closer to the bridge support than I realized. The current was pushing us sideways into it. "You're going to hit the bridge!" Sue screamed. I gunned it and slammed back into the passage, our rear side narrowly missing the support. The current caught us, pulling us through the passage almost sideways before our forward motion could run us into the opposite support. We dodged a bullet, I mean bridge, there.

Sue and I had been piloting our boat for less than two months after our training captain had left us. Sharon and Paul had come to travel with us, and we all learned a basic lesson. Whoever has the following current at a drawbridge has the right of way and should always go first. We learned a lot more as we traveled north on the Atlantic Intracoastal waterway that first summer in 2014.

In late 2013, I learned about the Great Loop. It was a trip of six thousand miles or more taken by boat that visited ports all along the East Coast and throughout the eastern third of the United States. Sue and I had seen much of Europe and Asia, but outside of New York City and Washington, DC, we had not seen the United States east of Texas.

We had a traditional viewpoint and liked to see museums

and the old part of cities. The cities we'd visit would be on waterways whose purposes were originally commercial, although some of them were now used for recreational boating. Traveling by boat, we would naturally be docking in the older parts of the waterway cities and towns.

I emailed Sue, who was in India at the time with Keith and Gayle, to tell her my plan to buy a boat we could live on for the long trip. Sue thought I was nuts and showed the email to Keith and Gayle, who told her, "You're nuts! Buy the boat and see your country, it will be a wonderful experience. We'll come over as often we can and go with you," and so it happened.

We bought Star Gazer, a used three-bedroom, two-and-a-half-bath boat, and spent six months refitting it. It was fifty-two feet long and twenty-five tons. We had owned personal watercraft and a nineteen-foot runabout when we lived in north Idaho but piloting this boat as much as eighty miles offshore was a different experience. The twenty-five tons meant that once that boat got moving, it wanted to keep moving, which we learned to deal with, especially when docking. We did learn, and thanks to modern weather reports, electronics, and GPS systems, it was easier than it was in older times.

That first 2014 summer was our learning trip. We did the full Great Loop in 2015. I suppose the cliché "Trip of a Lifetime" best describes it, as does the blog "jackandsuesimpson.com" we kept.

We lived on our boat, always in motion around the Eastern United States, full-time for three years, and most of the time for another year and a half. We got better at piloting and saw a lot of America. It was great to take out that time for something completely different. Keith and Gayle, Paul and my sister Sharon, and others came and traveled with us from two to six weeks at a time.

AFTERWORD

But how could you live and have no story to tell? — ***Fyodor Dostoyevsky****, White Nights*

Sue and I agree we've had a great life. Our tragedies have been mostly normal or expected. Parents die earlier than anyone likes — my dad at age seventy-six and Sue's dad at eighty were the worst for us. I was an oldest child while Sue was a youngest, so she lost her dad a few years before I lost mine. Our moms died at ninety and ninety-three. One exception was when Sue's older brother came to live his last few months with us in the Big House before his death from colon cancer in his 50s. The good part of that was we "inherited" his son and son's fiancée for a time. They married at the Big House and then went on to both earn degrees at the University of Washington.

My cousin Dianna died just after I finished the first draft of this book. For a brief time, she was in poor health and then got the coronavirus. Being three years older than me, she was always off elsewhere when I visited her brother Jim, so I did not see her much when growing up. When I did see her, it was in the presence of Jim, our parents, and often others. Later, we usually lived far apart, so I was never able to get to know her very well.

The Good Stuff

None of our sons, our nieces and nephews, or even their kids, have had deaths or medical issues serious enough to spill out into our awareness except for our one son who was accident-prone in his earlier years. He did come out of that phase after some serious but recoverable close calls. My sister, her husband, and my cousin Jim, the son of Dad's twin, are all still living and doing reasonably well, although their mother, my Aunt Marge, died too early at age seventy. At seventy-four, Sue and I are in good health, with those few issues we have under appropriate maintenance so they will not affect quality or expectancy of life.

Our life saw many instances of unlooked-for good fortune:

- I had parents who loved me and always stood behind me. My sister and I were always number one in their lives. I can't answer whether they or I are more responsible for the good things that have happened in my life.
- My parents' desires for me were in no way specific: just do right as you are able, be careful with girls (no worries there, girls were more than careful with me), study hard in school to learn all I could, and that was

pretty much it. They did not limit me in any way. They had no particular career or other life goals for me. Those were for me to discover. Dad never said I should strive to be successful, he just said I would be. I think there's a difference.

- A best friend got me interested in architecture and then a dad let me design our new house as I was finishing high school.
- My education presented unplanned opportunities to learn and build software.
- My eye disability helped me avoid the draft.
- My autism helped me concentrate better on complex systems.
- I ran into Sue at a church party and was finally mature enough (barely) to keep her.
- Warren asked us to be partners on a great deal.
- The California real estate runup started just after we had acquired significant property.
- I learned house planning and construction with Warren and Al.
- Dad mentally set me up to start businesses and then financially assisted me.
- We blundered into our Atherton acre and the Big House, getting each for a very low price.
- I built a product ten times as efficiently using the new C++, used Windows 3 that everyone suddenly had to have, and had a friend who convinced me we could build a company from it.
- Another thing, that the new product could be sold to consumers as well as construction professionals, was something I recognized and maybe the only thing for which I can take full credit. I got that contract with

Broderbund and developed a consumer offshoot from the main Chief Architect software. Minimal effort gave us a huge gain there, especially near the start of our company.

- Finally, in every way my company's people and I can look at it, having moved our company to Idaho gave us a huge advantage over having it in California. Dad caused that move, giving me a final blessing, although not at all worth its price.

That's quite a list. My education turned out to be important. Learning software implementation and home design/construction were not at all planned; it just happened that way. The one basic thing I finally learned about myself is that scientific research, being a college professor, or any number of other activities would not work for me. I love to build things, whether physically like a house, or in a computer, or in my head as a design or model. These last months have been great because I've been building this book. Working on its structure and order has been most enjoyable. It is good to be building again.

I have read that luck is a huge factor in successful businesses. Certainly, hard work and education count, too, as well as being in a frontier environment where "things are happening." Many things could have gone differently, with a very different outcome, and I would not have known the difference.

There is one other thing I can't include in the "unlooked-for" category, since Sue had planned to be a missionary to India since high school. India, however, had outlawed foreign missionaries from the time she was born. Besides that, there was plenty of nationalistic opposition to foreigners coming in and imposing their beliefs in India. There were also laws passed to specifically prevent foreign missionary and NGO activity and that prevented foreign money from coming into the country. Sue went to India, "imposed" her beliefs about education, child development, and wife-beating, contended with local politicians as well as local terrorists, brought in financial support anyway, and was successful in starting a school that remains to this day.

Sue and I have had fifty years together. Our golden anniversary was July 2020, a month before I started this book. We could not celebrate at that time, unlike when we got together for Mom and Dad's fiftieth in 1992, only three months before we moved up to be with them. I was not what Sue was looking for, yet she chose me. I was not looking for anyone at the time, and as I've been saying, hardly had a choice in the matter! There was no other way for me.

It's hard for either of us to imagine being apart. We could not be more different and do different things, each supplying what the other needs but cannot do. When it comes to long-term goals in life, we both want the same thing and enjoy where that has taken us.

Peer Groups

According to my recent reading, the effect of peer groups on young people's development is often more important than their own family. I had no peer groups. I had friends one at a time. They knew me but not each other. For example, my best friends Rod and Terry in high school. They did not know each other. I never saw the two of them together.

There were my younger fellow employees at Albertsons supermarket when I was in high school, but I was never with them outside of work. I can't call them a peer group. We were different, and neither had any thought of being like the other.

I did enjoy being with the Nads of the second floor of Hill dormitory at Seattle Pacific College. Were they a peer group? Had they done a better job of setting up my first date maybe they could have got me into trouble – but, hey, they did try! Other than that, they were good guys, if trying hard to live on the edge. They were either sufficiently careful, or sufficiently inept, that they never caused anyone any real trouble. Me taking on some of the character traits I noticed in them would probably have been an improvement.

One more possible peer group would be the singles' group I became part of when I went to Sue's church. I can say nothing but good about that, except for its short life after I arrived. In sum, peer groups had little effect on my life, which I think is unusual for most people.

The Bad Stuff

There are no severe marital problems to report. Our most difficult time was a few years after our 1981 to 2000 stressful business starting period. Was there stress in the change of finally having more time for each other once the business was relatively secure and its call on my time not so severe? In other words, the stress of suddenly having no stress? I don't know.

We've come close to financial ruin. The closest was a lawsuit against our company about two years after we started selling the product. The plaintiff was a predator, and we were by no means their first time suing a company. It was their specialty, and they were good at it. They had tricked us into a bad contract that set us up for the lawsuit. Their past behavior, which we became aware of, was legal if unethical and could not be disclosed to the jury as it would be "prejudicial." This meant that even though they had cheated other businesses in this same way, these businesses were not related to ours and so could not be mentioned in our case. Certainly, if any juror would have known or suspected that the predator made its living by doing what it did to us, they would have voted the other way, and we would not have lost the case.

We lost a huge amount, which had to be paid in two weeks. For about a week, Sue and I thought all we had done in our business would be lost. We were finally able to get a loan from a local bank by putting up all company assets and all our personal assets, including the Big House. Our business did well, especially with the boost from our Broderbund consumer sales, and the loan was paid off in a little over a year.

The jury trial system in the United States for highly technical civil cases is badly flawed and easily hijacked by hired "experts." As an example, look at how many years the tobacco company experts "proved" in court that smoking was not harmful. Only when the anti-smoking attorneys could make enough money in lawsuits against smoking could the "proof" go the other way in the courts.

We've had maybe five other legal cases. None have been existential threats. In one, we gained a lot of money, but that was money we should have gotten without having to go through that case. Another was a specialty predator that asked for millions. We got them down to low five figures and paid them off. They probably spent more than they got from us and should go after easier prey in the future. Two others were really only threats. A few lawyer visits, a little time spent, and they went away.

Overall, however, while the US business environment is not perfect and certainly is stacked toward really big businesses and the legal industry, it still is the best in the world for someone with an idea to turn it into a profitable business. Anywhere else is worse.

Most importantly, all of our bad stuff was financial, with more than enough good financial stuff to compensate.

Other Stuff

Sue and I both have always wanted to do the right thing. Dad always did when it came to business, money, or anything that was important to him and others. We've been greatly helped by having so few temptations to do the wrong thing. It may be that the nature of our businesses and lives have made dishonesty or cheating so difficult that we just don't go there. For our company, 99.9 percent of its income is from credit cards. All our payroll, taxes, and everything else is computerized with so much documentation that it is quickly accessible by us or by the IRS. How could we cheat on taxes and ever hope to get away with it? We're profitable enough that we stand to lose much more than we could gain.

Another good thing is that we can't think of a thing that political influence would give us. We've had no temptations in that direction, so we've saved money on various lobbyists and campaign contributions, especially at the national level, where things get expensive.

Our employees are the most important part of our business. If we treated any of them shabbily, it would come back to bite us soon and hard. So what's good for our company and its profitability is also what's good for our employees. As a result, our employee retention for software engineers — famously the most mobile employees there are — and everyone else is over six times industry average, and double the other best example we've heard of. Once again, where does our good behavior come from — virtue or simply lack of opportunity to do anything bad? Our employees are just too good to lose. Maybe that's another indicator that many of the systems in the US capitalistic society are working well.

A Final Word on Decisions

If you're drowning, do you "decide" to grab onto a nearby floating log or just grab it? I think of a decision as taking your time to think about the advantages and drawbacks of each side and then deciding on the one with the best balance of these. There may have been times when, if I was someone else, I could have done such a thing, but my upbringing and experiences conspired to make one side obvious and the other unacceptable, having no apparent advantage. There was no choice.

"No decisions" came to me after I wrote most of this book. I was living that way but did not realize it. Would it be more accurate to say that life always presented me with extremely easy decisions? I realize that others can have tough decisions to make. What if I did? The closest I came was in chapter 34, when "Sue and I went west over the hills to walk the Half Moon Bay beach." We did try to decide. Maybe we could have in another day or two. Instead, the phone call from Professor Gio Wiederhold made that decision for us.

"No decisions" is easy if everything is handed to you, even houses. The Little Yellow House was from Warren. Malory was from caving into Warren's very reasonable decision. MacBain was a deal I could not refuse. The Big House was, "Well, if I could get it for this, I could not refuse it," and "this" is what I offered. After that, Sue selected our next six houses as well as our live-on boat, often when I was not around. Where and how we live is more important to her.

If choosing was happening, who was choosing? It did not seem to be me. Was it Dad? Was I just doing what I thought he would do? Maybe it was Mom in a few cases. More recently, it is definitely Sue. I think I would just stay home and read if I was alone. She gets me out, whether a meeting with friends, a Sunday drive to look at homes, or a two-month trip to Europe. At first, the idea is not welcome; I don't like change, but once out, I'm glad it happened. We've had many great times that way. The only big exception to all this was our four years living on a boat, which was well after retirement and my choice originally.

Remember that first river cruise in Myanmar, just a few chapters back, "which we unknowingly scheduled two months after the final crackdown for the Saffron Revolution?" "We" there did not include me. Sue set up that entire trip, schedule, and all, before she presented it to me, so there was only a yes or no answer. I had never given Myanmar a thought or a comment before, but she really wanted to go. How could I refuse her?

Does this help you understand how I get into these messes? That first trip led us to get involved with importing books into Myanmar due to our mutual friends talking to each other. Sue then noticed issues in the schools getting the books and got our friend Gayle involved. Then we hired an in-country employee. Now I'm busy almost every week, handling issues that come up with our teacher training program there. Try getting expenditure documentation acceptable to the IRS out of some village in northern Myanmar and you'll understand my situation.

It's like people won't let me live my own life. But then what would my own life be like, without these other people? Would there be anything there? Am I a passive person, letting others, whether or not they are still alive, decide for me? Maybe that is not such a bad way to live, depending on who those others are.

APPENDIX A: WEBSITE LINKS

Learn about the last, successful, home design company I started at its website:

https://www.chiefarchitect.com/

Plans, pictures, and videos of homes and interiors from this software at:

https://www.chiefarchitect.com/products/samples.html

Log, with pictures, of the Good Ship Star Gazer from June 17, 2014, to October 26, 2018 is at:

https://jackandsuesimpson.com/

Early years of founding Opportunity Foundation Thailand:

http://www.opportunityfoundation.org/ofblog/?cat=1

Nang Rong and the Isaan area of Thailand during those years:

http://www.opportunityfoundation.org/ofblog/?cat=6

Nargis Library trips to Myanmar from our fourth trip in November 2009 to January 2012 at:

http://www.opportunityfoundation.org/ofblog/?cat=30

APPENDIX B: HOME DESIGN

Object Orientation: A New Way to Design a Home

A book about a new way of programming called "object-oriented programming" really clicked with me, especially for building a program that represented items in the real world.

With the old way, I thought about the procedures, and secondarily about the data they manipulate. With the new way, I would think about the data and its organization, and secondarily about the procedures to process it. It was simply a change in viewpoint for what can be the same problem. Looking at things differently made a big difference.

The just-out Borland C++ language compiler implemented most of these new object-oriented ideas. With this, I used the newly released Windows 3.0 and this C++ programming language to build a simple Computer-Aided Design (CAD) program. It produced straight and curved lines, circles, rectangles, and some other items. Each circle, rectangle, triangle, line, or anything else was an object according to these new ideas. I learned enough from that project to try building something useful.[1]

My second practice program drew house floor plans. An object — say a window, door, or wall in a house — would be an object in my program. The wall in the plan I'm drawing would be a wall object in the software. Windows and doors in my design's wall would be window and door objects in the software. Window and door objects would be owned by their wall object; that means once you find the wall object, you can find its window and door objects from it. In turn, a door object could reference, or own, its doorknob, bolt lock, and hinge objects.

A problem: I have two parallel lines representing a wall. Normally a window is drawn as two short lines each from one of those wall lines to the other. A line between the two short lines represents the window glass. How are those three lines a window object?

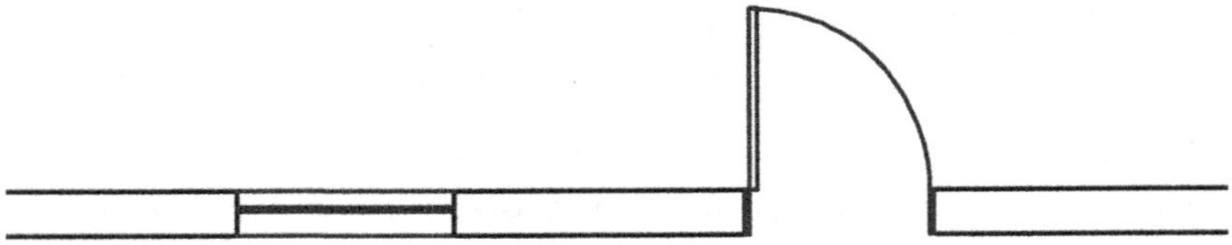

A wall with a window and a door in plan view.

The solution: you don't draw those lines to make a window. Click the mouse on an onscreen "button" to say, "I want to make a window now" and then click between the wall lines to position the window. Those two short and one longer lines appear in the wall. You can see that is your window. It is important that the program also knows that is your window. You can click on that window to resize it or move it along the wall. The program just erases its old lines and redraws them as you direct.

I can have a "library" of toilets, sinks, cabinet modules (you buy these in standard sizes and fit them together), and even furniture to finish things off. Each of these can be requested by clicking on its library entry, and then clicking in the plan where you want it to appear.

Since I'm not just drawing lines, but (somehow, with objects) making walls, doors, windows, and other things for a house, can't I think in terms of actually building that house from what you draw (for walls) or click into existence (for doors, windows, cabinets, toilets, etc.)? That's what I decided to do: build a house, really a model of a house, in the computer. How can I build a house from what you draw?

A problem: you are only drawing a floor plan, drawing walls, putting windows and doors into the walls, and putting cabinets, fixtures, and other items into the rooms of the house. We're trying to build a model of the whole house here. No information about the height of the walls or windows, the structure and framing of a foundation, floor or walls, or the steepness of the roof is anywhere in sight.

The solution: American home construction is amazingly standardized. We assume an interior ceiling of eight feet. If you want nine or ten feet, reset your preferred "standard" height before starting to draw or change it afterward. Framing is standard. If I give a builder a floor plan and a ceiling height, he'll know immediately how and where the wood framing pieces go for the floor and walls. He'll know how to frame around the windows and doors; it's always done the same way. The same for ceilings, roofs, etc. The rules of framing are straightforward, so they are straightforwardly programmed into the software.

Bottom line: you do "draw" each wall, starting at one end

and pulling its two parallel lines across the screen to its other end. Hit another wall and the two connect. You don't draw much else. You name it or select it from a library, and then click it into existence.

Anything about the house you did not specify as you drew the plan, the program would make a standard assumption, subject to any preference you originally entered into the software. That assumption could be modified at any time later. Of course, this modification might require a complete reframing and "rebuilding" of the house, but so what? The computer does all that in an eyeblink. In the real world, the hard work is actually building the house. In the computer, telling it how to build is the real work. The building takes no time at all.

All these objects are completely modeled by the program. Since a builder goes out and buys things like toilets, sinks, and furnaces and the interior designer goes out to buy furniture and accessories, data objects for each of these items are already produced and included in a library in the program. You shop for these items in the library and click them into your plan. When you later produce an elevation or 3D view, the model of that library item will appear.

This solved the problem I had designing that house for Dad before I left for college: never have the same thing in two places, remember? Don't draw a wall in one place and attach a dimension[2] to it that could say it's somewhere else. Don't position a window in a wall in the floor plan, and then put it somewhere else along the wall in the elevation view.

The floor plan, the elevations exterior and interior, the 3D views, and even the list of materials were all different views of one model of the house. In my software, only one house was "built." It would be a complete model the software could then "project" into a floor plan, elevation, 3D view, or list of materials. All views would come from the same single thing. Total consistency! Even if you try, you can't make it inconsistent.

~

The Fate of My First CAD Program

[1] I tacked that first CAD program onto the first few versions of our product. It allowed lines and other descriptive items to be in the plan view working drawings in addition to the "house" we built in the computer. We later replaced it with a better integrated CAD facility.

The other programmers, and also the tech support people who had to use it and explain it to customers, considered my original CAD not up to company standards, calling it "WackyCAD." So, when we announced we'd finally gotten rid of WackyCAD in a version release meeting, it was to riotous approval. The replacement helped drive our company's improving profitability, so I was fine trading a bit of self-esteem for that.

Dimensions

[2] I had a solution for that dimension that I drew wrong in the plan for my parents' house: I would not let you put the number in a dimension. The software knew where the walls were in the house model. It produced dimensions for you. Move a wall, window, or door, and a dimension locating it changed automatically. I later allowed the user to change the dimension number. When that number was changed, then the wall, window, door — or whatever the dimension line located — would automatically move to match the number. Consistency was always maintained.

I had looked at many plans and knew that dimensioning for any house plan was mostly the same: walls, windows, and doors located by two layers of dimension lines drawn around the outside of the house. The outer layer just located walls, the inner layer walls, windows, and doors. Since it was usually done this way, I had the software do it automatically. My plan was not just lines; it was walls, windows, doors, and other objects, and the software knew where all of those were, so anything could be dimensioned, and the dimensions could track it if you moved it or disappear if you decided to delete that object.

Other things were automated like this. Click and it drew all the dimensions, another click drew all the electrical outlets in all the rooms spaced as per standard codes. Another click would show a front, or a side, elevation that you never drew. Click to look through the ceiling to the interior. Did you place furniture and fixture symbols into your floor plan, each with just a click? If so, you would see them in 3D in your interior view.

Three-Dimensional House Pictures

Transforming three-dimensional coordinates of a model to two-dimensional coordinates on the surface of a display screen in order to produce a 3D view is easy. I found it in a book. Now you can look up "Camera Matrix" on Wikipedia. I learned matrices in twelfth grade.

Actually, screen coordinates are 3D; there is a dimension into or out of the screen, useful for determining which part of the model should display in front of or behind another part. This helps solve the "hidden surface" problem. Of course, today you don't worry about this. There are plenty of "3D Engines" and rendering systems you just buy and hook up. There are even graphics cards coming out now that do blazingly fast photorealistic rendering. Back then, it was a do-it-myself project for something closer to a watercolor picture than a photograph.

APPENDIX C: EXAMPLE THAI FOUNDATION CASES

We have received some truly horrible abuse cases. One of them reached the national news level, but I can't see the point of talking about any of them. These are some of our other cases. I changed names and a few identifying details for the usual reasons.

Chin's Case, years ago, just after our foundation started.

A call comes in from a woman located further north in our state. She describes a young girl of seven living with her maternal grandmother who is the caller's mother as well. The girl's mother and father are dead, both from AIDS. An older sibling was HIV positive and also died. This can place quite a stigma on a child, especially in a village, where everyone there knows about it.

The call passes to our social worker, Gatin. The aunt fears that her mother, who is pretty old now and sleeps much of the time, may not have the ability to protect the child from sexual or other abuse from certain villagers, especially a young uncle living in the same house. This abuse is more likely, almost a certainty, because this child is thought to be of little worth.

Most likely the girl has been HIV positive from birth. Gatin and another staff member travel to the village, which is several hundred kilometers to the east. They talk with the grandmother and meet Chin, who appears quite healthy, excited to see visitors, and talks a lot.

The uncle takes Chin to school and provides some other care since the grandmother has limited mobility. He drinks a lot and often entertains his friends where they will each take turns having Chin sit on their laps, hug her, etc. The grandmother is worried about this but is unable to protect Chin. She agrees to come with us back to Opportunity Village.

Once there, the grandmother spends much of the time sleeping on a couch while Chin, enthroned in the chair of an absent staffer, proceeds to take over the office, questioning everyone who passes her. They guess there has been no abuse yet. Abused children tend to be pretty quiet. Various appointments are made with the hospital and government social services offices. Another staff member verifies that the child's father, who left the family years ago and lived in another area of Thailand, has in fact passed away.

The most important thing we learn is that Chin is HIV negative! This is good news for all. Had she been positive, we can still take her. We have no strict policy against it. Certainly, if a child already living with us is discovered to be HIV-positive, she stays with us. If we know that from the beginning, however, it is often better to place her with a sister organization, Home of Hope, up in the north in Chiang Rai, which is better equipped to serve her.

Since the government has not intervened in Chin's case, we must get the approval of all close relatives before we can take her. Another aunt objects, saying she will send money to her mother to help with the child and will take her herself if necessary. We find she is on her third husband, is known to have a drinking problem, and apparently has no money for any kind of support. Still, as a private foundation, it is not our place to forcibly take a child from any situation, unless we see, and convince government authorities, that abuse has occurred. We leave it to the aunt who called to sort things out.

It turns out that Chin is remaining with her grandmother. We alert the social services authorities in that province regarding the situation. Will they have time to follow up? Gatin marks her records. She will follow up as well.

From social services, we found that Chin was eligible to receive some government support. Of course we must share this information with the family. Did this influence the aunt's objection? These amounts are never close to enough for us to make a "profit" by taking a child, but for villagers who, avoiding government supervision, can divert the money, it may be attractive.

Natcha Came Back to Us.

Natcha had been in more than five foster homes in all, often leaving because she could not behave well. We could not tell whether past behavior problems originated from the abuse that she received that got her into the foster home program in the first place, something that happened in some of the earlier foster homes, or from another source. When she came to us in 2010 at age thirteen, we did know she was sexually abused in each of her last four foster homes. She was easily our worst case, often out of control. We had some tough decisions. We wanted to help her but could not ignore her influence on the other girls. We came close to putting her back into the government system a few times. Then she turned finally, completely around. She completed high school and then two years of vocational school as well. From being our greatest problem, she became our greatest success.

Natcha left us to start her new life. She found work, but sadly she was sexually abused again by her best friend's father. We took her back in and were recently in process with a court investigation. When with us, Natcha got a job at a water factory nearby our foundation for decent pay. She also helped with our twenty-plus girls who lived on site.

I have personally been around Natcha over the years, the last time being at the foundation two years ago. She was assisting with the high school age "boot camps" we run with the Thai special forces from the Korat base. She has a very outgoing personality and is a kick to be around. She is a very hard person to miss. If she's around, you'll notice her.

It may be her recent troubles stem from not yet being all the way back to normal, whatever that is. Can she ever get there after what she has been through? We don't have records of all of that and she doesn't remember. She remains positive and is doing well. I'm wondering if she borders on the extreme for resiliency. I think she is going to be in good shape in the long run.

Chakan Is Simply a Great Kid

When Chakan was eight, his mother took him out of school to carry sand and concrete mix in a construction job where he earned about seventy-five cents per day. They lived in a small shack and ate rice with chili paste and some vegetables they could grow around their shack.

As with most Thai boys, he lived as a monk at the temple for a while and there received enough of the offerings to buy a bike he could ride to school. His mother soon sold the bike for a small amount.

Despite all this, Chakan was unusually well adjusted and outgoing and was noticed and befriended by neighbors in the village. When these neighbors learned his mother was trying to sell him to a stranger for a few hundred dollars, they called the police, the mother was taken into a program elsewhere, and Chakan was brought to us.

Chakan has been with us for two years now. His first few meals with us, he ate so much and so fast he would throw up. With a little effort, we convinced him that food would always be available every day. He has missed a lot of school, but his grades have reached 3.2 with no sign of stopping there. He was a hard worker before he came to us and this now shows in his schoolwork and in his school soccer team, where he has become captain.

The principal and teachers think he is the greatest and everyone can see how he applies himself and takes full advantage of whatever good things come his way. He is an example for our other children. When asked recently where he would like to be, he said he wanted to be where he is. Life is a responsibility. He is certainly holding up his end of that well. It's a joy for us to hold up ours.

ACKNOWLEDGMENTS

Acknowledgements

"To nine out of ten of you the choice which could lead to scoundrelism (Meaning: baseness, dishonesty, double-dealing) will come, when it does come, in no very dramatic colors... Obviously bad men, obviously threatening or bribing, will almost certainly not appear. Over a drink or a cup of coffee, disguised as a triviality and sandwiched between two jokes, ... the hint will come." — **C. S. Lewis**, *The Inner Ring.*

I must be the one out of ten.

It should be obvious by now that the term "self-made man" can in no way apply to me. I'd naturally keep to myself ninety percent of the time if I was allowed, but there are too many things in the world to mention that have prevented that. I'll try to focus on the people.

Dad, Mom, and Sue have been the three big ones. Beyond them are my grandparents on Mom's side, Harold and Maggie Kirkland. All five of these set an unquestionably strong moral example. I could not do better than any of them in this department. Note that I'm not talking about manners and etiquette, so Dad is off the hook there. A great misfortune is that I never met Dad's father, "Steamshovel" Bill Simpson, and his Mother Alice, although Alice held me a week before she died. I do wonder how Bill would have affected me had he lived longer. I bet I would have been tougher than I turned out to be.

Next in line would be Mom's cousin Clarence and Uncle Jim and Aunt Marge Simpson. Marge was more assertive than Mom, which was a probably good thing given the twins' behavior. Her example may have helped prepare me for Sue, who came to match her in that department.

Before high school, I was with my cousin Jim and sister Sharon a lot. For junior high and on, it was best friend Terry and also Rod, who turned me on to architecture.

I wish we could have had more time with Sue's father, Bernard. We have had great times, more recently, with my sister Sharon and her husband Paul. Asking Sue's father for her hand was not so hard. Paul had a bit more concern about confronting my dad, but made it through fine.

At my conservative Christian college, at Stanford, and my boss and the coworkers I knew at my SAI job, all were people of integrity. The same goes for our many friends, including Don, Carol, Jerry, and Susan, who we met through our churches in California. Finally, it has taken several chapters to cover the influence on me that Warren and Al had. Warren remained my best friend until his death.

How could I go wrong?

Even once I was more set in my ways up in Idaho, I have continued to be with people who either have a stellar character or if not, hide their deficiencies well. I'm talking about Greg, Scott, Bruce, Peter, and the Chief employees. There are Naveen and Sravani with our Indian foundation; and Papitchaya and Warut with our Thai foundation. Also our longtime friends Ruth, Shirley, Richard, and Gene.

Sue meeting Gayle in a Bangkok gift shop led to our best friends having to be all the way over in Australia. Gayle took over teacher training for Sue, is Chairman of our Thai foundation, and completely runs our Myanmar teacher education effort. When I think about "morals" and her husband Keith, the term "rock-solid" comes to mind. I'm especially thankful for Keith and Gayle's experience living and working with aboriginal people in violent places. It has made getting along with us for extended periods of work and travel easy for them.

There are things about people that I don't notice due to my limitations. Various issues may have passed right by me even if noticeable to others. So, in case you don't trust my judgment, and maybe you should not at times, Sue knows many of these people and has dealt with them often, and backs what I say here.

This does not make me perfect, but I can say that for the evil and failings that I have experienced, I can't find anyone to blame but myself.

I realize that many have not had my privilege in this way. They have been around others who have dragged them down. How can I say I would have resisted that, if even one of those I've mentioned above would have been that way? I've read how well others have responded to deaths of spouse or children, or worse, serious crimes against them. Could I have made it through something like that? Who knows?

Finally, I want to thank professional editors Howard Lovy and Anna Paradox, who edited this, my first book. Gayle, Ruth, Jim, and other friends did further editing. I stole the cover background from the Chief Architect user's manual.

Made in the USA
Monee, IL
04 November 2026

67375796R00207